A VERY BRITISH MIRACLE

A VERY BRITISH MIRACLE

The Failure of Thatcherism

Edgar Wilson

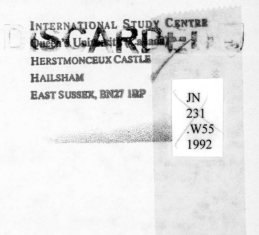
PLUTO  PRESS
London • Concord, Mass.

To Aby and Mary, my parents

First published 1992 by Pluto Press
345 Archway Road, London N6 5AA
and 141 Old Bedford Road,
Concord, MA 01742, USA

British Library Cataloguing in Publication Data
Wilson, Edgar
  A very British miracle: The failure of Thatcherism.
  I. Title
  941.085
  ISBN 0–7453–0653–5 hb
  ISBN 0–7453–0654–3 pb

Library of Congress Cataloging in Publication Data
applied for

Typeset by Stanford DTP Services, Milton Keynes.
Printed and bound in the United Kingdom
by Billing and Sons Ltd, Worcester.

CONTENTS

ACKNOWLEDGEMENTS

I have received invaluable assistance from numerous friends and colleagues. Help with research was volunteered by Freda Maxfield, Gwyniera Cox, Liz Smith, Gareth Beavan, Tom Barfield and Nicole Wilson. I am grateful for the help given to me by Lewis Amery of Labour Research, Christine Coates of the TUC Library, and John Crudas of the Labour Party's Research Department. John Raybould of the Institute for Economic Affairs was of great assistance in procuring literature. I was also courteously received and assisted by the Conservative Party Central Office, the Adam Smith Institute and the Centre for Policy Studies.

I am indebted also to Patrick Cormack, Sir Reg Prentice, Lord Beloff, Lord Chalfont, Sir Kingsley Amis and Lord Hugh Thomas of Swynnerton for correspondence on the subject. All the more so because I share few of their views. Sir Ralph Robbins, Deputy Chairman, and Charles Coltman, Director of Strategic Planning and Marketing Development, of Rolls-Royce plc kindly provided assistance with the sections on that exemplary company.

I am especially grateful to Professor Stephen Haseler, Dr Michael Singleton and Peter Doughty who have commented on drafts. Marjorie Foy, Diane Plant and Caroline Davies refused to be beaten in the processing of my low-tech script.

PREFACE

I started work on this book in 1988 when it was widely assumed that the New Right Conservative Party had succeeded in establishing its authority and its values in Britain. The idea that it had failed comprehensively seemed then to be a highly contentious thesis. While the book has been in preparation the world has moved on. The main character in the story, Margaret Thatcher, has been politically assassinated. At the time of writing, in August 1991, her successor John Major has been established for eight months as leader of the party and Prime Minister, and is preparing in the middle of a recession to fight a general election. It is not yet clear whether Thatcherite policies have been rejected by the party along with the leader.

It was originally intended that the work should include a critical examination of the New Right philosophy, and an exploration of what might replace it. As it has turned out, the account of the emergence of the New Right to government and its record during twelve years in office is a story sufficient in itself, and one that needs to be told. It needs to be told above all because, although there must inevitably be uncertainty about the policy direction to be taken by the Conservative Party after Margaret Thatcher's departure, it is likely that it will pursue broadly the same policies.

I regret that it has not been possible to include in the same volume an extended philosophical criticism of New Right ideas. That is a task that I, along with some others, have well in hand (and not before time).

Edgar Wilson
August 1991

INTRODUCTION

One way or another extraordinary things happened in British politics and government in the period called the Thatcher years from May 1979 to November 1990. What happened has been variously described as a 'revolution', 'the Battle for Britain' and a 'miracle'. Less grandiloquent words would not reflect the scale of the ambitions pursued and the achievements claimed by and on behalf of Conservative governments during this period. The miracle ventured was to halt and reverse Britain's seemingly irreversible decline in the spheres of economics, politics, society and general culture.

It was widely accepted that the postwar political consensus was proved in the 1970s to have failed. During twelve continuous years of Conservative government there was established the widespread belief, shared by many political opponents, that Margaret Thatcher's brand of 'New Right' Conservatism succeeded in substantially solving the problems and in establishing a new consensus based on New Right ideas. The central political debate in Britain has been about the failure of political opposition, particularly the Left. The economic, political and cultural changes made after 1979 are rooted in a distinctive and dominant philosophy, 'Thatcherism', from which success has supposedly been derived. Policies developed on this basis and implemented by government since 1979 were said to have been so effective in solving Britain's problems that by 1989 there was nothing left to do but for the Adam Smith Institute to export the philosophy. After 1989 the certainty became qualified. In November 1990 Margaret Thatcher was removed from the leadership of her own party because her uncompromising pursuit of policies was proving to be an electoral liability. Perceptive observers began to suspect that the reputation of the Thatcher governments could melt like the snows of spring. Against this, however, there is a tendency, not confined to New Right evangelicals, to magnify and mythologise the record of the Thatcher governments so that it amounts to nothing short of a miraculous transformation of British life, and one conspicuously motivated by distinctive ideas and values.

Twelve years of continuous office is as fair a test of philosophy and policy as any government can ever expect, particularly when it has been largely unaffected by opposition inside or outside Parliament. With the departure of Margaret Thatcher, it is timely to ask whether the New Right conservatism propounded and practised by her has been as successful as has commonly been supposed. A study of the political events in this period has not only the intrinsic interest that a study of most other periods has but also provides the opportunity to reflect on how the influential doctrines of the New Right fared in Britain when tested by practical experience. Also, there are lessons to be learned that have immediate relevance to the prospects for success of any other government, in Britain or elsewhere, which pursues policies derived from the same ideas and values. What follows, therefore, is a narrative of events, an exposition of the main ideas and policies informing them, a critical review of the results achieved in practice (both those claimed and actual outcomes), and finally a judgement as to success and failure.

There is a more particular reason for providing a review of the record of the New Right than the ones already given. British politics is now, at the time of going to press in 1991, at an especially important juncture. The extent of revision to be made by the Conservative Party to its New Right ideas and policies, following Margaret Thatcher's departure, is still uncertain and will be discussed presently. It is unlikely, however, that a substantial counter-revolution will take place. Whatever transpires in the way of change in Conservative Party policy it is anyway important to have a true record of the results in practice of New Right thinking during the twelve years of the Thatcher government.

This book comprises two parts. The first part recounts the circumstances in which the New Right emerged in the Conservative Party and the development of its ideas until the election victory of 1979. An account is given of the economic, political, social and cultural context of the postwar period. This includes an account of the perceived failures of the Left and the Old Right in responding to the intractable problems of Britain after the Labour administration of Clement Atlee. In this way the problems addressed by the New Right are identified. These include economic performance – industrial decline and uncompetitiveness; social disorder – the threat to the rule of law; bureaucracy – loss of individual liberty and the growth of welfare-statism; and ungovernability – the growth of corporatism and syndicalism (especially the trade unions threatening the sovereignty of Parliament). In this way criteria for successful change are established, the foundations for the new philosophy are identified, an analysis of the problems on this basis outlined, and the agenda for action drawn up. The main thesis advanced in this part of the study is that, in Britain, New Right ideas came into prominence by default out of a catalogue of errors, and their persuasiveness has been grossly exaggerated on the Left as well as on the Right.

The second part is a critical review of the record of the New Right in office: its dominance, and its successes and failures. This includes an account of the economic, political, social and cultural changes made by the New Right based on a shift from a consensus Social Keynesianism towards an "enterprise and individualist culture founded primarily on the economic and social philosophies of Milton Friedman and Friedrich von Hayek. As well as particular initiatives in industry, employment, education, inflation, health and welfare, housing, etc, the overriding ambition to bring about an irreversible shift in popular attitudes towards individualism is considered. This review suggests that there have been achievements of a lasting kind, including success in advancing (in some spheres) individual liberty, securing the rule of law, promoting enterprise, and generally confronting basic issues evaded by the old consensus. On the other hand, most of the old problems remain unsolved. By objective standards the Conservative economic record is unsuccessful. Many major government policies were rejected by most of the electorate. Electoral support for the governments was always weak and support for opposition parties twice as great. Substantial parliamentary majorities are attributable to a flawed electoral system. The main thesis advanced in this part of the study is that, even by its own standards and criteria, the record of Conservative governments under Margaret Thatcher has been one of comprehensive failure, with a few mitigating achievements.

It would be surprising if a study of this kind did not have shortcomings, if only because no such work can do everything. Among the issues that could with profit have been pursued further than I have been able to here, North Sea oil, gender, race, and relations with the United States are the most important. The record on most of these, however, is not significantly different from the rest. What is required for a comprehensive evaluation of New Right thinking is a critique of the philosophy, in order to extend the test provided by practical experience of its policies.

Many of the shortcomings of this study can be remedied by referring to the copious literature on the subjects discussed, only a fraction of which is cited in the notes and bibliography. Among the most useful sources are the collected speeches of Keith Joseph (1975, 1976) and Margaret Thatcher (1977, 1989a, 1989b). The seminal ideas are set out in Friedrich von Hayek's *The Road to Serfdom* (1944) and *The Constitution of Liberty* (1960). The decisive development of the ideas is well described in many publications of the Institute for Economic Affairs, notably Ralph Harris and Arthur Seldon's *Not from Benevolence* (1977) and *Hayek's 'Serfdom' Revisited* (1984). Useful reviews of New Right thinking are provided by David Green *The New Right* (1987) and Norman Barry *The New Right* (1987). Stephen Haseler provides a sympathetic account of the Thatcher Revolution in politics and government in *The Battle for Britain* (1989). At the highest level of political journalism Hugo Young's *One of Us* (1989) gives the most judicious account of the events of the period. Among the various works of Conservative politicians Francis Pym's *The Politics of Consent* (1984) has the great virtue of redefining the traditional Conservative view through the experience of being a conspicuous 'wet' in a 'dry' cabinet. Among economic commentators Samuel Brittan is distinguished by having anticipated the Thatcher revolution, and he provides a sympathetic and very illuminating exegesis of its economic ideas in *A Restatement of Economic Liberalism* (1973 and 1988). I have been exceptionally impressed by the writings of William Keegan of the *Observer* and have found his weekly column to be consistently enlightening and prescient. So far as I can recall he has been right all along. His book, *Mrs Thatcher's Economic Experiment* (1984), is an excellent account of the effects of 'Sado–Monetarism' on the British economy and industry. Extremely useful synoptic accounts of the record of the Thatcher governments are given in Madsen Pirie (ed) *A Decade of Revolution* (1989) (sympathetic); Robert Skidelski (ed) *Thatcherism* (1988), and Dennis Kavanagh and Anthony Seldon (eds) *The Thatcher Effect* (1989) (both 'eclectic'); and Labour front-bench spokesman Gordon Brown's *Where There is Greed...* (1989) (critical). Ideological analysis and criticism from the Left is available in canonical form in Stuart Hall and Martin Jacques (eds) *The Politics of Thatcherism* (1983) and Bob Jessop et al. *Thatcherism* (1988). Andrew Gamble's *The Free Economy and the Strong State* (1988) provides what I believe to be the most penetrating and useful account of the politics of Thatcherism.

In view of the extraordinary emphasis put by New Right evangelicals on the importance of ideas to their programme it is surprising that there has been comparatively little attention devoted by critics to the philosophy of the New Right. Some excellent criticism is provided, however, in Nick Bosanquet's *After the New Right* (1983), Ruth Levitas's *The Ideology of the New Right* (1986), Geoffrey Deakin's *The New Right: Images and Reality* (1986), Desmond King's *The New Right: Politics, Markets and Citizenship* (1989), and Jim Tomlinson's *Hayek and the Market* (1990). Ted Honderich's *Conservatism* (1990)

addresses the broad tradition after Burke but offers telling criticisms
of the New Right as well. This list is almost exhaustive. Finally, two
works of political psychology are of particular interest. John Rentoul's
Me and Mine (1989) explores the changing attitudes and values of
British voters in connection with the most fundamental aim of
Thatcherism, to capture the moral high ground. Leo Abse's *Margaret,
daughter of Beatrice* (1989) is an exercise in political psycho-biography
unique to British politics. Psycho-biography may be extremely
dubious methodologically, but it is impossible to read this book
without realising that the psychology of politicians has considerable
significance which in most political analysis is usually overlooked.

Although it is too early to be sure how far, under John Major's
leadership, the Conservative Party will move from the ideological
position of the New Right, it is instructive to consider the evidence
that is already available under the new leadership. There are factors
which suggest that significant change may be in the offing, and that
the change of leadership marked a return by the party to the middle
ground traditionally occupied by 'one nation' conservatism. The
change of style is very striking. John Major's 'decent drapery' of
manners is everything Burke could have wished, in contrast to
Margaret Thatcher's confrontational approach. He seems concerned
to consult and deliberate, whereas she valued single-mindedness and
decisiveness. A generally more democratic way of doing things is
indicated. In the economic sphere of local government finance the
party was quick to change its electorally disastrous policy on the Poll
Tax, and to replace it with a property tax (similar to Labour's),
related to ability to pay. The status of public services seems to be
secure in a way it was not during the Thatcher years. John Major's
first significant, possibly symbolic, act as Prime Minister was to
approve the award of state compensation to haemophiliacs who
had contracted the AIDS virus through NHS blood transfusions, a
measure which Margaret Thatcher had resisted. A Citizen's [*sic*]
Charter introduced in July 1991 embodied many measures designed
to empower members of the public to seek redress from public corporations for unsatisfactory service. Significantly, it presumed the
continued existence of public services as a 'good thing'. A shift in
transport policy was announced designed to transfer much traffic
from road to rail, with commensurate investment of public money
proposed. Such measures go against Margaret Thatcher's every
inclination. Among the signals of change that only *cognoscenti* would
appreciate, one of the most significant was the new Prime Minister's

association with the 'One Nation Group' of Conservative MPs and his distance from the 'No Turning Back Group' of Margaret Thatcher's New Right supporters. To crown all, John Major publicly avowed in Germany his desire to see Britain at the very heart of Europe where it belongs, whereas his predecessor had set her face against any such thing. If this picture of change is correct, well might Margaret Thatcher think she had been deceived into supporting John Major in the election for her successor as leader of the Conservative Party.

In contrast to this picture, other evidence suggests that in John Major Margaret Thatcher really did find her true political heir as well as her successor as Prime Minister. In the fundamental matter of economic theory and policy the evidence is that John Major's Conservative government is like its New Right predecessors. Its priority continues to be countering inflation, using monetary means (especially interest rates) to do so, regardless of the destructive effects on industry and employment. Consultation and deliberation do not necessarily yield significantly different policies. The replacement to the Poll Tax, the Council Tax, is a hybrid that makes allowance for ability to pay but retains an element of universal compulsory taxation, like the Poll Tax. The change was more likely driven by electoral prudence than by principles of fairness. There is no plan to change central government control over local government spending, that is, to restore local democracy. Public services, in education and health particularly, continue to be restructured as competitive commercial markets, by provisions for 'opting out' of public control, rather than as social services; this, in the teeth of bitter opposition from educators and the medical professions.

The proposed Citizen's Charter (John Major's 'big idea') spells out more effectively than a Marxian analysis could the capitalist free-market conception of individuals as essentially customers and consumers. The political and social dimensions of citizenship are conspicuous by their absence. The radical agenda for citizenship drawn up by Charter 88 and other groups calls for electoral reform, freedom of information, reform of public institutions, a Bill of Rights and a written constitution. The Conservative's Chartered-Citizen may complain about inconvenient road cones but not about these things. Most significantly no money is provided to ensure that 'citizens' rights' are really secured. It is perverse and futile, as proposed, to impose financial penalties for delays to services which are delayed in the first place because of lack of finance!

Economic and social rights such as those set out in the European Community's Social Charter – regarding minimum wages, equal pay for equal work, and worker participation in management – are also totally absent from the Conservative charter for the rights of citizens. The promising proposals to shift traffic to the railways and to invest public money in them turn out to be a preparation for privatisation. It is planned to continue the New Right policy of privatisation by selling off not only British Rail but the British Technology Group, British Coal and even the Post Office as well. In the move to closer monetary union with Europe it is intended to retain the essential sovereignty of the United Kingdom within a federal structure suitable for the purpose. Margaret Thatcher was able (however perversely) publicly to endorse John Major's view of this. By this account there is no evidence that John Major's Conservative Party plans to change the all-important New Right policies in economics, industry and politics. Moreover, continuation of the New Right policy of non-intervention by the state, and a continuing reluctance to finance public services, will ensure that provision of social welfare will not change substantially. Thus, although there is evidence to support both the view that Conservative Party policy is changing significantly, and the view that it is not, the balance of evidence strongly suggests that it is not. The New Right ideas and policies championed by Margaret Thatcher continue after her departure to exert a decisive influence on the Conservative Party. As Oliver Letwin explained to *Sunday Telegraph* readers (2 December 1990), instead of abandoning Thatcherism, John Major, by making clear the true aim of Thatcherite policies, will have done a service not only to Britain but also to the progress of political science. The greatest 'miracle' of the Thatcher years was that rhetoric triumphed over reality for so long.

PART 1

CRISIS? WHAT CRISIS? THE EMERGENCE OF THE NEW RIGHT

... a wholesale counter-revolution ... is not ... in the nature of the British Conservative Party – it lacks the essential attributes of a counter-revolutionary party – a faith, a dogma, even a theory'

ANTHONY CROSLAND (1956, p27)

'I have changed everything'

MARGARET THATCHER
(quoted in Cosgrave 1979, p197)

1 CRISIS

It is widely agreed that there was a crisis in Britain in the 1970s and that this led to the rejection of the established political order which had prevailed since the end of the Second World War in 1945.[1] The 'order' that replaced it is conveniently called the New Right. The record of the New Right since 1979 is a matter of dispute, and it is the purpose of this study to examine the record and to reach a verdict about its successes and failures.

Now, there are people of an unusually portentous disposition who are prone to see crises where most others would not. Politicians (especially in opposition) and political commentators are more prone to 'crisismongering' than most, certainly; and it is well to bear this in mind from now on. That said, it will be useful to proceed by reviewing some of the main events and issues that led in the 1970s to the emergence of the New Right in Britain. Something of the nature of the crisis can quickly be gathered by an attempt to locate some of its origins.

The emergence of the New Right could simply be dated 3 May 1979 when the Conservative Party led by Mrs Margaret Thatcher won a general election with a clear majority over all other parties. However, the result of the election was greatly influenced by the events of the winter of 1978–9 leading up to it. This has become notorious, as 'the Winter of Discontent', because of the widespread strikes. The most notorious involved public service workers who for months left mountains of refuse uncollected on the streets, and even corpses unburied in the mortuaries, in protest against a government-imposed pay limit of 5 per cent. The strikes were presaged in the summer and autumn of 1978 when three years of voluntary, anti-inflationary wage restraint by trade unions were formally terminated. The Trades Union Congress and the Labour Party Conference both resolved that government pay norms should be rejected and a return made to 'free-collective bargaining'. For reasons related to strikes and wages, Margaret Thatcher had been elected leader of the Conservative Party in 1974, because she was committed to the New Right philosophy and policies that the party adopted after two electoral defeats that year. These defeats came after strikes by unionised workers, particularly the mineworkers, at a time when oil prices had been multiplied fourfold, severely threatening the nation's trade and economy. The election of February 1974 was intended to decide 'Who Governs Britain?' – the

3

democratically elected government in Parliament or the trade unions? The electors decided it was not to be the Conservative government, which had put the question. Such confrontations had been in train ever since the nation's economy had crossed a crucial watershed in 1958 when, for the first time, the increase in incomes exceeded the increase in production.[2] These events were occurring in a political order that had been formed during the wartime coalition government of Winston Churchill where the Conservative and Labour parties tacitly settled on common policies for employment, social welfare and even to a degree public ownership and state direction of industry. Recurrent economic problems of inflation, adverse balance of trade, strikes and unemployment are determined by the performance of British industry which has been in relative decline ever since the heyday of Britain's industrial supremacy: Sir Henry Playfair had been dismayed to have to report that at the Paris Exhibition of 1867 Britain was definitely among the lower ranks of the exhibitors, whereas at the Crystal Palace Exhibition only 16 years earlier British manufacturers had won a majority of the prizes.[3]

Here then, in brief, are the salient features of the political scene which the New Right entered: electoral success; strikes; unemployment; inflation and incomes policies; the role of trade unions and their relations to government and to the Labour Party; democracy; the sovereignty of Parliament; world commodity prices; public opinion; political consensus; industrial growth, efficiency and competitiveness; international trade; and Britain's preeminence. In order better to understand the context from which the New Right emerged in Britain it is necessary to look a little more closely and elementally at the problems that led to the crisis and with more systematic regard to distinguishable economic, political, social and cultural factors. A conventional account follows in Chapter 2.

2 BRITAIN'S PROBLEMS

ECONOMICS

Inflation, Interest Rates, Exchange Rates and Trade

Inflation, the rate of increase of retail prices, erodes the purchasing power both of incomes and of wealth, especially in cash savings, and so is often taken as the single most important indicator of overall economic health. Britain had enjoyed ideally low levels of inflation in the postwar period. In 1959, for instance, it was just 1 per cent. During the term of the 1974–9 Labour government inflation exploded to unprecedented 'Banana Republic' levels of 28.7 per cent in 1974 and 24.2 per cent in 1975.[4] A second leading indicator of economic health is the bank interest rate on borrowing. Low levels of interest are conducive to economic activity. For long periods after the war interest rates were low. For example, during 1962 the bank rate fluctuated only slightly between 4 and 5 per cent, a rate roughly comparable to those in countries which are leading competitors in international trade. Whereas, as a general rule, interest rates in double figures are considered a clear sign of economic trouble, such rates became commonplace, and reached the previously unheard of annual average of 14.25 per cent in 1976.[5] Interest rates are linked directly to the fact that the pound sterling is an international reserve currency. Pounds can be exchanged for dollars 'on demand', at a rate that maintains the 'value' of money. If the exchange rate with sterling falls substantially because Britain's economy is generally weak, then the value of deposits in sterling falls accordingly. Basically for this reason a fall in the exchange value of the pound could have catastrophic consequences. Such consequences almost happened in 1976 when the pound was valued at less than $2 for the first time, and there was speculation that its exchange value could fall as low as $1. If this had happened the consequences would have been 'the collapse of the currency, the collapse of the government, and even the destruction of the stability of the western world'.[6] In order to prevent this the British government was obliged to secure a loan of £5 billion from the International Monetary Fund (IMF) for the purpose of buying its own currency so as to restore the exchange value of sterling. This act once again located Britain and its economy among the 'Banana Republics' as it pushed interest rates to 15 per cent. The salient indicator of a strong economy for industrial nations such as Britain is the balance of trade, and Britain's share of world trade in manufactures had been declining continuously since the nineteenth century. But whatever the share of world trade it is clearly desirable for a trading nation, as a general rule, not to buy more than it sells. In November 1967 the trade deficit of £153 million was then the largest recorded in peacetime. In June 1969 the Labour government committed Britain to achieving a surplus of £300 million by March 1970 in order to secure a standby loan from the IMF. This target was achieved with a balance of payments surplus of £387 million for 1969. It proved, however, to be only a benchmark of solvency from which to measure persistent deficits in trade throughout the 1970s, ranging from £302 million in 1978 to £2,348 million in 1973. The record of overall balance of payments was generally even worse, with deficits under the Labour government ranging from £224 million in 1977 to £3,591 million in 1974.[7]

Unemployment, Industry, Profit and Investment

Unemployment is the conventional measure of the extent of utilisation of the economic system, specifically its capacity to deploy the human resources of a society. In the years after the Second World War until 1970 there was never more than 2.5 per cent of the working population registered as unemployed. Levels of this order can be accounted for by residual factors, such as a proportion of workers always being in the process of changing employment. In the late 1970s rates of unemployment rose continuously to much higher levels: 4.2 per cent in 1975, 5.7 per cent in 1976, 6.2 per cent in 1977, 6.1 per cent in 1978.[8] In human terms there were in Britain in 1977 1,483,600 persons counted in the working population but not in work. At least one million of these would have been involuntarily unemployed. Although there was nothing new in either high levels of unemployment or high levels of inflation, there was something new and very significant about the occurrence of the two together. The Philips Curve succinctly captures the co-variant, specifically inverse relationship between inflation and unemployment that had until then been the long-established trend. When unemployment increased, inflation decreased (presumedly unemployment tended to reduce pressure for higher wages and so prices). The novel occurrence in the 1970s of high inflation and high unemployment together was called stagflation, and defied the explanatory powers of the prevailing conventional economic theory and practical remedy. Utilising the working population profitably is clearly dependent upon employment, particularly in manufacturing industry, but unfortunately Britain's manufacturing industry had proved to be chronically unable to compete effectively with foreign firms, not just internationally but increasingly in home markets as well. A variety of explanations is available for industrial failure.[9] There are two main types: (i) structural and managerial, and (ii) trade union practices. The main structural and managerial problems are the inadequate skills of the workforce (reflecting inadequate education and training), unsatisfactory industrial relations, and inadequate research and development.

Other significant factors included the scale of manufacturing plant, the (excessively wide) range of products, the relative size of the home market, and capital investment. The consequences of these factors turned out, inevitably, to be low productivity and low profitability. Profits, that is net rates of return on capital, for all industrial and commercial companies fell dramatically from 14 per cent in 1960 to 4 per cent in 1975.[10] This fact can be linked to another: a comparatively low rate of capital investment. From 1960 to 1979 Britain invested a lower proportion of its gross national product than any of the eleven other countries in the European Community – 4.4 per cent less of GNP than the average; over 18 per cent less than the average of the others.[11] The direction of causality as between low profitability and low investment is a matter of dispute, but the two are undoubtedly connected.

Profit, Loss and Ownership

Nationalised industry came in the public mind to be associated with unprofitability. As early as 1965 it was announced that the National Coal Board had a capital debt of £1 billion, of which £450 million was to be written off. In December 1972 a further £475 million of NCB debt was written off and additional grants and payments totalling £540 million provided. In the same month it was reported that £2,934 billion of debts of nationalised industries had been written off since 1946. However, it was by no means only the public sector that was in debt. Private company failure became an overfrequent result of low productivity, uncompetitiveness and operating losses. No private company received more government financial aid than the car and truck manufacturer British Leyland, which in April 1975 alone received £1.4 billion. Nevertheless the list of casualties in the private sector of industry was still impressive including, in 1972, shipbuilders Cammel Laird (£3 million) and Harland and Woolf (£49 million), and British Aircraft Corporation (£225 million). In 1975 Ferranti (£15 million) and IRD Industries of Liverpool (£3.9 million) were among the various recipients of government aid. Faced with the disintegration of much of British manufacturing industry, the Labour government after 1974 was impelled by its political philosophy, as well as its general concerns about unemployment and its links with the trade unions, either to take failing firms into public ownership or to set them up as worker cooperatives with government funding.

Upper Clyde Shipbuilders and Norton Villiers Motor Cycles were in the latter category. Both subsequently failed.

The Case of Rolls-Royce

The most salutory and instructive government retrieval of a bankrupt private company occurred in 1971, under a Conservative government. Edward Heath's government had set out in 1970 to force British firms into facing the cold winds of market competition without government assistance. Companies which failed the test were to be treated as lame ducks, left to their fate. The acid test of the policy came when the company with the most illustrious name in British industry, Rolls-Royce, turned out to be a lame duck in the meaning of the act. The briefest account of the events leading to the company going into voluntary liquidation on 4 February 1971 will serve to exemplify much that is said about Britain's crisis. More will be said later (in Part 2).

In the late 1960s Rolls-Royce was faced with the need to have its aero-engines installed as original equipment in a large aircraft with mass sales. That meant an American aircraft. Failure to achieve this goal would certainly have led to the company losing its place of technical preeminence in the aero-engine field to its two American rivals and, possibly, eventually to the loss altogether of this advanced-technology business. Urgency inspired invention and the engine developed for the purpose of winning an American contract was of exceptionally advanced and innovative design. This design, together with extraordinarily low price estimates and the Labour government's backing, secured the desired order, potentially worth as much as £1,000 million, from a leading American manufacturer, Lockheed. The order was hailed by everyone as a triumph of British ingenuity and business acumen against fierce competition: a model for British industry. Bad news came later. The great technical innovations ventured by the engine's designers took considerably more time and trouble to develop than had been planned for. Launch costs escalated from £65 million to £175 million. Penalties for late delivery were conservatively estimated at another £50 million. The new (Conservative) government refused to pay the (revised) sums required to fulfil the terms of the Rolls-Royce contract with Lockheed. The company was allowed to go bankrupt.

The bankruptcy of Rolls-Royce was described as the most shattering financial disaster to hit British industry since the Second

World War. Some of the explanations offered for the failure confirmed the doomsday view of British industry. Demonstrably the company had failed because it was not competitive in international markets. Its management was not sufficiently concerned with costs, profit and loss (they were mostly long-serving engineers preoccupied with engineering excellence). Market research was deficient, because important European opportunities had been neglected. Because of its industrial and strategic importance the aero-engine division of the company was nationalised and reconstituted as Rolls-Royce (1971) Ltd. Other divisions, including the famous Rolls-Royce Motors, were sold off privately.[12]

The City of London

Manufacturing industry is in the business of making the things that modern life depends on. In Britain's market economy industrial development depends on investment of funds by financial institutions of which banks and savings institutions are the most significant. There has been a general lack of investment of funds by financial institutions in British manufacturing industry, which has led to a cumulative cycle of decline. Failure to invest has undoubtedly been due to a reluctance on the part of financial institutions to accept the risks involved in lending to industry. A key measure of willingness to invest is the 'gearing ratio', which measures the level of borrowing regarded as acceptable in relation to the assets of the company. In the 1970s capital gearing in major competitor countries was several orders higher than in Britain, where it was about 55 per cent. In Germany it was 25 per cent higher; in France three times higher; in Sweden four; in Italy six and Japan seven times higher, at 300–359 per cent.[13]

A positive aspect of the City is its generation of 'invisible earnings' through the exploitation by bankers, brokers and insurers of financial management skills to earn significant sums of foreign currency at minimal cost to the British economy.[14] The City's 'invisibles' have certainly generated more favourable estimates of Britain's economic health, but their value has been a matter of dispute.[15]

Although the City does not make things, it is supposed to make the making of things more likely and more efficient. Unfortunately in practice the City's activities often appear to provide funds for real investment only as a by-product of financial manipulation. The Labour Party study group on financial institutions reported that many people in the City are employed on unproductive activities. 'They are unproductive because, while they may generate financial returns to the "investor", they do not increase the real production potential of the economy.'[16] The dealings of the City's speculative markets have been largely self-regulated and have left substantial scope for incompetence and fraud. Among numerous examples of this unacceptable face of capitalism is the case of the financial 'enterpriser' Mr Jim Slater.[17] One of the simplest unregulated methods he employed was to use his privileged positions as a share 'tipster' on the *Sunday Telegraph* and investment counsellor to manipulate the market by recommending purchase of shares he had already secretly bought himself. When the value of shares increased with the buying on his advice, he then sold at a profit. The attitudes prevalent in the City that make such practices possible prompted Lord Thompson to remark that 'there must be something wrong with this country if it is so easy to make money in it'.[18] One concern is that capitalism can only be compatible with democracy if there are sufficient safeguards for ordinary people. Another is the question of how an economy can flourish when its basic financial institutions are so readily and assiduously devoted to making easy money for financiers in the short term rather than useful things in the longer term.

The Trade Unions, Strikes and the Closed Shop

Trade unions have since 1871 been recognised as the legitimate means of workers promoting their collective interests especially with employers.[19] On the assumption that the powers of employers and unions were unequal, trade unionists were given special legal protection in their pursuit of members' collective interests, notably by the Trades Disputes Act (1906). This Act provides protection for members against legal prosecution when engaged in official union activities, including the inducement of others to break contracts of employment. In the postwar period the collective morality of trade unions generated widely recognised problems in industry. Demarcation disputes were prevalent because of the overspecialised nature of different unions, each of which claimed a right to the same work. Restrictive practices arose out of a desire to ensure that no more work was done than the minimum (thereby prolonging employment), and out of a fear that new technology and methods would lead eventually to unemployment. Unions used their power to negotiate manning levels that were often based more on a conception of the union's own solidarity and interests than on any objective assessment of the needs of the job. None of this was conducive to the efficient conduct of business.

Organisation and coordinated control has always been a problem for the unions themselves, reflecting the fact that the movement in Britain has developed haphazardly. There are numerous unions organised at different levels in different ways and not all of them are members of the loose federation that is the Trades Union Congress. Consequently there is no clear and concerted control over much union activity. In the 1950s industrial disputes became a source of increasing public concern. Wildcat strikes, organised locally by shop stewards without the approval of the unions permanent officials, became a particular cause for concern because of their effect on pro-ductivity and workplace discipline. Successive governments attempted to impose discipline by legislation. After prolonged discussions of its proposals in the document 'In Place of Strife', the Labour government abandoned its Industrial Relations Bill in 1969 because of threatened opposition from the trade unions which proposed their own self-regulation instead. The Conservative government's Industrial Relations Act (1970) was directed to the same purpose as Labour's Bill and was also rendered unworkable by the Trades Union Congress which in 1973 expelled 20 member unions for registering with the Industrial Court according to the requirements of the Act. The passing of the Act had precipitated an extraordinary sequence of strikes, with states of emergency being repeatedly declared throughout the period of Conservative government from 1970 to 1974. From a postwar average of less than 3 million working days lost annually in strikes, the level rose dramatically to 11 million in 1970, 13.6 million in 1971, 23.9 million in 1972, 7.2 million in 1973 and 14.7 million in 1974. The first actions of the new Labour government in 1974 were to settle the (major) strike by mineworkers, and to repeal the Industrial Relations Act (1970). The incidence of strikes was reduced but never to postwar norms. In 1977 10.1 million days were lost, in 1978 9.4 million, and in 1979 29.5 million: a postwar record. This is the main foundation of the view that Britain had become a union-dominated, strike-bound, almost ungovernable society.

By 1976 the influence of trade unions on government had grown so far that a Trade Unions and Labour Relations Bill was enacted securing in law the closed shop, which effectively required all workers employed in companies with such arrangements to be members of approved unions, excepting only those who could demonstrate religious grounds for exemption. The refusal of the unions and the government to allow sincere conscientious grounds for exemption was widely condemned as a violation of basic individual liberties (the former Deputy Leader of the Labour Party, Lord George Brown, an erstwhile trade union leader himself, resigned from the Labour Party over the issue). The Labour government's relationship with trade unions was brought further into question when MPs, including leading cabinet ministers, joined trade union pickets during a protracted and violent dispute on the issue of permitting unionisation of workers at Grunwick during 1976–7. The closed shop legislation and the Grunwick dispute were regarded as raising basic issues of constitutional government, civil liberties and the rule of law that went far beyond the workings of trade unions themselves.

Economic Consequences

The economic consequences of this combination of factors are illustrated by the following statistical data. Table 1 summarises the relative decline of the British economy in relation to other industrial nations by comparing gross national product (GNP) per capita over the 'crisis' period of the 1970s. Table 2 compares key indicators – unemployment, inflation and interest rates – of various economic competitors for 1978.

TABLE 1   GNP PER CAPITA (UK = 100) 1970–8

	1970	1978
United States	178	182
OECD	131	136
Japan	101	116
United Kingdom	100	100

Source: OECD Main Economic Indicators June 1980 (author's calculations)

TABLE 2   COMPARISON OF KEY INDICATORS: 1978

	Unemployment *(%)*	*Consumer* *prices* *(1975 = 100)*	*Interest* *rates* *(%)*
Canada	8.0	126.5	10.75
Australia	6.1	137.6	8.75
United Kingdom	6.1	146.4	12.5
United States	6.0	121.2	9.5
Germany	3.9	111.3	3.0
Japan	2.2	123.3	3.5
Sweden	1.6	135.4	6.5

Source: OECD Main Economic Indicators June 1980

Table 1 shows that the United Kingdom started the decade with the lowest GNP of the leading nations compared and, more significantly, had slower growth rates than the others, particularly Japan which began the decade almost on a par. Table 2 shows that, although some other countries had comparable levels of unemployment and others had comparable levels of inflation, none had the uniquely bad combination of all three indicators being adverse to a high degree.

POLITICS

The Corporate State: Government and Trade Unions

During the Labour administration of 1964–70 the trade unions' traditional links with the Labour Party were developed in new ways that gave cause for concern about the integrity of parliamentary government. At one level the new significance of trade unions amounted to little more than informal talks with beer and sandwiches at 10 Downing Street. Also senior trade union leaders were appointed to conspicuous quangos. Much more significantly the unions as well as the Confederation of British Industry were formally called upon to endorse the Labour government's National Plan of 1965. Again in 1974 the Labour government's economic policies were underwritten by an agreement with the Trades Union Congress. According to the conventional criticism these developments were interpreted as compromising the authority and autonomy of elected governments. On this interpretation the latent dangers even for a Labour government were made manifest when a major strike by seamen in 1966 in pursuit of a wage claim broke the restraints of the National Plan. The events of the winter of discontent in 1979 were merely a recurrence of this earlier episode. In both cases, apparently, attempts to govern with the unions led to the breakdown of government altogether. When, in 1974, the Conservative government tried to assert the autonomous authority of the elected Parliament over the trade unions 'the triumphant miners trampled over the prostrate body of Ted Heath',[20] the Prime Minister. The country, it seemed, could be governed neither by enlisting the support of the unions nor by opposing them.

The Legitimacy of Government

It is commonly presumed that democratic government practically implies majority rule (with, in the spirit, due regard to legitimate minority interests and basic human rights). The British constitution invests the elected government with absolute powers, but the electoral system does not ensure that a majority in Parliament corresponds to a majority of the electorate, or even a majority of voters (since 1922 only the Conservative government of 1931 was supported by a majority of voters [55 per cent]). So long as government does not enact legislation against the clear wishes of the majority the question of legitimacy is merely academic. In practice, however, governments frequently pass laws which would not be acceptable to a majority of the electorate. The radical innovations of the 1945 Labour government were enacted by a party with the support of less than half of the voters (48 per cent). The controversial nationalisation of the steel industry in 1950 was carried out by a Labour government with just 46 per cent of votes and a majority of just eight MPs. Anomaly was piled on anomaly in the election of 1951 when Labour's greater share of the vote (48.8 per cent, to 48 per cent for Conservatives) yielded only a minority of seats (296 to the Conservatives 320). The anomalies persisted in the 1970s and led to riots in the Commons in 1976 when the Labour government forced the enactment of an extraordinarily controversial bill to nationalise the aircraft and shipbuilding industries. It had no clear working majority at all, calling at one stage on the casting vote of the Speaker, but eventually it succeeded with a majority of one.[21] At the time of the previous general election a large majority of the electorate (68 per cent) were not in favour of further nationalisation.[22] In Britain people can be given what an unrepresentative majority in Parliament decides whether the majority of people want it or not.

As a consequence of such experiences many Conservatives began in the 1970s to confront the essentially undemocratic nature of the electoral system and the constitution. In 1976 Lord Hailsham delivered a disquisition to BBC TV viewers on 'The Dilemma of Democracy', in which he reflected portentously on the subject of the impairment of liberty and its chief cause: the absolute legislative power confided in Parliament concentrated in the hands of a government with a parliamentary majority. 'Elective dictatorship' he said was not a contradiction in terms to describe what we in Britain have by way of political authority.[23] Another consequence, just as striking as a Lord Chancellor and senior Conservative criticising the constitution, was that many businessmen were contributing to the cause of electoral reform and the Liberal Party, instead of to Conservative Party funds in the time-honoured way.[24] At the Conservative Party Conference in 1978 a resolution was proposed to commit the party to proportional representation, although this was defeated.

Manifest deficiencies in the democratic process tend to encourage the view that parliamentary democracy in Britain is not indispensable. In 1978 the former Conservative cabinet minister, Ian Gilmour, explained that Conservatives do not worship democracy; it is only a means to an end not an end in itself.[25] According to the leading Conservative philosopher, Roger Scruton, democracy is nothing better than a menacing disease.[26] The high-Tory journalist Peregrine Worsthorne went as far as to seek to persuade *Sunday Telegraph* readers in 1977 that if a radical left-wing government were elected then treason would be right.[27] On these matters, at least, Conservatives are in agreement with the international socialists, who explain that 'power cannot lie in the ballot box',[28] and with the Revolutionary Communist Party of Britain (Marxist–Leninist), which stated that a radical transformation of society cannot be achieved through Parliament, through reform; it can only be achieved through a revolution.[29] When, in the 1970s, these views moved from the lunatic fringe of politics on to the main agenda it is understandable that many believed that Britain was in a state of crisis.

SOCIETY

Social Issues

In the 1970s, no doubt induced by economic stresses, the contours of the endemic problems of British society became clearly discernible. It will suffice to indicate some of them here just briefly. Perceived problems of the trade unions were taken by critics on the Right to be indicative of a more general bias towards collectivism and against individualism. The trade union leader Hugh Scanlon disconcerted individualists when he said on television that: 'Liberty in my view, is conforming to majority opinion.'[30] The prevailing climate of expectation appeared to be that the government, the state, was responsible for solving basic social problems from the cradle to the grave: in health, housing, education, employment and welfare. The predominant relationship between state and citizens was paternalistic. Criticism of the 'client' status of individuals and communities came from all political directions, not least from the radical Left. No political party or government seemed to take seriously the emerging problems of race, gender and the environment.

The rule of law appeared to be under threat more from politicians and trade unionists than criminals. Notoriously, Labour councillors at Clay Cross refused to obey the courts, either to implement legislation or to pay the penalties for not doing so, and the Deputy Leader of the Labour Party denied that it was his duty to urge people to obey the law.[31] Responsibility for the breakdown of public order was traced, as was so much else, to the schools. Indiscipline in schools was one of the main criticisms levelled at educators of a progressive sort who were proud to attach more importance to self-expression than to self-discipline in their pupils. The main failures discerned in the education system, however, were a deterioration of academic standards, which was linked directly to the introduction of comprehensive secondary schools, and a lack of practical relevance in the curriculum, which was linked indirectly to the country's poor industrial performance. The Labour Prime Minister, James Callaghan, himself made the second link in 1976 in a seminal speech at Ruskin College Oxford. The National Health Service, the proudest legacy of Labour's postwar social reforms, had contracted its own form of British disease, with growing waiting lists, inadequate facilities, dissatisfied doctors and strained industrial relations. Even those favourably disposed to a public health service considered it foolish to deny that a crisis existed in the 1970s.[32] The System of Social Security and Welfare grappled with similarly intractable problems of trying to meet infinitely extendable demand. Inevitably, the worst off members of society fared most badly.[33]

Class

The social climate of the 1970s was manifested most obviously in bitter and often violent strikes. But strikes only gave expression to deep-rooted and persistent social class antagonisms. David Marquand, an academic writer not given to hyperbole, has accurately described how

> Britain's class politics have a peculiarly sour, suspicious, dog-in-the-manger, chip-on-the-shoulder quality which does not seem to be found elsewhere. That, rather than class politics *per se* is the chief emotional obstacle to class collaboration and cross-class coalition building.

He opines that the roots are to be found in a prevalent British conception of the prerogatives of property, and in the resentments and hostilities which that breeds.[34] Anthony Crosland retails the perceptive view of the celebrated Sherpa Tenzing, which located the roots of the British class system elsewhere than property. Tenzing worked with Swiss and British climbing expeditions in the Himalayas. In his autobiography he explained his reservations about his decision to climb with the British Everest Expedition of 1953 rather than wait for a year to join a Swiss team.

> I would rather have gone back to Everest with the Swiss ... With the Swiss and the French I had been treated as a comrade, an equal in a way that is not possible for the British. They are kind men, they are brave; they are fair and just always. But always, too, there is a line between them and the outsider, between the sahib and the employer.[35]

There is little doubt that Tenzing would have found a later generation of plebeian British climbers (such as Don Willans and Joe Brown) more congenial, but he had experienced and accurately described the best that can be said for British ruling caste attitudes, and his honest response is indicative of the human distance they cause. There are far snottier and less admirable varieties of complacent and groundless presumption of personal superiority than Tenzing records. Typically these evoke less respectful responses than Tenzing's among the British natives who are exposed to them routinely.

What is illustrated here anecdotally is related systematically to pervasive class differences in life expectancy, health, education, employment, wealth, income, even equality under the law.[36] The findings of comprehensive studies of class mobility in Britain conducted at Oxford University show that nothing much changes. John Goldthorpe and his co-workers studied data of half a century during which there were important developments favourable to class mobility such as expanding economy and educational provision. The conclusion reported in 1980 was that no significant reduction in class inequalities had been achieved. In Britain the transmission of social status is a kind of closed circuit. As the report explains, there is a

> situation of no change in relative mobility chances (as between different class origins) ... in which the inequalities in such chances that prevail are of a quite gross kind ... it is here that the reality of contemporary British society most strikingly and incontrovertibly deviates from the ideal of genuine open-ness.[37]

These findings refute the commonly expressed view that class distinctions were a thing of the past by the 1970s.[38] The most astounding and significant misconception of all was that of Conservative cabinet minister and celebrated intellectual Keith Joseph who asked in 1979, 'Is there mobility between classes?' and answered himself, 'the blessed answer in this blessed country is that there is almost infinite mobility.'[39] Not the least significant feature of Joseph's case was that he claimed that the Goldthorpe studies supported his assertion, whereas the very opposite was true.

Although some of Britain's rulers did not perceive class to be a problem, most British people had no doubt that it was. A *Times* survey in 1980 showed that a large majority, 71 per cent, believed that Britain's problems were completely or at least partly due to social class distinctions.[40] Informed foreigners had no doubts either, even when they could see virtues in the class system.[41] One effect of the class system which everyone, except some of Britain's rulers, recognised was its destructive effect on industrial relations, efficiency and productivity.[42] Several independent studies of Britain's economic problems reached this clear conclusion. The Hudson Institute of Europe reported in 1974 that

Britain needs economic and industrial modernisation, but also a modernisation of a rather different sort. The country needs a fundamental improvement in class relations and social attitudes as they relate to work and trade; and indeed *the claims here are of justice as well as efficiency*. Britain today maintains its grip on the imagination of Europeans and Americans exactly because, as a society, it seems to them in crucial respects pre-modern.[43] (Emphasis added.)

The Institute for Economic Affairs (IEA), a body not noted for its left-wing tendencies, published reports making the same points, drawing comparisons with Japan where social mobility and industrial relations are as different from the British as are efficiency and productivity. In particular it was pointed out that the authoritarian type of leadership favoured in Britain (where managers manage) was a thing of the past in Japan.[44] Another IEA report, which focused on the effects of the education system, notably private schools, on class divisions, concluded that

certain British Institutions and attitudes ... are incompatible with the needs of a modern, high technology economy ... If the British are determined to cling to them, then they must be ready to accommodate their aspirations towards material progress to the mediocrity of their economic performance.[45]

CULTURE

It will be useful to conclude this sketch of Britain in the 1970s by mentioning some of the broader cultural features discerned by commentators, for their particular relevance to the emergence of the political Right. The extraordinary tendency to institutional rigidity has just been mentioned. Pervasive attitudes manifest in confrontational industrial relations were seen as typical of a more generalised 'zero-sum' mentality institutionalised in the adversarial traditions of the Courts, in the government circles of Westminster,[46] and in the conduct of Parliament (indeed in the very construction of the Chamber of the House). The prevailing expectation was that in all matters of dispute there must be outright winners and losers, and compromise was equated with weakness.

In contrast to this was a tendency in some circles to reject competition altogether. It was easy for tabloid newspapers to lampoon zealots of this persuasion who would abolish school sports days on the grounds that they resulted in losing as well as winning (with more losing than winning). Some observers made the connection to the serious business of classrooms where increasingly pupils were not grouped by ability, for similar reasons. The doctrine of equality of esteem that motivated these developments was often associated with an iconoclastic rejection of traditional schools altogether, along with other established social institutions.[47] Industry and trade were particularly unpopular institutions of competition. Work in industry was regarded as unfit for human beings.[48] This attitude was acquired by the multitude from the example of its leaders.[49] The rejection of materialistic values and crass consumerism often went with a scorn for profit even in industry.

The cultural climate of the 1970s was imbued with many of the values of the 'Swinging Sixties'. One commentator portrayed these celebrated times as a collective fantasy of youth, energy, classlessness and an iconoclastic rejection of all tradition.[50] Self-assertiveness prevailed over self-discipline. In the view of critics of prevailing norms, by the 1970s, a generation had matured, many of whom rejected their parents' conventional values of job, traditional family and social responsibility, in favour of new conventional values that went with idleness, single parenthood and state Social Security payments. What was lacking was any sense of economic realism. The new liberal climate of the 1960s and 1970s was welcomed in some unlikely quarters. Samuel Brittan, an assistant editor of the *Financial Times*, approved of many basic aspects of the new permissive society. As he pointed out in 1973, 'doing your own thing' was really what classical market capitalism had always been about; and a capitalist market economy is a powerful agent for disrupting existing class barriers and official hierarchies.[51] The central dilemma facing the new individualism was that it depended on an economic system that was subject significantly to state control whereas only a capitalist market economy is capable of actually producing more of what people really want.

3   CONSENSUS AND THE END OF IT

It must be admitted that sometimes in a crisis only an existential upsurge of force will suffice to secure desired results. (Count Stauffenberg's briefcase could well have done the trick in 1944.) That is all that needs to be said here on the subject of violent revolution. Since the present subject is something else, parliamentary democracy, the problem to which it is an imperfect solution is how people who want to do very different things for very different reasons are to live together in the same place with the minimum of trouble. Either one or another group gets it all its own way, or a course is pursued which most can at least acquiesce in.

The crisis in the 1970s and the problems associated with it occurred in a political order formed by a consensus on policy sufficient to have provided political stability in Britain since 1945. It had four essential elements. Commitments to full employment, comprehensive state social welfare provision and foreign policy were the broadly agreed ends. The principal means was a mixed economy managed according to principles derived from the theory of John Maynard Keynes.[52] The experience of mass unemployment of the 1930s and a determination not to repeat it was common ground on employment policy. After the privations and sacrifices of the war, neither leading party was inclined to dispute the recommendations of the Beveridge Report on social welfare and the 'Equal Opportunities' Education Act of 1944. The consultants' teeth were filled with gold, as Aneurin Bevan said, to secure the National Health Service. Labour's decision to dissolve the Empire, beginning with the granting of independence to India in 1947, was also, surprisingly, endorsed by the Conservatives. After the basic industries of energy and transport had been nationalised by Labour as a matter of doctrine, the Conservatives found no sufficient reason to de-nationalise them.

The formula of Keynesian economics that is essential to the workings of a mixed economy is basically simple enough. Involuntary unemployment can be reduced if the demand for goods is increased. Demand will be increased if money is made available for the purpose. Governments are able to make money available. Ergo, when excessive unemployment threatens it can be staved off by government spending. The answer to the question of where the money comes from is that it comes from taxation and from borrowing. This is justified because people in work pay tax and make a bigger 'cake'; such deficit spending by government is by the theory an investment in high production. A reversal of the process will evidently have reverse effects. This, together with the axiom, 'full employment tends to produce higher wages and so prices, that is, inflation', provides governments with a theoretical macroeconomic lever for controlling inflation. Keynes's revolution in economic theory thus showed how governments could manage a national economy and if necessary 'spend themselves out of economic trouble'.

On the economy the Conservatives accepted more public ownership, government intervention and 'incorporation' of trade unions than true doctrine would prescribe. Labour set limits to the extent of public ownership, accepted the essential financial institutions of capital, accepted limitations to trade unions' legal privileges and actions, and limits to spending on social welfare. Politically, Conservatives accepted the results of the electoral system when they were adverse and inequitable to themselves, and when in government they had refrained on principle from reversing many of the measures they had resisted in opposition. Labour accepted constitutional forms that more often than not systematically disadvantaged the interests of their natural supporters, and upheld the sovereignty of Parliament and the rule of law, often against trade unions affiliated to the party. On social issues, Conservatives against much dogma accepted the goals of full employment, state welfare, and the principle of equal opportunity in education. Labour (in practice) tolerated substantial unemployment, accepted class-based private sectors of provision of health, education and welfare, and imposed limits to the standard of living of workers, through statutory wage restraint.

From 1948 on, Britain was evidently in economic difficulties by the various criteria of inflation, economic growth, the balance of trade and the value of sterling. The measures taken by governments of both parties to remedy problems were derived from the Keynesian theory that became orthodox in political, treasury and academic circles. The task was to produce a bigger economic cake while steering a course between the Scylla of inflation and the Charybdis of unemployment. When inflation tended to run away, the brake was applied to government spending, and wages (and sometimes prices) were controlled either by voluntary or statutory means in a variety of pay pauses and wage freezes.[53] When involuntary unemployment increased to worrying levels, and economic growth was pursued, the 'accelerator' was applied, either directly by government spending or indirectly through reducing interest rates on borrowing. A cycle of (failed) attempts to control unemployment and stimulate economic growth followed by (failed) attempts to stabilise inflation became recurrent. In a synoptic view, each time the cycle recurred the amplitude of the problems became greater, suggesting a runaway system yawing out of control. An analogy favoured by critics of

Keynesian theory was with drug addiction. As a junkie needs a fix, so the British economy needed bigger and bigger injections of government spending to fix its problems, but each time the withdrawal symptoms of inflation or unemployment were more acute. In the 1970s, both occurred together. By then the political and social problems caused by the chronic economic problems amounted to a crisis that undermined faith in the principal values and goals of the consensus, and in the theory underlying the attempts to control the stalled economy. The compromises and constraints inherent in the consensus were dissolving, and the circumstances of radical change established.

4 ALTERNATIVES TO FAILED CONSENSUS

SOCIAL DEMOCRACY: READJUSTED CONSENSUS

Faced with the failure of consensus policies (and leaving aside extra-parliamentary options) there were three possible alternative strategies. First, the option of interpreting the failure as a very unfortunate, but not necessary, consequence of consensus policy. Social Democrats looked to Sweden and Austria, where policies of full employment, a welfare state and a mixed economy continued to provide the basis of flourishing economies and stable humane societies. In this view the problems of the 1970s needed to be put in perspective by allowing for the effects of external conditions such as world recession, and then they could be seen to be solvable by applying the consensus methods more efficiently. Economic growth could be forthcoming if resources were deployed to private industry discriminately, in the manner of a laser, instead of indiscriminately, in a blunderbuss sort of way. On this view, if the pay norm of 5 per cent had been raised to 8 per cent in 1978, at least for the lowest-paid workers, then the winter of discontent could have been avoided, and better use of the other controls could have done the rest economically. Socially, problems could be solved by humanising politics and work, and promoting cross-class collaboration.[54] Drastic problems, however, seem to require drastic solutions, and the breakdown of consensus was welcomed both on the political Left and the Right as an opportunity to pursue policies and goals that had been frustrated by the compromises imposed by the consensus: policies more likely to solve the problems.

DEMOCRATIC SOCIALISM: THE OLD LEFT

The second option, democratic socialism, comprised the residual essentials of the political Left's compromised ideals. For the economy, state planning with either nationalisation of key financial institutions or the setting up of a state bank; for industry, nationalisation of the 'commanding heights' – 25 of the most profitable companies; for politics, an end to the moribund authoritarian traditions of the constitution with, instead, full accountability of government to Parliament and to the people and, in the workplace, self-management by workers; for society, an end to class privilege.[55] This shift leftward by dominant elements in the Labour Party was taken by one Conservative theorist to prove that the postwar consensus had not been a socialist one.[56] There was, however, no clear evidence that a large majority of the electorate favoured a radical socialist programme, especially a great extension of public ownership. Aneurin Bevan, keeper of Labour's socialist conscience, had rejected centrist planning.[57] Indeed, theoreticians of the Left, faced with evident public scepticism and the various manifest failures of socialist systems in Eastern Europe, turned to basic critical re-examination of socialism.[58] The two socialist options do not concern us directly here because they were not implemented.

THE NEW RIGHT: FREE-MARKET CONSERVATISM

The third option emerged in the Conservative Party: the New Right. Its policies were implemented and it requires further scrutiny. A full and detailed examination of the philosophical basis of the New Right is not necessary for the present purpose. A concise definition of New Right thinking is liable to mislead because there are so many elements and shifting emphases. Still, it is not too misleading to say simply that New Right thinking is a novel amalgam of traditional Tory-Conservatism and free-market liberalism. They share beliefs in hierarchy, a strong state, the rule of law, private property, individual freedom, and a scepticism about democracy. They differ in that traditional Tory-Conservatism is committed to community (of a paternalistic sort), state power, patriotism, tradition and the ultimate priority of social cohesion and stability, whereas free-market liberals give priority to individual autonomy, the rule of law even above the state, innovation, the primacy of the free market and the rights of private property over patriotism and social cohesion. The New Right analysis of the problems and its prescribed solutions is discussed in Chapter 5. Before that, some of its main sources can be identified.

Maurice Cowling helpfully distinguished five amalgamated elements of the New Right.[59] First, and by far the most catalytic and important, there was theoretical opposition to Keynesianism propagated from missionary institutes of free-market competition. Secondly, there was a substantive movement in the parliamentary Conservative Party that had been in evidence at least since 1959 when the Conservative Chancellor of the Exchequer, Peter Thorneycroft, and three junior ministers, including Enoch Powell, resigned because of their dissatisfaction with Keynesian consensus policy. Keith Joseph and Margaret Thatcher became the leaders of this movement in the 1970s. Thirdly, there were influential journalists notably on the *Telegraph* newspapers, the *Financial Times* and *The Times* who disseminated the doctrines of competitive markets and high Tory dogmatics. Fourthly, there was academic opposition of various kinds emanating notably from the London School of Economics (where the views were likely to be Whiggish-liberal) and Peterhouse College Cambridge (where the views were likely to be 'monastic' Tory-reactionary). The Conservative philosophy group developed to publish the *Salisbury Review*; its meetings were attended by Margaret Thatcher. Fifthly, there was a movement in education, publicised in a series of Black Papers, that generated wide controversy over the evident failure of the education system to preserve academic standards or to discipline pupils and over the priority given to social engineering before teaching and learning. A sixth element was the influence of single-issue pressure groups, such as the National Viewers' and Listeners' Association, devoted to establishing conservative standards of public morality and taste, and the Freedom Association (FA, formerly the National Association for Freedom [NAFF]), which works mainly through the legal defence of specific individuals against coercive majorities. All of these elements were interrelated and contributed in their various ways to the thinking of the New Right.

5 THE NEW RIGHT VIEW

AGENCIES AND IDEOLOGY[60]

Most political movements heralded as 'new' turn out on closer inquiry to be nothing of the sort. The New Right is a perfect example of this. Among the agencies promoting the 'new' views, the Economic

League was formed in 1920. In addition to prosyletising the virtues of capitalism, its activities include 'the assiduous monitoring of subversion' and the compilation of an employers' 'blacklist' of persons (secretly) deemed to be politically undesirable. AIMS was founded in 1942 as 'Aims for Industry'. Its influence on the New Right government has been described as 'preparing the menu for the kitchen cabinet' (*The Times*, 1 July 1987). The Mont Perelin Society is an international organisation formed in 1947 by Friedrich von Hayek, the most significant thinker of the New Right. Its original aims were to provide mutual aid for individualists and a forum for economic theories of the free market. It was on Hayek's suggestion that the Institute for Economic Affairs was established in 1957, with the main purpose of challenging predominantly Keynesian analysis of the economic system and to promote free-market solutions to Britain's problems.[61] The Centre for Policy Studies was established in 1974 by Keith Joseph and Margaret Thatcher in the immediate aftermath of the Conservatives' two election defeats in that year. Its philosophy and aims are similar to the IEA's but it was generally more disposed than the IEA to stress the morality of markets and, unlike the IEA, it is directly associated with the Conservative Party. The Adam Smith Institute, founded in 1977, was not a major influence in the emergence of the New Right, although its subsequent influence on government policy has been considerable. All of these agencies have contributed to New Right thinking and policy formation. Most of them have engaged strongly in public criticism of Keynesianism and policies derived from it; all of them have positively promoted free-market capitalism. The New Right in these ways provides an ideology that competes with alternatives for persuasive power, popular support, electoral success and legislative enactment. It is to quite other issues to do with ideas, their coherence, plausibility and truth, that the present inquiry is addressed.

NEW RIGHT IDEAS AND POLICY

New Right ideas include all the various elements identified earlier. Without doubt, however, economic ideas that challenged the Keynesian consensus were the main elements in the amalgam distinguishing it from consensus-Conservatism and Tory traditions. It is not too misleading therefore to take the economic analysis as central to the New Right thinking.[62] The most salient features of New Right ideas can be summarised as follows.

Economics

Inflation. The problem of inflation provides a convenient point of departure for the New Right analysis of Britain's chronic problems. Self-evidently, when consumer prices rise more money is paid for the same goods. The monetarist explanation offered by the New Right economics has two versions. The simple version, due to Milton Friedman, is that 'inflation always and everywhere is a monetary phenomenon'.[63] That is to say, inflation occurs when governments increase the money supply by the simple expedient of (literally) printing it, but without any commensurate increase in the quantity of goods. More money chasing the same amount of goods: this is a succinct definition of inflation. The more complicated version, due mainly to Friedrich von Hayek, adds a crucial causal explanation for the increase in the money supply.[64] Governments in effect 'print money' when wages are paid to workers who do not produce goods to the value of their income. Such wages add to the costs of goods and so to their (real) price. Evidently, when governments are committed as a matter of policy to maintaining full employment at any cost and, following Keynesian theory, inject money to stimulate demand, they cause inflation. This is only part of the picture, however. Government commitment to a full-employment policy unconnected to productivity is in practice the result of the influence of trade unions, which constitute a 'lobby' promoting a vested interest, not necessarily in the broad public interest. Trade unions cause inflation in other ways, by the use of their collective power, especially the legally protected power to strike. Trade unions secure for their members wages higher than real productivity warrants. British unions, in this view, have persistently acted so as effectively to increase the money supply disproportionately to production, and so have caused inflation. The cure for inflation according to Friedman is simply to reduce the money supply. The cure according to Hayek is more complicated. It is to reduce unproductive government-promoted spending, and to curtail the power of trade unions to secure uneconomic wages for their members. What constitutes an economic wage is a question that leads to the taproot of New Right thinking.

The Market, Income and Employment. The simple fact is that in economic affairs there is no objective way of establishing the money value either of goods or of the work that produced them, other than what people are prepared voluntarily to pay. This doctrine is at least as old as Adam Smith but was forgotten when, in the nineteenth century, governments began to intervene in the 'market' process. When people are allowed freely to choose what they buy and what they are prepared to pay, the goods available and their prices will always tend to reach some 'natural' level. If the price of labour and goods is so high that people are not willing to pay then the price will fall until they are. If demand increases and people are willing to pay more then the price will rise. In the long run the price will be set at a level that reflects supply and the relevant buyer-demand. Market prices and sales in this way determine income. If demand for goods is high, then demand for labour is high and incomes will be high. If there is no demand for goods then prices and sales may fall so low that it is impossible to subsist on the income. When this happens the market is indicating that there is not sufficient demand to warrant the production of the goods, and producers should redirect their efforts to producing what people do want. Problems arise when workers are paid incomes greater than the 'natural' market level, and when prices are lowered below their natural market level. One critical problem is that the information provided by market prices, about what people want and how much they want it, is distorted or lost. The provision of goods and employment, and the level of wages, can come to bear no relationship to real supply and demand. In so far as it matters whether what people do for a living satisfies a demand, and whether incomes are related naturally to what is done, then intervention by government in the market process is a disservice to free citizens.

The cure for unemployment cannot be for the government to employ people to do things for which there is no demand. The remedy for low incomes cannot be to provide incomes higher than the natural market rate. Workers who are no longer needed in one industry (shoe-making, say) should be redeployed to another where they are needed (glove-making, say). As to low incomes: either workers should transfer to jobs in which the market level of income is higher; or else they should acquire more realistic expectations of the income they can command in the market for their services. Problems in Britain have been created by governments struggling to keep people in employment for which there was inadequate demand, and also by a failure to instil in people sufficiently realistic (that is low) expectations of income. The single factor most inhibiting to the market's efficient operation is the trade union.

Competition, the Hidden Hand and Innovation. The market process of establishing prices and incomes does not work if there is a monopoly in either selling or buying. Buyers may be forced to pay more than they can afford if there is only one supplier who won't sell at a lower price and is not obliged to because the buyer has no alternative (other than doing without altogether). Sellers may be in a similar position if there is only one buyer who will not pay more and is not obliged to because the seller has no alternative (other than going out of business altogether). Governments can frequently put themselves in the advantaged monopoly position which clearly disadvantages citizens, whether they are consumers or producers. The only solution to the problem of monopolies is to ensure that there is more than one seller and more than one buyer, and preferably innumerable ones. Competition between sellers ensures that prices will not be higher than buyers can afford, otherwise they would buy from other sources. Sellers will tend to minimise prices to encourage sales of their products. This in turn is an incentive to reduce costs. Competition between buyers ensures that prices will not be lower than suppliers can afford.

The competitive market is, according to this New Right account, a mechanism that automatically adjusts the supply and the price of goods to the level of demand. The (competitive) market price is the essential information that determines the natural level of demand, and incomes. Each buyer has in mind only the utility of what is purchased. Each seller has in mind only the utility of their sale. None has in mind the overall adjustment of demand and supply of the market which may be international in its extent. Nevertheless supply and demand, prices and incomes, are adjusted to one another by an invisible hand.

Competitive markets have the vital character of encouraging people to develop innovative products, methods and services. A seller who by the exercise of ingenuity offers an improved product – or a product at a lower price – benefits from it with increased sales and profits. The buyer and the community at large also benefit. The competitive market in this way provides powerful incentives to innovation and efficiency. Enterprisers benefit themselves, but so do others. This is the only source of genuine and sustainable economic prosperity.

The problem in Britain has been that governments have intervened in and controlled the market process by creating state monopolies, by setting statutory minimum wage levels, so inflating costs and prices; and by imposing such punitive levels of taxation on profits and the incomes of enterprisers that the incentive to innovation is greatly diminished. This has adverse consequences, directly in the market, and eventually on employment. Everyone loses out in the process. The remedy lies in withdrawing government from the market, because the market works without intervention.

Politics

Authority and Government. A strong state is not the same thing as an all-pervasive one. The 'politicisation' of society, the tendency to transform all interests, activities and institutions into political ones, does not necessarily strengthen the state, which becomes over-bureaucratised and over-burdened. The proper scope of state authority in a free-market economy was, in Adam Smith's view, restricted to maintaining law and order, a sound currency, defence against external threats and provision of such public goods as it would not be profitable for individuals or smaller groups to provide. Within this limited scope the authority of the state should be uncompromised and unchallenged. This is consistent with the traditional Conservative view that established state authority should be submitted to unquestioningly because it provides the indispensable framework of any social life.[65] Change and state action itself should be minimal,[66] since normal economic and social life can be conducted only in a framework of strong and durable law supported by the unchallenged authority of the government. The role of government in society in this view is analogous to that of the referee in a game. The referee's authority cannot be challenged without subverting the game, and the best referee is the unobtrusive one who interferes least with the flow of play, and who certainly doesn't work towards some preferred and predetermined outcome.

The problem in Britain, in the view of the New Right, has been the over-politicisation of social life. The scope of state activity needs to be reduced. Compromises to the supremacy of state authority, particularly the incorporation of trade unions into government, should be curtailed. Government should impose its authority and the rule of law emphatically and unequivocally, but desist from the pursuit of particular social objectives, such as promoting equality.

Public Choice, Private Interests and Government Spending. A major obstacle to the solution of economic and social problems is the (Keynesian) presumption that problems, such as failure of industry and business, can be and must be remedied by government. This explains why, for example, governments intervene in the economy to reduce unemployment by subsidising failing companies or taking them into public ownership. The presumption that government does not suffer from problems the same as, or worse than, private institutions is highly suspect, according to the Virginia school of public choice theory subscribed to by the New Right.[67]

An economic analysis of political process shows a strong tendency for goods and services to be supplied more because they win votes or support for politicians and build empires for bureaucrats than because the wider public interest is served. A business might be given government aid because it is located in a politically salient place such as a marginal constituency. Similarly, influential pressure groups, such as trade unions or universities, may succeed in their demands for government expenditure that does not serve the wider public interest. In all such cases there is a tendency for the cost of the intervention to be discounted because it is not properly assessed or because it is not borne by beneficiaries of expenditure. It is evident that in a democracy even a majority can act against the basic liberties of minorities and individuals and against the long-term general interest when it votes for benefits the cost of which is borne by a minority. The propensity for politicians and bureaucrats to serve vested interests is all too evident in Britain, where industrial employers and employees alike have been subsidised by government and where public services (in health, social welfare and education) have expanded indefinitely at taxpayers' expense without check. By the 1970s public expenditure was commonly reported to be 50–60 per cent of GNP.[68] It is commonly the case that the government alternative is inherently inferior to the market, not because politicians and bureaucrats are corrupt, but because the institutional imperatives, structures, rules and procedures themselves are flawed. The remedy is to reduce drastically government expenditure and to privatise the provision of public goods as far as possible so as to expose the processes of both supply and demand to the economic discipline of the market. This is not a matter of dispute about the *ends* to be served but about the *means* to achieve them.[69] 'Government does not work, markets do' is an apt slogan for the New Right's economic policy.

Society

Social Issues. The big idea behind most New Right thinking on social issues is that individuals making rational choices in free markets of whatever kind will always produce better results than collective solutions arrived at by government planning.[70] Studies of market alternatives to state welfare, pensions, housing, medical care and education proved, to the satisfaction of the New Right at least, that they were more likely to solve recognised problems than the failed consensus policies for collectivist state provision. In housing, for example, it was evident that collectivist policies of rent controls and council housing subsidies, and the exclusion by local authorities of private builders from the supply of housing, had produced a shortage of housing for purchase and for rent. The market solution proposed was twofold, first to put an end to rent controls and subsidies, returning home-building to the market and thereby encouraging home-building for rent; and secondly to sell existing local authority houses to sitting tenants at discount prices in order to return such houses to the market, to promote home-ownership and to develop tenants' independence into the bargain. Significantly, this second measure had been proposed by a Labour MP.[71] In education, the problems of institutional isolation and inertia were soluble by shifting the locus of control from government to users. This meant for schools a shift to greater parent control and more involvement of local industry and business. For higher education it meant a shift to non-government sources of funding, including industry and commerce, and student loans instead of grants. Concern was repeatedly expressed by New Right politicians over the brain drain from research and development because of the great disincentives in Britain to excellence and enterprise.

Class. The New Right view of class is composed of two parts not obviously compatible. First, there is the Conservative presumption that class differences are the natural result of differences between people that are simply normalised in organic social and institutional arrangements. Secondly, there is the Liberal view that individuals of ability, energy and enterprise should if they choose be socially mobile in an open class system. The two views converge in the influential doctrines of Friedrich von Hayek. According to Hayek: 'All human differences ... create unfair advantages. But since the chief contribution of any individual is to make the best use of the accidents he encounters, success must to a great extent be a matter of chance.'[72] Roger Scruton explained how it is important for a society to ensure that as many intelligent persons should be confined to the lower orders ('of life') as the satisfaction of its members may require, and not 'siphon away by education intellectually gifted people to the point where they no longer wish to do what in fact they might otherwise have done willingly and well'.[73] Hayek links this insight with the question of political stability when he observes that: 'There are few greater dangers to political stability than the existence of an intellectual proletariat who find no outlet for their learning.'[74] The consequences for policy were to 'let our children grow tall and some grow taller than others'.[75]

Culture

The culture of consensus politics was informed by shared collectivist ethics. On the left, the egalitarian ideal of mutual responsibility and mutual aid prevailed. On the right, the aristocratic ideal of mutual responsibility and *noblesse oblige*. Each in its own way took altruistic concern for others' welfare to be the moral foundation of society: a foundation on the moral high ground of Christian theology. It is true that collective provision of welfare by the state may tend to encourage 'free-riding' or 'scrounging', but this for society at large is a matter of prudence rather than morality. There is still, according to the New Right, the basic problem of dependency created by collective provision in the welfare state, which negates the principle of individual autonomy essential to morality.

Against the ideal of altruistic (or 'compassionistic') mutual aid the New Right looked to Adam Smith for guidance and to self-interest. In a very influential passage in *The Wealth of Nations*, Smith suggests that:

> man has almost constant occasion for the help of his brethren, and it is vain for him to expect it from their benevolence only. He will be more likely to prevail if he can interest their self-love in his favour and show them that it is for their own advantage to do for him what he requires of them ... Nobody but a beggar chooses to depend chiefly upon the benevolence of his fellow citizens.[76]

The ideal of self-interest combines the moral virtue of autonomy with the practical virtue of promoting the common good, though unintentionally by way of the invisible hand that regulates mutually self-interested market transactions.[77] The moral high ground, in this view, has been too readily conceded to the mere good intentions of collectivism and mutual aid. Individualism and self-help are more in keeping with efficiency and even morality, though a duty of charity remains to be discharged by successful individuals. This shift in the moral ground is the most profound and important objective of New Right doctrine. Instead of the deadly levelling climate of collectivism and chronic guilt feelings about the needs of others, there is warrant for triumphant competitive individualism, enterprise, a buccaneering (or Samurai) spirit and a robust refusal of the strong either to shoulder the problems of the world or to be ashamed of not doing so.

The elevation of self-interest to moral primacy, together with individualism and liberty, risks debasing morality and liberty to licence. This tendency is counterbalanced by another derived from traditional Conservative doctrine. That is the view that self-interest and the exercise of liberty are constituted in social and cultural contexts. If this is understood then there is no conflict between individual freedom and social order because in Conservative individualism they are not contraries but are inseparable.[78] Indeed, Conservative individualism provides the necessary rationale for opposition to the permissive society in all its manifestations. Liberty is rescued from licence by the exercise of it within the intelligible conventions, rules and institutions that constitute an established order at any given time. Child-centred learning, expressive arts, alternative and classless lifestyles and such like, divorced from any cultural context, milieu, order or authority, are not really learning, art or living at all.

The Political Agenda

In the aftermath of electoral defeat in 1974, Keith Joseph succinctly summarised the issues from the New Right perspective. Compared to our neighbours in western Europe, Britain had the longest working hours, the lowest pay and lowest production per head. We had the highest taxes and the lowest investment. We had the least prosperity, the most poor and the lowest pensions. We had the largest nationalised sector and the worst labour troubles. Our education, our social services, our health services, our cultivated barbarisms, all gave cause for concern. We did not give right treatment to the disabled and good rewards to such groups as teachers and nurses. We were a disinvesting nation. The problem most generally was that we had had too much socialism. More specifically, we had relied too much on government: the public sector, like 'the lean kine', had been draining away the wealth created by the private sector; the trade unions had been unenlightened in their pursuit of self-interest; and we had conducted a vendetta against free enterprise and profit.[79]

Against the Keynesian consensus, it was argued that the aim of full employment was incompatible with the control of inflation, and the welfare state was costing more than the economy could support. Keynesian solutions had failed. Wage controls always proved ineffective and price control without wage control was not sensible. Demand-led growth had proved to be a will-o'-the-wisp. Nothing less than the abandonment of the consensus and a new, right, direction could solve Britain's problems.

6 THE NEW RIGHT ESTABLISHED IN THE CONSERVATIVE PARTY

New Right, free-market, views had had some currency in the Conservative Party since the 1950s, though they were excluded from the mainstream and intractable believers excluded from office. After defeats in two general elections in 1974, the party could not avoid major self-examination. The leadership of Edward Heath was called into question by MPs of a New Right persuasion. He had embarked on a programme of New Right-style reforms in 1970 (this had been drawn up at a seminal policy conference in Selsdon Park while the party had been in opposition). But after two years in office, he had abandoned the programme 'at the first sound of gunfire' when bankruptcies multiplied and unemployment increased. MPs led by Keith Joseph challenged Heath's leadership and what they believed were the failed policies he adhered to. When Keith Joseph proved in the process to be an unlikely leader of the party (because of impolitic remarks about eugenics), Margaret Thatcher replaced him as the leader of the New Right tendency. Her challenge to Edward Heath's leadership was unprecedented in the Conservative Party, being the first under the formal procedures for the parliamentary party to elect its leader (which had replaced the antediluvian method of 'soundings' that had been the norm until 1964). On 11 February 1975 Margaret Thatcher was elected leader of the Conservative Party, and New Right ideas and polices were put on the political agenda of a 'party of government' in Britain.

Margaret Thatcher's election as leader was a remarkable event in many ways (not least the fact that she was the first woman to be elected to the leadership of a major party and so potentially the first woman to be Prime Minister in Britain). Her gender was, apparently, doubly remarkable in so far as it was the Conservative Party that had done a radical thing in electing a woman. This fact proved to be less remarkable than it seems at first sight. The reason for this is that her gender was scarcely an issue. It was said at the time that Margaret Thatcher benefited greatly from the fact that she was not Edward Heath. His personality was not congenial to everybody and he had led the party to two election defeats. MPs were reacting against Heath's personality, and the fact of electoral defeat. This allows a different construction to be put on the emergence of the New Right from the one suggested in popular histories of events. Conservatives were not moving positively to a New Right position, any more than they were to a feminist one.[80] Consequently, in the first ballot of the leadership election, Margaret Thatcher did not have an overall majority of votes, nor was her margin over Edward Heath a large one – a balance of only six (the result was Margaret Thatcher 130 votes, Edward Heath 119 and Hugh Fraser 16). Only after Edward Heath's resignation was her victory (over William Whitelaw) decisive. The answer to the question of how far the New Right ideas prevailed in the Conservative Party in 1975 can be looked for in other indicators. Most of the shadow cabinet was opposed to her and (in so far as they were an issue) the new ideas; indeed her only strong supporter was Keith Joseph.[81] The chairman of the party did not support her. The former Prime Minister, Alec Douglas-Home, who still had considerable personal influence, was against her. Perhaps more significantly, Conservative Party Central Office estimated that the great majority of Conservative Association members in the country (70 per cent) supported Edward Heath. Indeed, Margaret Thatcher and her ideas were hardly known among Conservative activists in the country. This is not so surprising, considering that she was a stranger to many of her fellow MPs as well. After 15 years in parliament the new leader needed to introduce herself to her own back-benchers,[82] as well as to the constituency associations. All of this was reflected in 'informed opinion' among political journalists and commentators, which regarded her as a rank outsider in the leadership election with little chance of success.

It is doubtful whether Conservative MPs, not to mention ordinary members of Conservative Associations, knew of and agreed with the New Right ideas Margaret Thatcher now stood for. She later spoke of the 'iron that entered her soul' during her experience of strikes and crises in the cabinet between 1972 and 1974, but in 1978 Ian Gilmour was still confidently explaining that the Conservative Party did not believe in the infallibility of capitalism, was in no sense wedded to an ideology, and that it must shun not only all extremism but also doctrines that are the mirror image of those of its opponents.[83] With the benefit of hindsight it is possible to see quite clearly that the election of Margaret Thatcher to the leadership of the Conservative Party was more like a political aberration than an indication of a significant and massive shift of ideas. Whether or not the ideas were objectively what Britain needed is another matter.

7 SOME RIGHT TURNS

An old saying has it that if you aren't a socialist when you're young then you have no heart, and if you aren't a Conservative when you're old then you have no sense. A surprising number of prominent figures of the New Right would agree; they had embraced socialism in one form or another in the course of their lives but rejected it later. Alfred Sherman, the first chairman of the Centre for Policy Studies, had been a Marxist and fought on the Republican side in the Spanish Civil War. Kenneth Minogue, a director of the Centre for Policy Studies, was a student Marxist in Australia, a sophomoric socialist (he later explained to the tabloid press that left-wing women were easier to bed). Rhodes Boyson, an editor of the Black Papers on education, had been a Labour councillor. One prominent tabloid journalist to the New Right, William Woodrow-Wyatt, had been a junior minister in a Labour government. Caroline Cox was disabused of socialism at the Polytechnic of North London before entering New Right orbits. John Vaizey, a distinguished economist, was a Labour councillor. Alan Walters, a leading professor of monetarism, was an ex-Labour voter, as was David Young before he became a successful property developer and special adviser to the Conservative Prime Minister.[84]

One significant group of converts to the New Right thinking published their views in 1978 in a volume edited by a Conservative MP, Patrick Cormack, and it is instructive to mention some of them here.[85] Some of their retrospective views after twelve years will be discussed in Part 2. These authors included Reg Prentice, a Labour minister until his resignation in 1976; Professor Graham Knight of Cambridge University, a former Labour supporter; Alun Gwynne

Jones (Lord Chalfont), a former Labour Minister of State; Kingsley Amis the author, another one-time Labour supporter; Edward Pearce, sometime Treasurer of the Oxford University Labour Club and Labour parliamentary candidate; Paul Johnson, who worked for and edited the distinguished left-wing periodical the *New Statesman* for 15 years until 1970; and Max Beloff, Gladstone Professor of Government and Public Administration at Oxford University and an active member of the Liberal Party.

Such a variety of individuals inevitably provides a wide variety of views, but there were reiterated themes which illuminate both the intellectual attraction of New Right Conservative thinking for people who had been strongly identified with the Left and the corresponding repulsions of the Labour position. First, there was the theme of individualism: whereas the old Labour Party had been tolerant of, indeed devoted to, the value of human individuals, the drift in the Labour Party had been strongly towards uncompromising collectivism, and closed-shop legislation proved this. Secondly, there was the concern to promote excellence, especially in education and academic research: had not Aneurin Bevan said that nothing was too good for the working class? Instead, the Labour Party had become obsessed with a levelling-down sort of egalitarianism, especially in education, which had been debased to something more like social engineering. Closely connected with individualism and excellence was a third concern, with freedom: in the past the Labour Party had tried to increase freedom by education and social welfare, by an enlightened attitude to civil liberties and, in external matters, by maintaining strong defences. By the 1970s, conversely, the Labour Party's actions were of a more coercive authoritarian Eastern-European kind. Worst of all was the intention to bring about irreversible changes in British society (as declared in Labour's programme 1976), and a willingness to diminish substantially the commitment to strong defences. A fourth concern was with private enterprise. It had always been possible in good conscience to support the Labour Party when it accepted a substantial place for private enterprises, alongside state-owned ones. By 1976, however, the Labour Party Annual Conference received a resolution from Newham proposing that the state should nationalise 250 private companies which together earned 80 per cent of the national income and to nationalise the banks and insurance companies. Paul Johnson believed that the aim was eventually to make self-employment impossible. Many of the writers expressed concern about the rule of law and, related to it, personal style and conduct. The old Labour Party had proved its commitment to the established institutions of Parliament and the law as its chosen means of achieving its openly declared political and social objectives. This commitment was reflected in the character and conduct of Labour leaders (such as the exemplary Fenner Brockway), who were congenial and humane. In the 1970s the Labour Party did not demur at the most militant trade union action, indeed even a respected 'moderate' cabinet minister like Shirley Williams was willing to join picket lines during a violent strike at Grunwick. Labour councillors were prepared openly to defy the courts, while leaders of the party would not condemn them but would seek to indemnify them retroactively. Instead of the benevolent pacifist Fenner Brockway, the changed spirit of the Labour movement became embodied in the person and style of Dennis Skinner, who was described as the Beast of Bolsover. As perceived by disillusioned former supporters such as Edward Pierce, the changed Labour Party was the home of 24-hours-a-day, humourless, perpetual-motion zealots who alienated traditional Labour Party activists.

Perceiving a perilous economic, political, social and cultural state of the nation and an evident inability of the Labour Party to provide tolerable solutions, these one-time opponents of Conservatism turned Right and joined Conservative MP Patrick Cormack in looking optimistically to Margaret Thatcher and to the New Right road she offered to a solvent, stable and free society. In this they may have been like many others who were concerned about the same problems, experienced similar disillusionment and sought the same remedy. That remains to be seen and is the subject of further discussion in Part 2.

Before leaving this excursus it is worth noting the personal histories of the 'right turns'. The project was, significantly, inaugurated in a London gentleman's club, the Reform. Six of the eight contributors had attended public schools, and the other two (prewar) grammar schools. Seven of the eight were university graduates, six of them from Oxbridge. One, Hugh Thomas, had been president of the Cambridge University Conservative Association. The one non-university man, Alun Gwynne Jones, had been a career soldier after leaving school. Whatever else might be said of this articulate group of disillusioned Labour supporters, their life experience was inevitably very different from that of the Labour Party's working-class constituency. In this connection the observations of Adam Smith and John Stuart Mill should be recalled, to the effect that no one is in a better position to know the circumstances of a person's life than the person themself.

It is salutary therefore to reflect on the lives of most ordinary people, and on the substance of the previous commitment of the Right Turns to the values they rejected. As the idol of Paul Johnson's youth, Aneurin Bevan, wrote: 'Disillusionment is a bitter fruit reaped only by the intellectually arrogant.'[86]

8   THE ELECTION TO POWER OF THE NEW RIGHT

THE PRELUDE: THE WINTER OF DISCONTENT

An atmosphere of crisis began to mount in the winter of 1978 when for the first time ever members of the Fire Brigades Union went on strike for higher wages. In the spring of 1978 the recommendations of a 'top people's' salary review had been implemented, with increases of over 30 per cent for senior civil servants, heads of nationalised industries, forces chiefs and judges. The police were awarded a pay increase of 40 per cent. For other workers, including public service workers, the norm of 5 per cent was still imposed. Significantly the Conservatives voted in December 1978 against the continuation of the 5 per cent limit on wages in the public sector. In January 1979 local authorities were instructed by the Labour government to restrict wage increases for public sector workers to single figures when 15 per cent was common in the private sector and inflation was 9.3 per cent. The Labour minister, Roy Hattersley, told the unions that a price freeze was just not possible. Following resolutions in October 1978 at the Trades Union Congress to reject the government's pay norms, members of numerous unions went on strike. The winter of discontent that ensued has already been referred to, with the number of days lost in 1979 setting the postwar record of 29.5 million. When Labour Prime Minister Callaghan, on his return to Britain in snowbound, strikebound January 1979, was asked about the crisis and was reported to have replied 'Crisis? What Crisis?', the nation was outraged.

THE CIRCUMSTANCES

Edward Heath's failure to rally decisive popular support for his government against the mineworkers in 1974 proved to be a watershed. After that many observers, particularly on the Marxist Left, perceived public opinion to be moving decisively in the direction of the New Right thinking. Real life problems and the New Right rhetoric of authoritarian populism were bringing the forward march of Labour to a halt. Other factors were identified as affecting the outcome of the general election of 1979. The traditional electoral base of the Labour Party in the working class had been eroded (through disproportionate mortality rates among the 1945 generation of stalwart supporters, and with general affluence). There had been growing disillusionment with the state services associated with the Labour Party (because of the cumulative effect of everyone's numerous bad experiences in health care, housing, transport and problems *ad infinitum*). The policies of the Left, like many of those who framed them, were out of touch with the views of most ordinary people.

By the time the general election was held on the 3 May 1979 it was possible for the New Right Conservatives to exploit a pervasive climate of failure, disillusionment and crisis. As their election manifesto proclaimed: 'This election is about the future of Britain – a great country which seems to have lost its way.... today ... [it] is faced with its most serious problems since the Second World War ... During the industrial strife of last winter confidence, self-respect, common sense and even our common humanity were shaken. At times this society seemed on the brink of disintegration ... We cannot go on, year after year tearing ourselves apart in increasingly bitter and calamitous industrial disputes.'

THE RESULT

The result of the election was a clear victory for the Conservatives, who obtained a majority over all other parties.

TABLE 3 ELECTION RESULT 1979

	Number of votes recorded (as % of electorate)	Members of Parliament elected (numbers)
Conservative	33	339
Labour	27.7	268
Liberal	10.4	11
All others	4.8	17

TABLE 4 MANUAL AND NON-MANUAL WORKERS' SUPPORT
FOR POLITICAL PARTIES (%)

		Labour	Conservative
Manual:			
October	1974	57	24
General election	1979	50	35
Non-manual:			
October	1974	25	51
General election	1979	23	60

Source: Heath et al (1985), cited in King (1987) p131

The significance of the results shown in Table 3 is in the clear majority of MPs returned four years after the New Right leadership had been established in the party. The significance of the data shown in Table 4 lies mainly in the substantial loss of support for Labour among manual workers (down 7 per cent) and the even larger increase of support for Conservatives from that group (up 11 per cent). It was remarkable that only half the manual workers voted for Labour. In 1966 it had been 69 per cent. It was also remarkable that the swing of manual workers' votes to the New Right Conservative Party, at 11 per cent, was even greater than the swing of non-manual workers' votes, at 9 per cent. This data evidently leaves no room for doubt that the New Right ideas and policies found a receptive audience, especially of people who had previously been regarded as 'natural' Labour supporters. No more evidence seems necessary to establish the case for the electoral success of the New Right.

THE PROGRAMME: THE FIVE TASKS

The Conservative election manifesto of 1979 set out its proposed programme. It provided 'a broad framework for the recovery of our country, based not on dogma, but on reason, on common sense, above all on the liberty of the people under the law'. More specifically an agenda comprising five tasks was given, and these provide one set of convenient criteria for assessing the record of New Right in office. The tasks were:

1. To restore the health of our economic and social life, by controlling inflation and striking a fair balance between the rights and duties of the trade union movement.
2. To restore incentives so that hard work pays, success is rewarded and genuine new jobs are created in an expanding economy.
3. To uphold parliament and the rule of law.
4. To support family life, by helping people to become home owners, raising the standard of their children's education, and concentrating welfare services on the effective support of the old, the sick, the disabled and those who are in real need.
5. To strengthen Britain's defences, and work with our allies to protect our interest in an increasingly threatening world.

The ambitions of Margaret Thatcher were much higher than these specifically economic and political goals. Nothing less was required than the creation in the country of a wholly new attitude of mind.[87] Ultimately it was not a matter of economics but of morality. As she explained to the Zurich Economic Society in 1977:

> The economic success of the Western world is a product of its moral philosophy and practice; the economic results are better because the moral philosophy is superior. It is superior because it starts with the individual, with his uniqueness, his responsibility, his capacity to choose.[88]

The moral foundation of the programme involved rejecting the egalitarian 'politics of envy' and pursuing instead individual freedom. Whether individualism is morally superior, whether economic success is the test of moral superiority, whether the country has acquired a whole new attitude of mind – these are the most fundamental questions to ask of the record of the New Right.

9   CAVEAT EMPTOR

What has been presented thus far has been a conventional descriptive account of the circumstances that led to the emergence of the New Right, New Right thinking, the manner of its achieving power; and its programme of action. Before buying this yarn at the recommended retail price it will be instructive to take a closer look at some reasons for supposing that it may be flawed, perhaps grossly so.

POLITICAL CHANGE

A direct inference could be drawn from the fact of electoral success to the superiority or greater persuasiveness of the ideas of the victorious party. But there is another way of viewing the matter. Everyone knows that voters periodically switch their political allegiances. Periodic or cyclic change might be explained in a variety of ways,[89] two of which are relevant here. Change may be the determinable result of numerous factors significant to changing ideas converging at a particular time (a 'conjuncture'). Or it may be due to mundane factors with people opting for change for no particular positive reason of new ideas. Faced with chronic problems people may be, in a mood of exasperation or hope, prepared for someone else to have a try at solving them. Such change is a triumph of hope over experience, not evidence of the positive superiority or persuasive force of ideas and values.

The Conservatives' election victory in 1979 was achieved with the support of just 33 per cent of the electorate, the lowest level since 1945 (with the exception of the recent defeats of 1974). Support from manual workers at 35 per cent was not unprecedented, being similar to what it was in 1951 (34 per cent) and 1970 (33 per cent), during the heyday of the consensus. There is no convincing evidence from electoral results or opinion polls that public support shifted positively to the Conservative Party.[90] Such a view is highly implausible. An alternative view, that voters were looking for change without concerning themselves very much about the option they were choosing, is highly plausible. Indeed, Margaret Thatcher herself recognised this when she told her party conference after the victory that: 'Some of (the people who elected us [had]) taken the ... step ... more in hope than belief.'[91] Most of the rest were Conservative voters on 'reflex'. There is little need to look into the bowels of political culture for the most plausible explanations of the Conservatives' electoral success in 1979.

THE PRESTIGE FACTOR

Britain's chronic economic problems are attributed by doom-sayers to almost any factor but one very decisive one: the financial cost of prestige. The Conservative historian Robert Blake suggested that, although Britain had ceased to be a world power in 1945, for another ten years the country (or rather its rulers) suffered from the illusion that she still was.[92] In fact the illusion, really a delusion, continued into the 1970s and still exercises a powerful influence. Its manifestations are various. They all contribute to the chronic problems. They are largely ignored.

The Cost of War

An Adam Smith Institute author suggested that Britain's war losses were not as great as Germany's so the postwar economic record should have equalled the Germans'.[93] This neglects the contribution made to German recovery by the Americans for strategic reasons, whereas American Marshall Aid to Britain, perceived as a victorious imperial power, was quickly curtailed after the war. Even more significant was the price the Americans exacted for the wartime lend-lease agreement that Winston Churchill had called 'the most unsordid act in history'. In fact the price included Britain surrendering valuable world markets, including South America, to the United States. In addition Britain surrendered patent rights and royalties on many important technological innovations, including radar, antibiotics, jet engines and nuclear power. As Harold Wilson said, had Churchill been able to insist on adequate royalties for these inventions, both our wartime and our postwar balance of payments would have been very different. When lend-lease was ended, Britain was obliged to negotiate a loan from the Americans which placed a burden of national debt repayments on the British economy into the twenty-first century. Britain was handicapped in international competition by its prestigious victory in the war.[94]

Defence

Britain's defence expenditure reflects national delusions of grandeur rather than realistic priorities. Only the superpowers spend a greater proportion of their national income on defence (Israel is a very peculiar exception). Typically, following the imperatives of prestige, Anthony Eden volunteered in 1954 to station considerable British forces in Germany for fifty years in order to retrieve the European Defence Community. This was presented to our allies 'as an unconditional free gift of military aid for half a century' with no regard to the cost to British taxpayers, the balance of trade, or its effect on Britain's economy.[95] Some comparisons with defence expenditure and investment expenditure of other countries in relation to GNP and population illustrate the nature of the problem (see Table 5).

TABLE 5 DEFENCE AND INVESTMENT EXPENDITURE 1974

	Military expenditure (% GNP)*		Industrial investment per capita ($)+
Britain	5.24	Sweden	988.9
West Germany	3.58	Japan	775.8
Sweden	3.10	West Germany	744.0
Japan	.83	Britain	560.7

Sources: * US Arms Control and Disarmament Agency (1976); World Military Expenditures and Arms Transfers 1965–1974, in Labour Party Defence Study Group 1977.[96]
+ United Nations Department of Economic and Social Affairs Statistic Office, Statistical Yearbook 1975; OECD, *Main Economic Indicators December*, 1978.

Evidently Britain's defence expenditure was, and is still, disproportionately large and, by international comparisons, in inverse ratio to its investment in industry. Japan in particular has benefited from its extraordinarily low expenditure on defence, which is correlated with correspondingly high investment in industry. As one author from the Institute for Economic Affairs observed in 1974: 'If we consider how much first-class scientific, industrial and administrative talent has been applied in Britain to defence since the war, we may gain some inkling of what this has meant to the economy.'[97] Britain is handicapped by defence expenditure incurred from delusions of grandeur, not realistic priorities.

Sterling

Since the end of the war, governments have struggled to maintain the exchange value of the pound in order to sustain sterling as an international reserve currency. In 1958 Andrew Shonfield described the position graphically: 'Britain, a gentleman banker much reduced in circumstances, with clients who continue to deposit their money with the firm largely because of tradition and habit, has to keep up appearances by handing out certain amounts of largesse each year. Meanwhile, because of the expense which the banker cannot any longer afford, there is no money to pay the bill for repairs on his own house, which is now in danger of falling down.'[98] Governments repeatedly resorted to borrowing from international bankers in order to maintain the value of sterling: in 1964, 1966, 1968, 1969 and again, as recorded in the demonology of the New Right, in 1976. At that time the Prime Minister, James Callaghan, said 'I would love to get rid of the reserve currency – from Britain's point of view I see no particular advantage in being a reserve currency at all.'[99] Alas, in 1990, while the reasons for divesting itself of sterling multiplied in new forms, Britain's economy continued to be burdened by the demands the reserve currency makes on it.[100]

Prestige has sometimes been exercised effectively for worthy ends. British diplomacy has influenced events in a way that has preserved peace and stability and thereby secured the wellbeing of other nations. Governments have at times had ethical motives for committing the country to expenditure for such purposes. It was then a question of having to afford the economic costs. But the effects on the lives of most ordinary people have not been adequately assessed. Worse than that, working people, including, by any reckoning, the vast majority of trade unionists, have been reproached and vilified for their failure to out-produce the workforces of other countries, as if their leaders had imposed on them no financial burden of prestige.

THE 'FAILURE' OF SOCIALISM

Britain's difficulties, especially economic ones, are routinely attributed by the New Right to the intrinsic deficiencies of socialism. The bankruptcy of socialism was long taken by the New Right as proved on the evidence of Eastern Europe. The economic weakness, political repression, social conformism and cultural rigidity endemic there were taken to be the inevitable consequences of the socialist theory by which it was supposedly governed. Fear that the Labour Party was moving in the 1970s towards the Eastern European model of state ownership of industry and planned economies was one of the main impulses to New Right thinking. Since the autumn of 1989 the Soviet bloc of nations including Russia has quickly abandoned the political forms of state socialism and moved towards market economies along with commensurate social and cultural changes. It is widely assumed that the request by Russia for financial aid during this period was proof that socialism had failed, and failed because it is unsound in principle.

Without denying any of the facts, it is necessary to keep in mind some factors that are easily neglected in the excitement of momentous events. First, it is as well to recall that Soviet state socialism, especially the Stalinist variety that prevailed until 1985, bears the same relationship to Marx's teachings as Torquemada's Spanish Inquisition bore to the teachings of Jesus Christ; that is, very little, and none directly. It bore none at all to the rich variety of other variations of socialism including Marxist humanism. Secondly, Stalin's doctrine of socialism in one country, with its awful consequences for Russians, was born out of post-revolutionary events including the landing in Russia of British and American forces. The circumstances in Russia reflect its national history as much as its political philosophy. Nations like the United States and Britain which haven't suffered the effects of two world wars on their home soil see things in a more complacent light than Russians who suffered the loss of more lives than all the other combatants. Russians have had good reason to be defensive. And the cost of defence proved to be destructive of their economy and way of life.

It is instructive to recall some basic facts about the Russian economy. In 1917 the GNP of Russia was just 15 per cent of that of the United States. The effects of the revolution and counter-revolution were such that by 1920 the GNP was reduced to 2 per cent of that of the United States.[101] Subsequently the Russian economy suffered the effects of a German invasion (with massive industrial dislocation) and a protracted cold war that imposed an embargo on trade in advanced technology from the West. In these circumstances the Russian economy generated parity with the United States in arms, and in nuclear and space technology. The financial cost was in absolute terms astronomical and, as was revealed in 1990, amounted to 25 per cent of the GNP, compared to 6 per cent of that of the United States.[102] In 1988 the GNP of the Soviet Union was estimated at between $1,900 billion and $2,487 billion; about 40 per cent of the United States' $4,425 billion GNP.[103] Evidently, despite hot and cold wars and trade embargoes, the Russian economy expanded approximately twentyfold between 1921 and 1988 in relation to the United States. Growth of that order is unheard of in Western economies. It cannot be denied that Soviet Eastern Europe was a model of a repressive and dismal society. But this had a lot to do with Russia's being a siege economy developed from nothing in a hostile climate. It is far from obvious how much, in the circumstances, it had to do with socialism. Significantly, the recent changes effected in Russia and Eastern

Europe have been endorsed and promoted by the Soviet Communist Party during Mikhail Gorbachev's administration. This fact confounds New Right thinkers who supposed that it was obvious that a dictatorship would not be transformed into a democracy without a system of private capital.[104]

DECLINE, RELATIVE AND ABSOLUTE

Most assessments of Britain's economic performance derive their pessimism from statistics showing that Britain's position is deteriorating relative to other countries, notably by the measures of rate of increase of GNP and share of world exports in manufactures. Yet there has been continuous economic growth since statistics were first recorded. Between 1855 and 1945 GNP increased by an average of 1.7 per cent annually. Between 1945 and 1975 it increased by an average of 2.5 per cent annually.[105] It was simply growing more rapidly in other countries, most of which were starting from a much lower economic base. Similarly the steady decline of Britain's share of world exports in manufactures started from a position where Britain was the only significant exporter of manufactures and continues through the progressive industrialisation of the world. The reduction in the share of world trade might be a cause for great concern if there were also an absolute reduction in production or in trade but there has not been. An industrialised country would be likely to have a share of world trade roughly commensurate with its size among other industrialised nations. Nobody uses this criterion. Two old-fashioned philosophical issues attach to the 'problem' of slow economic growth. First, there are excellent ecological reasons for questioning the almost universal assumption that continuous and unlimited economic growth is necessarily a good thing.[106] Secondly, there is a very strong case for the view that there is far more to life than getting and spending. As Bernard Nossiter has forcefully argued, the British propensity to prefer leisure to hive-like activity in factories and offices may be, in human terms, more like a solution than the problem it is supposed to be by indefatigable politicians and professional enthusiasts of competitive markets in consumer goods[107] (most of whom work neither in factories nor in offices themselves).

THE CONVENTIONAL WISDOM CORRECTED

The conventional account rendered above of the circumstances in which the New Right emerged is misleading. It is necessary, therefore, to correct various errors and misconceptions before judicious assessment of Britain's problems can be made together with the New Right solutions to them.

The Economy

*Inflation.*It was claimed that inflation in Britain in the 1970s was the highest in the industrial world. In fact Japan experienced the same level of inflation in 1974 and for the same reason, a fivefold increase in oil prices. Continuing high levels of inflation in Britain in 1975 are attributed to Labour government policies, whereas, according to the New Right's own preferred monetarist theory, they were the effect of large (26 per cent) increases in the money supply by Edward Heath's Conservative government in 1972 and 1973. Largely as a result of trade unions volunteering to restrict wage increases for four years, inflation in 1978, the last year of Labour government, was 8.3 per cent compared to 24.2 per cent in 1975.[108]

Profitability. It was claimed that in the 1970s the Labour government pursued a 'vendetta' against profit. In fact companies' real profits (net rates of return on capital) increased by 100 per cent, from 4 to 8 per cent between 1975 and 1978 (reversing a precipitous decline between 1972 and 1974 under the Conservatives). Britain's banks were easily the most profitable in the world .[109]

Unproductive Employment. An influential analysis by Eltis and Bacon claimed to establish that there were too few producers in Britain and too many people employed in services. New Right politicians made a similar claim: that public-sector employment (of 'lean kine') was an unproductive burden on the productive, meaning the private, sector. The presumption that people in employment other than industry or commerce are an unproductive burden is simply an error. For example teachers of engineers and businesspeople are indispensable to their productive capacity as are the nurses and doctors who maintain their health (and so on). Most persons who are employed in the provision of services, such as, typically, part-time women workers, are not suitable candidates for full-time jobs in industry and commerce. Moreover, the general trend in other advanced industrial nations, such as the United States and Sweden, is also for employment to grow in the service sector and diminish in the manufacturing sector.[110]

Public Expenditure and Taxation. A factor that contributed very strongly to the sense of crisis in the 1970s was the repeated claim that public spending in Britain had risen to intolerable levels of up to 60 per cent of gross domestic product (GDP), and that this was placing an intolerable burden on taxpayers and was a major factor contributing to economic problems generally, by siphoning off money from productive uses and by removing financial incentives to individual enterprisers. The main basis for these claims was data published in the Treasury Blue Book of 1974. There were errors in the statistics which were later corrected. The corrected figures showed that public spending in Britain was about average for European and OECD (Organisation for Economic Co-operation and Development) countries. At its highest in 1975 it was 46.9 per cent of GDP, compared to 47.1 in West Germany, 48.2 in Denmark, 48.9 in Luxemburg, 49 in Sweden and 55.9 in the Netherlands. The level was progressively reduced to 43.7 per cent in 1978 when only Greece, Spain and Finland among European countries spent a lower proportion of GDP on social security. Outlay on welfare in Britain at 7.7 per cent of GDP was substantially lower than average for the other nine Common Market countries, at 10.6 per cent, and less even than the free-market United States at 8 per cent. Taxation in 1975, though relatively high at 36.8 per cent, was lower than in France (36.9), Denmark (43.1), Norway (44.7) and Sweden (46 per cent). Since these countries were more prosperous than Britain, evidently public expenditure and taxation were not decisive factors distinguishing them from the British.[111]

Strikes: Incidence and Consequences. New Right politicians and their supporters took it as axiomatic that the record of strikes in Britain was extraordinarily bad. It was said that in the 1970s the unions were more militant than ever before. This was far from the truth. Although many days were lost in strikes in 1979 and 1972, many more days were lost in 1926, 1921, 1919 and 1893, when the workforce was much smaller. International comparisons show that Britain has no more strikes than the average for industrial nations, and often far fewer than some countries with much higher productivity, such as Canada, Australia and the United States. As one professor of industrial relations has observed:

> The evidence suggests, then, that Britain is not unusual in the dimensions of its strike record but in the attention which the latter attracts ... The direct consequences of strikes are no more serious

in Britain than in other countries; it is not so much the strikes as the hue and cry which they attract which is the real problem.[112]

It has also been suggested that it is not the total number of days lost in strikes that causes economic damage, but the effect of prolonged strikes by large numbers of workers in mass-production industries which occurs in Britain.[113] This argument misses the point that strikes in the United States and Canada are usually of this sort also.

Strikes: Causes. It is widely believed that strikes are caused by irresponsible trade union militancy. Hayek attributes half of strikes to a pursuit of the closed shop. The Royal Commission on Trades Unions reported that in the period between 1964 and 1966 just 1.3 per cent of days lost in strikes were in pursuit of the closed shop. In fact major strikes, of the sort that generate belief about trade unions being an uncontrollable power in the land, were likely to be the last resort of workers with no record of militancy, in pursuit of wage claims after incomes had been eroded over many years to bare subsistence levels or below. In 1966, for example, the National Union of Seamen's strike was the first by them since 1911. The dispute was about employers enforcing a 56-hour working week for £60 a month. The miners' strike in 1972 was the first for many years, and was caused by the fact that wages had been eroded to the point where this most hard, dangerous and dirty work was paid only the average for manual work. Adam Smith knew that wages two to three times the norm were equitable for mineworkers, but this had been forgotten in 1972 and mineworkers' claims were repeatedly ignored until strike action was resorted to. Again in the events of legend in 1974, mineworkers' claims were dismissed, although they reflected prevailing market conditions (including oil and labour shortages). The union went to that strike by due process and a ballot of members showed that an overwhelming majority of 81 per cent favoured strike action. The Trades Union Congress undertook to treat the miners as a special case, and not to use any wage increases awarded to them as a criterion for other union claims. This offer was rejected by Edward Heath's government and the consequences proved not to be advantageous to them. In 1979 the most conspicuous problems were caused by the strikes by the lowest-paid workers, members of the National Union of Public Employees, which had a long record of non-militancy. After years when their real wages, which were already the lowest, had been eroded by hyperinflation and voluntary wage restraint, they could see no reason to exercise further restraint when they knew that 'top people' and politicians were receiving substantial increases. The Labour Chancellor of the Exchequer of the time, Denis Healey, later expressed the view that the winter of discontent would probably have been avoided if recognition had been made of the special problems experienced by the lowest-paid workers by awarding them an 8 per cent wage increase, at the level of inflation, instead of insisting on a 5 per cent limit. It is difficult to avoid the conclusion that the worst strikes have been caused by a failure or refusal to acknowledge real financial hardships endured and real inequities, so that workers who by their strike record have proved not to be generally militant have felt compelled to resort to strike action. Also, trade union members have felt that sacrifices they have made during periods of wage restraint have not been matched by commensurate measures to increase investment or to control prices. There is truth in this, and this explains much of the dissatisfaction of workers and the resultant industrial militancy.[114] As the Hudson Institute observed, 'the claims here are of justice as well as efficiency'.

Nationalised Industries. It was commonly assumed that nationalised industries and public utilities were uniformly inefficient and merely a drain on the economy. In fact the great mass of productive capacity, 80 per cent, was owned privately in the 1970s. Industries which had been nationalised, including coal mining and railways, were of a sort that were unprofitable almost everywhere else in the developed world. A point never acknowledged by critics is that state industries which make operating losses are very likely to be subsidising private companies which pay less than realistic prices. Even so, state enterprises did make profits, sometimes very large ones! For example, in 1977 record operating profits for 1976 were reported by the Post Office (£392 million) and the Electricity Council (£206.5 million). Other profitable state industries included British Airways (£35 million) and British Rail (£13.7 million). Even the National Coal Board reported a profit of £27.2 million. If British industries were failing, they were mostly private companies; and publicly owned enterprises were not by any means always a burden on the taxpayers.

Investment in Industry. The failure of British financial institutions to invest adequately in industry was in striking contrast to other countries. The explanation offered by Keith Joseph for this was that the practices of other countries, such as West Germany, could not be used in Britain. 'A little learning is a dangerous thing,' he said. 'The institutional, legal and historical situation is quite different and the German banks' influence over industry cannot be transferred here where traditionally industry has been much more independent.'[115] What the New Right wanted, obviously, was the economic success achieved by other countries, without British financiers and industrialists having to do anything about their traditional institutions, laws and historic practices; rigidities in the workforce, however, could not be tolerated.

Trade Unions. In the demonology of the New Right, trade unions are represented as the most potent of all forces for national failure. Such assessments stress faults to the exclusion of manifest merits. Leaving aside the considerable moral traditions of the unions as agencies of equity and mutual aid, there are more pragmatic matters that are overlooked. It is now forgotten that for four years after September 1974 trade unions voluntarily restricted wage claims to a fraction of inflation levels; cooperation that was formally approved of by the Conservative Party Annual Conference in 1976. Unions have cooperated in the implementation of change. The mineworkers' union, for example, cooperated in considerable reduction in employment as a result of modernisation: in 1965 alone the decision to close 150 mines was negotiated with the NUM, with the loss of 120,000 jobs. There is an informed view that, far from being too powerful, British trade unions are too weak. The evidence is in the relatively poor benefits British unions have won for their members compared to their European counterparts. One industrial consultant told union leader Jack Jones that tough unions should provide management with a powerful incentive to greater efficiency. This happens in the United States. In Britain, workers often in effect subsidise management inefficiency with their low wages. It is a fact that Britain's relative economic decline was well advanced before unions were highly developed. The New Right's vendetta against trade unions neglects other evidence such as that provided during the Second World War, when union–management differences were sunk, and from the good labour relations that foreign (especially Japanese) companies enjoy with an ordinary British workforce. Such evidence strongly supports the view that industrial relations are as good as the quality of management.[116]

Management. Insistence that trade unions are inherently bad for the economy commonly goes in New Right thinking with a denial that management is a problem. Typically, Keith Joseph dismissed the idea when he said in 1974: 'People who could not tell a lathe from a lawnmower and have never carried the responsibility of management never tire of telling British management of its alleged inefficiency.' This view conveniently discounts evidence of the kind provided by the free-market Institute for Economic Affairs, that the education, training and style of British managers generally leaves much to be desired in comparison to their foreign competitors such as the Japanese. It is impossible to resist the temptation, by parity of reasoning, to ask how refugee Austrian economists and All-Souls-oriented politicians without real experience of unionised workers' situations can claim to know better than the workers themselves how to order their lives.[117]

Politics

Ungovernability and Trade Unions. A prominent place is reserved in the New Right account of events in the 1970s for the way that the strike of mineworkers 'brought down' Edward Heath's Conservative government in 1974. But this is a plain misrepresentation. Edward Heath did not resign office under political pressure. He decided to call a general election specifically on the issue 'Who governs Britain?' – that was to say, a choice was presented between his government and the mineworkers' union. If the issue had really been as simple as that it would have been no contest, but it wasn't: the Conservatives lost a general election in February 1974. A clear majority of the electorate voted for an alternative government (48.4 per cent), a minority abstained (22.1 per cent), and only a minority of less than one third of the electorate (29.5 per cent) supported the Conservatives. After the plain truth that it was a general election that the Conservatives lost, not an industrial dispute, the most significant fact about the choice of the great law-abiding British electorate was that it showed a remarkable lack of resentment against mineworkers and their union. Evidently, the British electorate in February 1974 saw some justice in the mineworkers' case that the government had not recognised.[118]

The Mandate and the Democratic Constitution. The constitutional difficulties that exercised the Conservative Party in opposition and led to Lord Hailsham decrying Britain's elective dictatorship violated the spirit of the democratic constitution. As the former Conservative minister Ian Gilmour explained (while he was in opposition), 'A party which failed to get the support of as many as 61 per cent of the electorate may fairly be said to have obtained a counter-mandate: its controversial proposals have been rejected by the voters and should be dropped ... Not even a notional mandate can be said to have been given if a policy was not supported by a majority of the electors.' In the general election of May 1979 the Conservative Party was supported by just 33 per cent of the electorate (44 per cent of voters). By Gilmour's criterion it had a counter-mandate from the 67 per cent of the electorate who did not support it, yet Margaret Thatcher declared, after her election success: 'Those who voted Conservative knew the principal policies we stood for, and that in voting for us they were voting for those policies. That was, and is, our mandate. We have every right to carry it out and we shall.' Evidently the new Prime Minister's conception of a mandate was not Ian Gilmour's, and took no account even of the fact that Conservative voters could not be assumed to approve all policies. Even more significantly the large majority which was unsupportive of, or opposed to, Conservative policies was for her to count for nothing.[119]

Society: Inequality, Wealth and Income

By the 1970s the Labour Party had long since, to all intents and purposes, abandoned the aim of promoting social welfare by wholesale redistribution of wealth and income. It was common ground with Conservatives that improved welfare depended on economic growth (a 'bigger cake'): in this way people could be better off without the need to address the issue of class differences and their relationship to unequal incomes, wealth and welfare. Part of the common ground was the belief that there simply wasn't wealth and income enough to go around, to make much difference to the worse off. In 1976 Keith Joseph estimated that redistribution of incomes above £5,000 per annum would yield an increase to the whole population of under 70p per week. This does not square with data from the Blue Book of national income and expenditure, according to which the poorest 10 per cent of the population, for example, received 3 per cent of income. An equal distribution would, evidently, yield for its worst-off decile an increase in income of 223.3 per cent. Unless Keith Joseph supposed the poor in 1976 to have been living on 30p per week his estimate of the benefit for the worst off to be had from redistribution was, to say the least, grossly mistaken. The scope for redistribution is not obviously limited by the lack of benefit to the worst off 60 per cent of the population, whatever other disbenefits accrue.[120]

Culture

Dependence, Independence and Greed. A great deal is made of the culture of dependence that prevailed in the 1970s. The problems of 'dole-scrounging' and social-security fraud were given wide publicity. Some proportion can be brought to the order of these problems, however, by comparing them to two other factors: the scale of unclaimed benefits and tax evasion. The relative scale of these factors of cultural economics is most conveniently shown in figures from 1980–81 which indicate that, although losses due to false claims of unemployment and social security benefit were substantial, at £40 million per annum, benefits unclaimed by those entitled to them were of an altogether higher order, at £400 million. Losses to the Inland Revenue due to tax avoidance were of a higher order still at £4,000 million. In the clamour on the Right about the dependency culture very little attention was paid to the privations endured by those too proud to claim benefits. Nothing at all was heard about the 'avoision' of tax by the very wealthy. Nevertheless, avoidance inevitably increased proportionally the tax burden on the worst-off compatriots who were neither disposed nor able to avoid tax deductions from their incomes at source by the compulsory PAYE system. In simple quantitative terms, while talk of the culture of dependence occupied a great deal of New Right time, the ten times larger cultural fact of pride was overlooked, and the hundred times larger problem of dissimulation and fraud positively suppressed.[121]

Freedom and Trade Unions. The New Right is devoted above all to promoting and preserving individual freedom. Protecting individual freedom against coercive trade union practices, especially the closed shop, is a particular concern. One old-style Conservative, Lord Hailsham, confessed that he tended to regard those who refuse to join a union in factories as eccentric, perverse or possibly wanting in 'public spirit' but would, he said, defend with his life their right to hold such a point of view and to act on it. The problem of the free-rider is not one that is easily solved in union matters, or in others, and the issue is much wider than simply the freedom of individuals. Freedom in practice must also embrace the freedom of individuals to join a union if they wish to do so. It is noteworthy that the Freedom Association was not concerned about the freedom denied to workers at Grunwick to join a union as they wished to do, and was silent about the rejection by George Ward, the owner of Grunwick, of the recommendations of an inquiry chaired by the Law Lord Justice Scarman. The freedom pursued by the New Right is liable to be a sometime thing that always just happens to serve the pikes and ignore the minnows.[122]

PERSONS

In a study devoted essentially to ideas and to whether or not they are true or otherwise warranted there is little place for a consideration of persons and their histories, but there is some. *Ad hominem* arguments do nothing to establish validity and truth. Nevertheless, even on the high plane of academic philosophy there is illumination to be had from an examination of the personalities and circumstances that have gone with important ideas.[123] On the lower plane of practical politics the interest is undiminished, but has a greater pertinence because politicians invite public scrutiny of the persons as well as the politics. This is especially true of politicians who attach paramount importance to the individual person, personal responsibility, the supremacy of moral values in their political professions, and who have thrust themselves forward in the vanguard of a crusade to transform the country's thinking and whole way of life.

Keith Joseph

Keith Joseph has been described as the leading economic evangelist of the New Right. This reflects his central role both in propagating free-market ideas within the Conservative Party, and in first leading the political revolt against the party's 'socialism'. He has also been described, by former Labour minister Denis Healey, as a cross between Hamlet, Rasputin and Tommy Cooper (the manic, catastrophe-blighted comic conjuror).

The Hamlet in Keith Joseph goes with his upbringing as the only child of a Lord Mayor of London; an education at Harrow and Oxford; and a thesis at All Souls on political, racial and religious tolerance (as a dark portent of things to come this was never finished). Acquaintances and civil servants have always found him to be a very charming man and, as a minister for social services, a compassionate and free-spending one. Indeed, he entered politics in 1954 because of his concern for poverty and with a reputation as a liberal-progressive. Playing cricket and captaining the second eleven at Harrow he found to be an 'absolutely intoxicating' experience, but he has been more of a lonely haunted rambler than a team player in his mature political career.

He is unusual among parliamentarians in being a don and more unusual in being a right-wing one. It is said that he follows the logic of an argument wherever it leads. He is prepared to accept the consequences if they are unpleasant, even to the point of always asking himself: 'Am I wrong in some way?' (As it happens, the answer, unfortunately, has frequently been 'yes'.) The streak of Rasputin was revealed in his preparedness to be disingenuous when it was politic for him to be so. The Centre for Policy Studies was set up by Keith Joseph and Margaret Thatcher in 1974 with the (albeit reluctant) agreement of the Conservative Party leader, Edward Heath. Heath was given to understand that the object of the centre was simply to undertake comparative studies of other countries' political and economic systems. He was not originally made aware of the centre's true purpose, which he strongly objected to, which was to develop free-market policies in opposition to those of the official Conservative Party Research Department.

Tommy Cooper's is the persona most illuminating with respect to the New Right thinking adopted by Keith Joseph. Joseph's career as a government minister was marked by a succession of radical innovations based on new-fangled ideas. They seemed to him at the time to be such good ideas that they were pursued with enthusiasm and zeal worthy of any boy scout. Repeatedly the ideas proved to be fatally flawed and the projects collapsed like Tommy Cooper's tricks (though unintentionally). At the Ministry for Housing and Local Government in the 1960s he promoted the construction of high-rise blocks of flats everywhere in the country because he had been convinced of their superior economy and technical merit by some theorists in the building trade (his family owned Bovis the building construction firm and he had been trained in the business before he was a director so he was supposed to know something about these things). These buildings proved to be uninhabitable and dangerous and they have been progressively demolished at enormous cost since the 1970s. During his time at the Department of Health and Social Services he discovered a theory about 'poverty traps' which he was obsessed by. He later attacked this theory after his conversion to market thinking. His main efforts at the DHSS were fired by another enthusiasm, this time a theory about the organisational and managerial efficiency of public administration. He saw to it that the National Health Service was reorganised in the 1970s along the approved lines by introducing a system of regional authorities between the area and national administrations. Like high-rise blocks of flats, this proved to be based on a 'bad' theory and the Regional Health Authorities were among the prime targets of bureaucracy and waste of public money to be demolished in the 1980s.

A very remarkable feature of Keith Joseph's character and history is how, like Toad of Toad Hall, he has failed to heed warnings about the impracticality of his enthusiastic ideas and schemes; then, when they have gone wrong he has outdone his critics with his self-reproaches (Leo Abse, the Labour MP paired with Joseph for 30 years, took the view that he so evidently enjoyed blaming himself and was so well-meaning a man that Abse rarely denied him the pleasure). It is astonishing, therefore, that recurrent failure to see things through or to do anything properly seems not to have dented the invincible certainty with which he has espoused his successive enthusiasms. In spite of his All Souls intellect he simply lacks common sense and certainly political judgement. It was some ill-judged remarks in 1974 about the need to control the breeding habits of the working classes that put paid to any possibility that he might have had of becoming party leader and Prime Minister.

So, to the New Right ideas. In fact, Keith Joseph was twice converted to New Right thinking. He first sought enlightenment from the Institute for Economic Affairs in 1964. This pre-dated his free-spending years at the DHSS, and the fiasco of his NHS reorganisation. He turned again in 1974 to the New Right analysis after he discovered that, although for twenty years he had been a Conservative MP, he had really been a socialist all that time. In 1975 he said, 'I include success as an index of virtue, in the puritan tradition, since the aim of politics is to succeed; if they fail there must be something wrong with them.' In so far as the character and competence of believers is evidence as to the worth of their beliefs then Keith Joseph is an unconvincing apostle of New Right thinking.[124]

Margaret Thatcher

The Person. When a person is the first woman to lead a party of government in Britain (the Conservative Party in particular), the first to become Prime Minister, the longest-serving Prime Minister of the century and possibly in history, it would be surprising if that person did not have extraordinary qualities. Margaret Thatcher has demonstrated political skill of the highest order. Her most impressive quality is her strong sense of conviction and a determination that goes with it. She is celebrated for possessing herself the courage she offers as a personal ideal for others. She has been described by someone who knows her well as 'a warm and very generous person, and someone who is genuinely interested in other people'. She acquired an enviable reputation as a politician of integrity and honesty. She frequently says that the Conservatives must win not just power but the battle of ideas; an indication, perhaps, of an extraordinary concern with the truth and with what is right (her participation in meetings of the Conservative philosophy group encourages this understanding). It would be misleading, however, to leave the matter of her personal character there.[125]

Conviction is not in itself a positive quality. It depends on what the conviction is about. Leaving aside the convictions of the Hitlers and the Stalins, Aneurin Bevan, the leading postwar figure of the Labour Left, was also a conviction politician. Democratic socialism is built on a conviction, he said, and it is better to risk a clear and definite rejection than to win uneasy followers by dexterous ambiguities. (Bevan it was who had described Tories as 'vermin' on one occasion and who, after Labour's victory in 1945, recommended the political annihilation of the Conservative Party.) For every political conviction there is an equal and opposite conviction, and single-minded adherence to one almost invariably invokes single-minded opposition from another. There is a question, then, of which political beliefs, if any, warrant conviction. The mere fact of conviction has little direct relevance to this question.[126]

Personal courage is not easy to assess but Margaret Thatcher's has not always been flawless. Faced with the risk of losing the election of 1979, she could have refused to promise to increase public spending by implementing substantial pay awards. That would have been an act of great political courage by a conviction politician. Instead she promised, against her convictions, to increase public spending considerably because, as a colleague said, 'Margaret wanted to win the

election as if there was no tomorrow.' Courage did not come into it
when personal ambition was at stake. The person who described her
as 'warm and very generous' was her own sister. Others have more
difficulty in detecting these qualities in the political persona. Her
admirers regarded as her 'good fortune' the fact that she was not
'emotionally hamstrung' by the prospect of mass unemployment
among her compatriots.[127]

Her intellectual integrity does not extend to paying attention to
views she does not already agree with. According to one admirer she
dipped into political philosophy not to find enlightenment but in order
to find the resources to bolster and defend her own intuitive view of
things. Therefore, when she speaks of the battle of ideas and of
winning the argument, she is really concerned with rhetoric,
persuasion and belief, not logic, demonstration and truth. It is unsurprising, therefore, that as leader of the opposition she attributed
hyperinflation in 1975 to the actions of the Labour government when
she knew it was the result of world oil-price rises and, as a monetarist,
she believed that inflation was caused by the monetary policies
pursued by the previous Conservative government of which she
was a member. Indeed, she and Keith Joseph had repudiated those
past Conservative policies precisely because they caused the problems
she blamed Labour for. Similarly she was saying in 1979 that Britain
had the worst strike record in the world, when official *Employment
Gazette* figures showed otherwise; unless, against standard statistical
practice, a conveniently narrow timescale was used to exclude long
strike-free periods. These examples show that Margaret Thatcher is
strongly disposed to state as true what there is no good reason to
believe to be true, or what is so partially true as to be seriously
misleading. This disposition goes beyond the politician's occupational
vice of conjuring with statistics, and is a large part of the explanation
of her extraordinary political success. To an extraordinary degree she
lacks candour. The most significant clue to Margaret Thatcher's
integrity is provided by a remark she is reported to have made to
explain her refusal to approve the publication of a history of the
wartime activities of the secret services which had been commissioned
by Edward Heath and James Callaghan, her predecessors. According
to a *Guardian* report she said: 'When I was called to the bar the first
and best piece of advice that I received was never to admit more than
you have to.' It is this standard of candour, and the belief in rhetoric
rather than reality, that must be borne in mind when assessing

Margaret Thatcher's own account of her activities and the record of her administration since 1979.[128]

The Politician. The purely personal character and style of the New Right Prime Minister is important but for the present purpose less important than the insight her personal history gives into the nature of her political commitment. It will be convenient to consider her personal history with reference to the time honoured mainstays of Conservative doctrine. In the matter of religion, Margaret Thatcher draws her moral standards from Christian teaching, although she said in 1978 that Christianity had not equipped her with a political philosophy. She identified two conflicting ideas in the New Testament which have political import: first the idea that we are all members one of another – the egalitarian doctrine of mutual dependence. Second is the idea that we are each and every one of us moral beings with a uniquely valuable personality and the responsibility to choose between good and evil – the individualist doctrine of free choice. For her part, she said: 'I am working for ... a free and responsible society' (not for her the injunction to equality as interdependence). It is significant that in an address on the subject of Christian teaching, compassion is mentioned only to remind us that it cannot be achieved simply by passing laws. Care and sacrifice are mentioned as things some commendable individuals do personally 'even [sic] outside the confines of the family'. Handing over (all) responsibility for others to the state would only make loving one's neighbour more difficult. Her emphasis lies elsewhere, and derives from the 'very rigid' standards of the religious environment she was brought up in. Christianity for her was a matter of diligent attendance at chapel, thinking it was wrong to spend very much on personal pleasure, and making up your own mind, not following the crowd, 'daring to be a Daniel'. In this view religion teaches above all that this life is to be made *use* of, as a preparation for the next. The nearest thing to a political doctrine she can find in the Bible is to render unto Caesar that which is Caesar's. But the 'devil is still with us, reflecting his successes in all the maladies of society, the state should treat people as Christianity wanted them to be: free and responsible'. It requires self-discipline and imposes great responsibilities on individuals – but 'such is the destiny of man and in such consists his glory and salvation'. In such too consists our national greatness. 'Righteousness exalteth a nation.' One word for this austere doctrine is puritanical. Another is pharisaical. Whichever it is will be easier to decide after considering other aspects of her life and beliefs.[129] There is no doubt that her public pronouncements were influenced by a moral conception of free-market economics. This was based on an unorthodox view of Christian teaching formulated at the Centre for Policy Studies and dispensed at 10 Downing Street by Professor Brian Griffiths, a God-fearing limited-liability Christian.

Fierce patriotism is one of Margaret Thatcher's best-known traits and Kipling, the poet of Empire, is her favourite. She believes in Britain's special superior place and destiny. It is all the more remarkable, therefore, that when it was usual for most young women of her age in 1943 to help in their country's life and death struggle against Nazism by joining the military forces or to work in factories or with the Land Army, Margaret Hilda Roberts chose instead to go to university. Also, strong allegiance to the 'small platoon' that Burke celebrated, to the locality and patrie of one's birth, is unknown to Margaret Hilda Roberts – who rarely returned to or had anything to do with her home town Grantham after she became Margaret Thatcher.

The family, according to Conservative doctrine, is the indispensable foundation of the nation. Margaret Thatcher is a good Conservative in her pronouncements about the paramount virtue of family life. But the conduct of her own family life left a great deal to be desired by traditional standards. In a rare remark about her mother she said she'd had nothing to say to her after the age of 15, and on another occasion disparagingly referred to her as 'a bit of a Martha' (the patron saint of housewives). She does not acknowledge her mother in her *Who's Who* entry, where she is identified only as the daughter of her father, Alderman Alf Roberts. Equally telling was her haste to put her ambitions to be an MP before what Conservative doctrine teaches were her duties as a mother when her twin children were only a few months old. As with so much else to do with Margaret Thatcher there is some disingenuousness in the later telling of these events. According to one 'enhanced' account by Russell Lewis, 'At the time of the 1955 election campaign the twins were too young to be left during the campaign.' This implies that Margaret Thatcher herself thought they were too young to be left. The truth was otherwise. Another sympathetic biographer, Patrick Cosgrave, tells how in fact she actively sought selection as a prospective parliamentary candidate for the safe seat of Orpington, for the by-election of 1954, as soon as the twins were born prematurely in 1953. In 1957 traditional family-minded Conservative Association selection committees at Beckenham and Maidstone found it necessary to point out to her that in their view she should be at home looking after the children. She was adopted by Finchley in 1957 when the children were barely four years old.[130] Later generations, of women especially, will have much sympathy with Margaret Thatcher's determined pursuit of a political career against the traditional doctrine and practice of her party. They might be less comprehending and understanding of the fear she later expressed, that a generation of 'latchkey' children were growing up whose mothers had left home to go out to work.

Conservatives have traditionally believed in hierarchy and this has increasingly taken the form of elitism based on merit. Margaret Thatcher has always believed in elitism, and the rewards due to superior talent and efforts. This did not altogether exclude inherited status. As an undergraduate she acquired the reputation of encouraging personal relationships only with those who could help her to 'get on'. One description of her progress provides an impressive case of meritocratic excellence winning through to success. The bright grammar school pupil became head girl of her school before going to Oxford where she fell short of the highest academic attainment in her field only because of the excessive time she devoted (successfully) to extra-curricular politics. The truth, again, was slightly different. At school she was not regarded as exceptionally bright. She did work extraordinarily hard. She was appointed head girl when she was one of two girls who stayed on for an extra year in the sixth form: both were made joint head girls. She had chosen Oxford entirely for reasons of its prestige regardless of what she was to study there. She chose chemistry as her subject because that offered her the best chance of gaining admission by minimising the competition against her – relatively few girls opted for science. Her tutors thought her incapable of achieving first-class standard.[131]

Private property, and the rights and privileges it affords, have always been the foundation of Conservative philosophy. Margaret Thatcher's political career has been devoted to creating the conditions for the flourishing of a property-owning democracy. Significantly, her own way of acquiring wealth and property was expeditious. At the age of 26 she married a wealthy company director ten years her senior.

According to Conservative doctrine one of the main virtues of property is its instrumental value in securing individuals' freedom, by providing financial independence from others and from the state.

Margaret Thatcher has persistently promoted individualism and freedom in a conventional way for Conservatives, but is married also to the Victorian virtue of independence through self-help. She constantly asserts that she came from an ordinary family and enjoyed precious little or no privilege in life. She believes she made her own way in the world by dint of ability and hard work. Dismissing feminism in her maturity she once said: 'Some of us [women] were making it by our own efforts long before feminism was even thought of.' Leaving aside the flawed history of feminism implicit in this remark, it shows a remarkable blindness to her own past advantages and personal dependencies. No doubt compared to aristocracy her background was not privileged. Having an outside toilet is a terrible privation! But by any objective measure relevant to the whole of society she had very considerable privileges. Few children have a father with his own business who is a Lord Mayor of a respectable-sized town. Few families could have afforded the special tuition in Latin and elocution her father paid for to prepare her for Oxford. Afterwards, she was able to study for the bar and to enter politics only because her husband was a wealthy man who could afford to pay for it. At crucial junctures in her life she was as dependent as dependent could be: first on her father, then her husband. Her failure to learn from this dependency and to empathise with those not in a position to depend on others as she was marks her out as an authentic Pharisee – to use an apt Biblical term. When these basic truths were drawn to her attention, she took the view that marrying money was no worse than acquiring it by speculating in the City or inheriting it; and anyway such observations were cheap. But the truth in this instance is not cheap at all. Contrarywise, how cheap her own disparagement of those not so fortunate as herself in having parents and husband to depend on? This is far more than a personal point. It is to do with the import of the religious and moral precepts that the champion of the New Right supposedly lives by.[132]

The Philosopher. Margaret Thatcher has frequently expressed her belief in the importance of ideas, especially political philosophy. Some of her critics dismiss this claim. William Keegan for example doubts that Margaret Thatcher wrestled with the ideas of the Nobel Laureate Friedrich von Hayek, he suggests that 'she was a simple provincial girl looking for an uncomplicated philosophy', and that she was much more at home with the simple homespun philosophy of William Simon (the United States Treasury Secretary). Anthony

Barnett went so far as to say that 'the political theory of Thatcherism is sub-zero'. The truth in these remarks may be that she is not an original thinker and she has never questioned her beliefs in the disinterested spirit of philosophical inquiry. Well, few thinkers are truly original and the Marxist Left does not question its beliefs in the disinterested spirit of philosophical inquiry either. To that extent Margaret Thatcher and some of her critics are engaged in a 'positional' struggle of rhetorical persuasion, not philosophical argument. Philosophy does not come into it.[133]

There is, however, a considerable philosophical theory at the root of Thatcher's New Right thinking about politics, mainly due to Friedrich von Hayek. It reflects no credit on her critics on the Left that they have offered very little criticism of this philosophy. Margaret Thatcher read Hayek's extraordinarily influential book *The Road to Serfdom* when she was 20 years old. She was already receptive to the criticisms of socialism he brought from Austria through her contact with an Austrian friend of her sister's, whose view of events there was like Hayek's. His linking of socialism in any form with Nazi totalitarianism is an unstated constant in Margaret Thatcher's thinking. Hayek's was always a philosophy for individual liberty and against collectivist conformity. By the 1970s Hayek had elaborated his basic ideas into a comprehensive system that even some critics thought to be 'magnificent'. In 1960, in the heyday of consensus, it was a magnificent dinosaur. By 1974, the ideas provided for some a plausible explanation for the events in the real live world of Britain. It was socialism and consensus which seemed to them to be antediluvian. The suggestion that she was able to remedy deficiencies in the philosophical logic of professional philosophers may be risible. But no greater mistake could have been made than to regard Margaret Thatcher's political theory as sub-zero. The manner of her defence of it might fail the tests of an undergraduate philosophy course, but the substance of the theory she subscribed to is anything but sub-zero. It is most appropriate, therefore, in assessing the record of the New Right in office, to bear in mind the philosophical ideas behind the policies.[134]

10   CONCLUSIONS

In 1990, with inflation at 10.5 per cent and rising, unemployment (on the 1979 basis) at well over two million and rising, and interest rates of 18.5 per cent and rising, but with no media clamour about crisis, it was difficult to credit the climate of crisis proclaimed in 1979 because inflation was at 8.4 per cent (though falling), unemployment at 1.3 million, and interest rates at 14.4 per cent. Evidently a climate of crisis does not depend on anything so simple as mere facts.

The crisis of 1979 was in part illusory and in part real. It was an illusion that the problems facing Britain were all unique or extraordinary. Some misconceptions were based on, let us say, honest errors (even though disastrous ones), such as the grossly exaggerated official estimates of public expenditure. Some popular misconceptions were deliberate falsehoods propagated by media sympathetic to the New Right, such as the record of strikes, and the causes of hyperinflation and the level of unemployment being in Labour policy rather than in earlier Conservative policy and world recession. Most of these misconceptions and thereby the illusion of crisis could have been dispelled. The success of similar consensus-based political economies in Sweden and Austria supports this interpretation.

The real basis of crisis had various aspects. Some problems were ignored or overlooked by both major political parties, notably the constitutional issue of absolute power being confided in an unrepresentative government. The assumption that economic growth is an unqualified good is still not seriously questioned by any major political party. Other problems were deliberately denied in the more or less overt pursuit of class interest: the Left denied the record of failure of statism and the problems caused by trade union practices, the right denied the failure of financial institutions and private enterprise management to develop the economy and refused to acknowledge the chronic class problems of British society. If there was a crisis in Britain it was a crisis of established institutions and leadership refusing to face the facts and to change themselves, although they were adamant that others should change. A major problem for Britain has been the delusion of grandeur that has thwarted best attempts at national renewal by squandering the fruits of labour, and sacrificing them by feeding them into the maws of sterling and 'big league' defence expenditure. Inadequate account was taken of the exceptional burdens of war and defence borne by Britain in contrast to the exceptional benefits enjoyed by Japan and Germany from having limited defence commitments.

None of this was really on the routine agenda in 1979. The electoral success of the New Right thinkers both in the Conservative Party and nationally was primarily a reaction against something rejected, not a positive shift to the new ideas. In any case in electoral terms the change was not great and impressive. Once the degenerate electoral process had delivered power to the New Right it was natural that their rhetoric and ideas would gain wider currency. It is important to bear in mind this order of priority. It is futile to look for some explanation for the ascendency of the New Right in its ideas (such as their greater simplicity) if the ascendancy of its ideas is secondary to and dependent on iniquitous electoral systems, iniquitous precisely because they deliver power to a minority whose ideas are ultimately not intellectually persuasive and not widely shared. There is philosophical interest to be found in such events, however. Kenneth Galbraith suggested that if the highly tendentious free-market theory of monetarism was to be tested experimentally at all on a real economy for a long time then Britain was the best place to try it because of its celebrated political stability. The record of the New Right during twelve years continuously in office would be the best possible empirical test of the ideas. As Keith Joseph said in 1975:

> We shall be judged by how resolutely and successfully we fight for our ideas. I include success as an index of virtue, in the puritan tradition, since the aim of politics is to succeed; if they fail there must be something wrong with them.[135]

The next task then is to assess the record of the New Right, as a practical test of its ideas.

PART 2

MIRACLE? WHAT MIRACLE? THE RECORD OF THE NEW RIGHT

'It is hard to persuade people for very long that you are on the right track if none of your policies deliver the goods'

NIGEL LAWSON (1988, p10)

11 THE DOMINANCE OF THE NEW RIGHT

The first thing to note about the record of the New Right in office is the exceptional dominance it has exercised. Most obviously there have been substantial majorities of Conservative MPs elected: in 1979, 44, in 1983, 143, and in 1987, 101. Then there has been the strong party discipline exercised, increasing with the duration of the administration. Finally there is the almost unprecedented period of continuous tenure in office of the same Prime Minster with the same fixed ideas. This had the effect of progressively excluding from power opposition to New Right ideas from within the party itself. Older-style Tories such as Ian Gilmour and Norman St John Stevas were not long in office. Other sceptics, such as Francis Pym and James Prior, were ejected later. During most of her twelve years as Prime Minister, Margaret Thatcher succeeded in establishing a cabinet dominated by true believers in New Right thinking, such as Keith Joseph, Geoffrey Howe, Nicholas Ridley, Norman Tebbit, Nigel Lawson and Cecil Parkinson. Parliamentary opposition throughout this time was divided and weakened, most especially through the formation in 1981 of the Social Democratic Party by four senior Labour politicians led by Roy Jenkins, former president of the European Commission. In the general elections of 1983 and 1987 the combined Labour and SDP share of electorate support was virtually the same as for Labour in 1979: 28.2 per cent and 30.2 per cent respectively against Labour's 27.7 per cent in 1979 (and Labour's 28.5 per cent in October 1974, when they won). This shows that, leaving aside the issue of the electoral system, the dominance of the New Right Conservatives in Parliament was due more to division in the opposition than to electoral support for new ideas. Internal constitutional disputes in the Labour Party further weakened opposition by distraction (doubtless these events reflected external factors as well, in the world economy and Britain's place in it).

Margaret Thatcher strengthened her position substantially in other ways. First, key decisions were devolved to sub-committees of the full cabinet that excluded dissenting opinion. Secondly, the role of special advisors was greatly extended, and was so increased in importance that in 1989 the long-serving Chancellor of the Exchequer, Nigel Lawson, resigned because his role was being taken over by an advisor, Professor Alan Walters, whom the Prime Minister described as a 'family friend'. Thirdly, the convention of observing political

73

impartiality in making appointments to senior civil service posts and to quangos was abandoned. Appointments were made according to the test, 'Is he one of us?' Fourthly, ministers were extraordinarily insistent on acting independently of their career civil service advisors. After more than twelve years of such developments, supposedly impartial junior and middle-ranking civil servants often have difficulty framing problems and issues in ways other than those prescribed by the approved New Right wisdom.

The New Right domination of Parliament and Whitehall has been extended to local authorities and beyond. By introducing rate-capping and strictly controlling central government financial contributions, local authorities have been subordinated to central government by the power of the purse. The intractable Greater London Council was simply abolished altogether. More general control has been exercised through such measures as invoking the provisions of the Official Secrets Acts and extending censorship on grounds of national security – to diminish the basis and possibility of criticism. Finally, there has been a proliferation of detailed techniques for securing desired results by plain gerrymandering. The most notable of these is the novel 'democratic' procedure of counting abstentions in a free vote as 'yeas'. In this way, for example, a simple majority voting against a proposal – such as a majority of residents voting against selling off council houses – can be turned into a majority in favour.

Whatever has been brought about politically and economically in Britain since 1979 has been due predominantly to the action of New Right thinkers in government, restrained neither by effective political and administrative opposition nor, as events turned out, by opposition from trade unions, industrialists or public opinion generally. More than usually, certainly, the proof of this pudding is in the eating.

12   THE PROGRAMME

The five tasks undertaken in the Conservative manifesto of 1979 serve as an agenda for the entire period from 1979 to 1990. For some purposes (of political science and sociology) it may be useful to 'periodise' the developing programme discretely. For the present purpose of assessing the practical success of New Right thinking this is not necessary. Although the governments formed after the 1983 and 1987 election victories were faced with different economic and political situations, there is no reason to suppose that the New Right programme was altered in any basic way. For example, privatisation of state-owned industries merely assumed a higher priority after 1987 than it had in 1979, when trade union reforms and inflation were the most pressing matters. Strengthening defence was one of the five main tasks of 1979, but after the Labour Party officially adopted a policy of unilateral nuclear disarmament in 1981, defence issues assumed a higher priority on the political agenda. In such ways the stress put upon various policies and the order in which they were addressed certainly reflected numerous contingent and variable factors. Nevertheless two basic aims were constantly pursued: the promotion of free markets and the assertion of the paramount authority of the state.

13   EVALUATION OF THE RECORD

The extraordinary dominance of New Right government has been noted. But even the most dominant government is heavily constrained by external factors beyond its control. World commodity prices, especially oil; the influence of multinational corporations; international financial markets; international commitments, such as membership of the EEC and NATO; civil disorder and war: these are only the most obvious constraints on the autonomous actions of national governments. The effect of such things should certainly be taken into account when judging the success of a political programme. In the case of the New Right in Britain we may be reassured. Over a twelve-year period there is a better than usual chance that such factors would tend to cancel one another out in their effects for good or ill. Also, most externalities of these kinds affect other nations in similar ways, so that comparisons lend objectivity to judgement.

If anything, external factors tended to promote the policies of Conservative governments during the period. Two major external factors which had undermined the efforts of the Labour administrations of the 1970s favoured the Conservatives in the 1980s. The cost of importing oil fuelled inflation in the 1970s and increased trade deficits, whereas North Sea oil revenues generated substantial trade surpluses in the 1980s, tended to reduce inflation, and insulated Britain from the effects of increases in international oil prices. Secondly, the New Right's commitment to monetarist theory and policies was approved of by the (monetarist) International Monetary Fund, whereas the Labour government had to be forced by the IMF

to adopt monetarist policies, regardless of their effects on industry
and unemployment. Powerful international financial institutions
and multinational corporations are natural allies of New Right
government, and are favourably disposed to support or promote their
policies, rather than frustrate them. The effects of other external
factors will be taken into account, where appropriate, in what follows.

14   THE ECONOMIC RECORD

ECONOMIC THEORY: MONETARISM

Notoriously, there is no consensus among economic theorists
comparable to those found in other disciplines with scientific
pretensions to explanatory power.[1] Samuel Brittan says that the key
to understanding many economic pronouncements is that they
belong at least as much to the entertainment as to the information
industry. What he means is that, in the absence of some universally
shared paradigm of economics within which questions of validity and
truth can be settled, readers of the economic runes are inclined to
resort to casuistry and rhetoric. This is especially true of the devotees
of monetarism, the economic dogma that is the taproot of the New
Right's thinking on all things economic. Milton Friedman is the
Nobel Prize-winning top gun among the 'Chicago Boys', as the
monetarists have been called. Friedman's version of the monetarist
explanation for inflation has already been mentioned (Chapter 5). Its
great simplicity recommended it to New Right politicians looking for
simple solutions to very complicated problems (the occupational
vice of autocrats and dictators down the ages). Although there are
more and less simplistic versions of monetarist theory, a version
based on the household finances of a 1930s Grantham grocer served
very nicely the needs of the New Right Conservative ministers (or
'Moonies' as they were called by traditional Tories). Milton Friedman
himself confidently proclaimed that monetarism is susceptible to
scientific proof, like gravity.[2] Let us, therefore, take him at his word
and see how monetarism stood the test.

Thatcher-monetarism can be given short shrift and longer shrift.
Short shrift comes from pointing out the simply false analogy it is
based on, and falsifying experience that discredits it. Contrary to
Margaret Thatcher's groceresque view, a national economy is not like
a Grantham family's budget (neither is a healthy business for that

matter). Among other differences, a family's income is not necessarily reduced if it doesn't spend, whereas a government's (or a business's) is, in all probability.[3] Also, from 1973 Chile provided a practical test of monetarist theories, the result of which (catastrophe) was studiously ignored in Britain. Milton Friedman, Friedrich von Hayek, James Buchanan, Gordon Tullock, all the stars in the firmament of monetarism and public choice, were on hand from 1973 as unhidden (hired) hands to guide General Pinochet's military dictatorship according to their economic theory.[4] After four years, the annual increase in Chile's money supply was reduced from 570 per cent to 130 per cent but the rate of inflation was greater with the reduced money supply. Inflation was reduced (to 50 per cent) by the further, theoretically simple, expedients of enforcing wage restraints, banning Trade Unions, consigning their leaders to concentration camps and submitting the Chilean people to all the repression typical of fascist dictatorships (this is called a 'free market in labour'!).[5] Friedman and Hayek wish to dissociate themselves from such unpleasantness, but the fact remains that without it wage repression would not have led to reduced inflation and the (spurious) success of monetarist policies. Even by 1979 it was clear that monetarism led to such insufferable social problems that only a dictatorial regime could sustain them.

The longer shrift to monetarism requires attention to Friedman's scientific pretensions. Textbooks tell us that successful scientific theories permit adequate conceptualisation, description, (causal) explanation, prediction and control of phenomena. Monetarism derives from a certain conception of money – of the clinking metal and rustling paper kind that Friedman's good old country folk stashed in bedsocks and mattresses for 35 years after 1920. In the modern, credit-ridden world the distinction is blurred between money of this sort and 'non-money', that is various kinds of credit and fiduciary and inspired financial arrangements.[6] 'Controlling the money supply' is then not a clear and distinct operation. Indeed credit is a vehicle for money *demand*. Describing adequately a relationship between money supply and inflation is another problem. Money supply is supposed by Thatcher-monetarism to be largely determined by government borrowing (the public sector borrowing requirement). But Nicholas Kaldor, who first described this relationship that held until 1969, also showed that after 1970 there was zero correlation between money stock and the borrowing requirement.[7] The explanation offered by monetarists for inflation involves causation from increased public spending to increased money supply to higher wages to inflation. Attributing causation to money supply and public spending in this way reverses the real order of causation, as if a high temperature were the cause of and so the explanation of a fever rather than an effect or symptom to be explained by the disease.[8] In reality, inflation is related to wage increases that require an increased money supply, and, among other things, increased public spending. The existence of a necessary causal relation from increased money supply to increased inflation is empirically disproved by the experience of other countries with similar increases in money supply without Britain's level of inflation.[9] Another aspect of the logic of explanation is also suggested by a consideration of causation, really multiple causality. Inflation, in reality, can be triggered by changes in commodity prices, wages, taxation, exchange and interest rates, and other financial controls. The causal explanations for inflation are as various as these distinguishable causes. The predictive powers of monetarist theory have proved to be negligible. Attempts were made to predict and so control money stock in the years between 1980 and 1984. Only by 'fiscal adjustments' (meaning *ad hoc* revisions to the targets) were 'goals' met.[10] As to controlling the money supply according to the theory, this proved to be impossible. For example, in 1980 the government set an annual target for increased money supply ('M3' is the Treasury label for money supply) of 8 per cent. The level was exceeded in just two months, July and August. Later shifts of emphasis to controlling demand for money through interest rates proved no more successful. In a devastating analysis in October 1988 of the government's economic forecasts, the Labour MP Gordon Brown drew attention to errors in all of seven predicted economic measures, such as inflation and money supply, up to the order of 50 to 100 per cent or more.[11]

When the Nobel Prize winning theory on which these calculations were based was subjected to careful econometric scrutiny at Oxford University, it was discovered that Friedman had performed 'simply incredible' manipulations of the empirical data he cited in support of his assertion of the link between money supply and inflation. In the absence of any evidence that money stock was low between 1920 and 1955, he assumed, *ad hoc*, that it must have been reduced by 20 per cent because war and depression cause people to hold more money in their bedsocks. When his theory required higher prices in the period after the Second World War, but prices were not higher, he argued that prices must have been higher than statistics showed (by an amount coincidentally confirming his analysis) because the money supply grew more rapidly. Since the theory that increased money supply causes higher inflation is only plausible when corroborated by the data, and since the 'adjusted' data is generated on the assumption that the theory is true, evidently the argument for Friedman's monetarist theory is circular, and not derived from data at all.[12]

The longer-term results of the Chilean experiment with monetarism showed extremely mixed consequences. On the credit side, inflation was reduced from a postwar 1000 per cent in 1973 to an annual average of between 30 and 50 per cent; economic growth of the order 6 to 8 per cent was recorded between 1979 and 1981; and Chile pays interest on its foreign debt promptly and in full. The debit side, however, is heavy: gross domestic product was reduced by 14 per cent in 1982 alone; 50,000 medium and small-sized businesses were bankrupted; unemployment increased to 35 per cent. Among other social consequences, 80 per cent of Chileans earn less than they did 20 years ago, the number of poor doubled to 43 per cent of the population, and according to United Nations criteria 60 per cent live below the poverty line. By 1988 public expenditure on health had been cut by 62 per cent and housing by 33 per cent. There has been a major redistribution of wealth in favour of the richest 10 per cent. Among numerous violations of human rights, thousands of people have been tortured, exiled or have disappeared altogether; political parties and trade unions were forbidden or their activities severely limited and almost total control was imposed on the media. A Brazilian general, himself a member of a military regime, summarised the situation in Chile: 'The economy is fine; it's the people who are suffering.'[13] Milton Friedman argues that his theory doesn't necessitate dictatorial measures, and cites the examples of Germany in 1948 and Japan in 1950 where it worked successfully. He does not reckon with such factors as American aid for strategic reasons, the provision in Germany of state welfare, and in both countries strong though indirect government-sponsored industrial development.[14]

The British experience showed all the same tendencies as in Chile, only restrained by greater institutional inertia. Unemployment escalated from 1.4 million in 1979 (when Conservatives proclaimed that 'Labour isn't working') to 3.5 million in 1986. This and other consequences will be discussed in more detail presently. In the face of overwhelming evidence of the practical failure of the government's monetarist policies, the Prime Minister continued to proclaim (like the 'donkeys' who drove the 'lions' of the British infantry to attritional slaughter in the mud of Flanders), 'There is no alternative.'[15]

Not only was monetarism not working, some of its former advocates began to acknowledge that it does not work. At least one enthusiastic apostle of monetarism, Professor Alan Bould of the London Business School, eventually conceded that despite 3.5 million unemployed and severe curtailment of trade union power the free market in labour was not working.[16] In 1991, nevertheless, monetarism, although showing signs of age, is not dead. It is very much alive in 10 Downing Street.[17] As William Keegan pointed out:

> The Thatcher experiment [in monetarism was] not really an experiment at all. The word experiment implies willingness to observe and to alter assumptions accordingly. There [is] little evidence that [the monetarist evangelists] changed their basic economic preoccupations.[18]

Leaving aside the wider question of the gap between rhetoric and reality and the invincible ignorance of particular persons, there is a philosophically significant explanation for this persistence of monetarist theory in the face of overwhelming disconfirmatory evidence. No less an authority on the matter than Ludwig von Mises, the ubiquitous Professor Hayek's mentor, denied the possibility of evidence at all. He said: 'There are in the field of economics no constant relations, and consequently no measurement is possible.'[19] On a question of this sort, in the absence of measurement, there can be no adequate empirical test. What we have then is not testable theory of a sort that treats monetarism like gravitational theory (as Friedman claims), but rather ideology which treats monetarism as an article of faith: a kind of economic religion.

As it happens, it is a religion with few adherents outside of Downing Street and Lord North Street. In 1981, 364 distinguished academics took the unprecedented step of publicly denouncing the dogmatics of the new religion. In 1990 the overwhelming opinion of 1,000 economists confirmed the judgement, with the benefit of twelve years of hard evidence to go by. For all the world like Adolf Hitler in his Berlin bunker – directing non-existent divisions and invoking the legend of Frederick the Great – the small band of die-hard faithful believe in economic miracles; and deny the evidence all around them of economic disaster and the disintegration of the social fabric.[20]

SUMMARY RECORD: THE RHETORIC

According to the New Right Conservatives' own account, between 1979 and 1989/90 a transformation took place in the British economy, and by extension the wider society and culture.[21] The miracle, they argued, was evident in greatly reduced inflation (of the order of 5 per cent from 1983 after a peak of 20 per cent in 1980), with increased industrial output, productivity and employment rising to record levels. Privatisation of many nationalised industries including British Aerospace, Brit-Oil, British Telecom, British Gas and the Water and Electricity Boards went with a great expansion of share ownership (from 7 to 14 per cent of the public) and improved profitability (rates of return on capital) from 3 per cent in 1981 to 13 per cent in 1988. Improved profitability transformed for the better the prospects for industrial investment. Public borrowing was greatly reduced from 10 per cent of gross national product in 1975–6 to nothing by 1986–7. Controls on the export of sterling were removed and (according to John Redwood of the Adam Smith Institute) this produced a positively embarrassing influx of funds to Britain, not a mass exodus. The ending of price and wage controls led to the reduction of both wage and price increases. Substantial reductions in income tax, with the top rate reduced from 86 per cent in 1979 to 40 per cent in 1988, provided both more incentives to individual enterprise and more scope for personal savings and investment. Industry was investing 30 per cent more 'in real terms' in 1989 than in 1979. Manufacturing output was in 1989 at record levels, with productivity increasing faster in the 1980s in Britain than in any other major industrial country. The average employee was producing by 1989 more than half as much again as they did in 1980. The transformed economic performance has been achieved through basic social changes (such as in work practices and normal expectations) and a fundamental cultural change in attitude towards a work ethic, self-reliance and an enterprise culture.

SUMMARY RECORD: THE REALITY

Inflation

The record between 1979 and 1986 stands as strong evidence against the monetarist theory that inflation is a purely monetary phenomenon. The government inherited an inflation level of 10.1 per cent in May 1979. This increased dramatically to 20.1 per cent one year later, not because of a dramatic increase in the money supply, but largely because of increased wages (awarded after comparability studies in 1978). Another factor was an increase of VAT from 8 to 15 per cent. Inflation was reduced substantially only after unemployment increased from 5.7 per cent of the workforce (1,300,500) in 1979 to 13.4 per cent (3,772,900) in 1986. Inflation rose to 8.3 per cent at the beginning of 1989 and reached 10.6 per cent in 1990. After twelve years the New Right's own chosen main indicator of economic health showed 'no improvement'.[22]

Industrial Growth and Output

The evidence for an economic miracle is all derived from statistics of comparative growth. For example, the gross domestic product grew by an annual average of 2.2 per cent between 1979 and 1988 compared to just 1.3 per cent between 1973 and 1979. Corresponding growth was recorded in output per head of the employed labourforce over the same period: in manufacturing from 0.75 per cent to 4.2 per cent; and in the non-North Sea oil economy from 0.5 to 1.8 per cent. In the years from 1986 to 1988 the growth of Britain's GDP was higher than those in almost all other OECD countries (including, in 1986 and 1987, Japan).[23]

These statistics give a very misleading impression of economic strength because growth rates are not indicative of absolute levels of growth, either the datum or current levels. High growth rates were measured after a catastrophic collapse of the industrial economy between 1979 and 1981 when 20 per cent of manufacturing industry was destroyed. The absolute level of production of early 1974 was not regained until 1988. Significantly, Samuel Brittan chooses output of the employed labourforce to show growth. The growth in productivity was achieved more by rising unemployment than by rising output. Those in employment just worked harder to produce less (with the spectre of over 3.5 million unemployed as an inducement). GDP per capita of population provides a more illuminating measure of economic prosperity: by this criterion Britain lags behind the United States, Canada, Switzerland, Sweden, Japan, Finland, Germany, Australia, France, Austria and the Netherlands. Among the nations whose growth was compared by the OECD in 1990 only Italy and Greece had lower GDP per capita (GDP per capita for Britain in 1988 was $8,988 compared to $11,807 average for OECD countries).[24]

Various other economic indicators show the same weak performance. For example, Japan's productivity per person employed (as opposed to per hour worked) is about 50 per cent higher than Britain's. Even using Treasury criteria (on a per hour basis, and at purchasing power parities) Britain lags behind the productivity levels of the USA (by 24 per cent), France and Canada (14 per cent) and Germany (5 per cent). Figures on the rise in manufacturing output in leading European economies between 1973 and 1988 show a 33.53 per cent increase for Italy, 17.75 per cent for West Germany, 13.26 per cent for France and 3.26 per cent for Britain – after ten years of miraculous New Right government. The result was that between 1979 and 1989 the contribution of manufacturing industry to the economy shrank from 28.4 per cent to 22.2 per cent.[25]

Profitability and Investment

Comparatively high productivity through more strenuous labour accounts for the substantial increase in profitability reported in 1989 – a 20-year high. This, as the government was careful to point out, 'transformed the *prospects* for business investment' but, alas, did not transform actual investment since, in the absence of controls, profits were dispersed as higher dividends, not invested. Between 1979 and 1988, total investment in Britain was 17.3 per cent of GDP, compared to 17.8 for the USA, 20.5 for Germany, 21.5 for Italy and 29.5 for Japan. In 1989, for example, the Koreans invested 28.2 per cent of their GNP, the Japanese 23.2 per cent, the Germans 12.8 per cent and the British 10.2 per cent. (The latest figures available in 1989 showed that by 1986 investment in British manufacturing had fallen to just 78 per cent of the 1979 level. In the north-east it was just half the level of 1979.) Between 1979 and 1989 investment in new plant and machinery in financial services increased by 300 per cent, that in distribution by 126 per cent, but in manufacturing by just 8 per cent – barely enough to cover official capital consumption. These contrasts are striking, especially since the net national income generated by financial services had fallen to nothing by September 1990. In June 1990, the Trade Secretary, Nicholas Ridley, denied that British industry was being undermined by the City's demands for short-term profits at the expense of long-term development (there had, he said, 'simply been a communication breakdown between companies and the investment community'). This was not in keeping with the view of the Conservative Research Office that firms are well advised to reduce their borrowing for investment (called simply 'debt'). The poor record of investment does not square with the government's claim that investment was by 1989 30 per cent higher than it was in 1979. This gratifying result was achieved by counting the proceeds from local authority council-house sales as 'positive investment' by the private sector. This is an achievement of creative accounting, not real investment. Claims of record investment are 'in real terms' unfounded.[26]

Trade, Foreign Investment and Financial Services

Whereas Britain had a trade surplus in manufactures of £5 billion in 1978, there have been sharply increasing deficits after 1983 rising to £20 billion in 1989. Government apologists sought to explain such figures positively, claiming that they reflected imports in materials and capital equipment needed to expand the economy. In fact most of the imports were consumer goods purchased with the proceeds of substantial tax cuts and a credit boom fuelled by uncontrolled borrowing against inflated house values. During this period Britain's share of world trade continuously declined from 8.2 per cent by value in 1979 to an all-time low of 6.8 per cent in 1988. This is truly a matter for concern because it also goes with a failure of absolute growth. In 1983 Britain became a net importer in manufactured goods for the first time ever – a most significant test of the New Right's failure to revitalise the British economy. Even the Adam Smith Institute commented: 'It cannot be a source of pleasure to note that Britain is now incapable of making its own machine tools and has to allow all of the activity to the Germans.'[27]

At one time it was common to seek consolation for declining trade in so-called invisible earnings from foreign investment and financial services. After removal of controls on overseas investment they rose from £12 billion in 1979 to £113 billion in 1986 but have since declined steadily, as current account deficits have been financed from them, to £94 billion in 1988. In 1989 British direct investment abroad was £20.76 billion, while foreigners invested £8.99 billion in Britain – less than half the outflow from Britain. The proportion of national product due to financial services grew from 11.6 per cent in 1979 to 19.8 per cent in 1989. That is, to the same order as a shrunken manufacturing sector (22.2 per cent). The surplus on trade in financial services, never very high, fell by about 40 per cent between 1985 and 1988 to £3.5 billion. By September 1990 the balance of trade in invisibles was zero. The negative trend in other sorts of invisibles was the same. The deficit in tourism and travel, for example, increased from £530 million in 1986 to £2,042 million by 1988.[28]

There is no evidence in figures for trade and financial services of miraculous economic recovery between 1979 and 1990. There is on the other hand considerable evidence of a deteriorating economic performance.

Industry

According to the government's own account, 'on *any* measure of performance British industry is in better shape than for years'. The measures they nominate are output, investment, profit and productivity. In fact the level of output in 1988 was the same as it was in 1973 – not a very impressive rate of progress by any account. As we have already seen, the record of investment in manufacturing industry is very poor. Increased productivity (and thus profitability) has been achieved by intensifying labour for the fewer people in employment, not by permanently increasing productive capacity through investment in new plant and technology. British workers are already among the lowest paid in the industrial world, and increased profitability is achieved in an increasingly low-waged, low-skilled industrial economy. Apart from the social and ethical dimensions of increasing productivity through a 'fear factor', the road to profitability through low wages and hard labour is economically unsound in the long term because, even though the labours of the unskilled be ever so Stakhanovite, they can never compete with a highly capitalised and skilled workforce.[29]

Three specific obstacles to fundamentally improved industrial performance have not been tackled by the New Right: management, research and development, and education and training. It is widely acknowledged that there is a need for British management to be less authoritarian. One leading American management consultant, Tom Peters, argues that in order to achieve performance and quality, management must develop 'beyond hierarchy' – to a workplace that functions in the traditional informal collegial style of the university, rather than the adversarial, no trust, style of autocracy. Japanese management methods are already closer to this. But enthusiasts of the New Right continue to believe that 'the failure of management control over the workplace has been identified as a significant constraint on enterprise'. If there have been changes they have been far too few to alter significantly the entrenched culture of British management.[30]

In 1990 British companies were spending less on research and development as a percentage of annual revenue than European competitors, and it was planned that government funding should be reduced still further. The result of a survey (conducted by the P and A Consultancy Group) showed that 71 per cent of German companies spend more than 5 per cent of revenue on research and development; in Japan it is 35 per cent of companies and in Britain just 28 per cent. Government spending of £4.6 billion for 1987–8 will be reduced to £4.3 billion by 1991–2. Throughout the 1980s Britain consistently invested less in research and development as a proportion of gross domestic product than any other EEC country, as well as others like Sweden and Japan. The USA invested a lower proportion, but of a very much larger product. In concluding his survey of British research and development in 1989 Tom Wilkie said: 'There is no plan, no overall scheme: above all no confidence in the future. And all the while our major economic competitors are investing a greater proportion of their national wealth in support of civil research and development.'[31]

Shortly after becoming leader of the Conservative Party in 1975, Margaret Thatcher pointed to the loss of highly trained personnel through emigration as evidence that Britain was unable to provide the incentives and rewards necessary to keep them here. During the 1980s British professional engineers have continued to be paid less and to be held in lower esteem than their counterparts in other countries. Their continuing emigration will certainly accelerate after the single market is established in Europe in 1992. The most spectacular loss of highly trained personnel has been of scientists pursuing basic research. One conspicuous emigrant to Australia was a professor of physics, Paul Davies, who left Newcastle for Adelaide in March 1990. As a schoolboy in Finchley he had been encouraged to pursue science by his MP, Margaret Thatcher, who assured him that science was what the country needed. The government's contempt for his basic research was the main reason for Davies deciding to leave. He is typical of innumerable others. In February 1990 a petition signed by 1,600 scientists working abroad (including 100 department heads, 200 full professors and 24 members of the Royal Society) was presented to the Prime Minster. The signatories were unable to get the government to acknowledge that there was a problem with emigration or with the morale of people involved in basic research. The nature of the problem is reflected in the reduction in the number of new ideas patented. In 1987, for example, Britain produced fewer patents per capita than Finland, Greece or Austria.[32] Here (again) the New Right's preoccupation with short-term market profitability leads to the sacrifice of basic values, and even purely financial interests, in the longer term.

The greatest failure of investment in industry is in education and training. Numerous commentators have drawn attention to the very wide disparity between the qualifications and skills of workers in British industry and their counterparts elsewhere. Compared with competitors there is a far smaller proportion of well-qualified people at all levels in British industry. The full picture is more complicated and even more worrying. Britain produces far fewer graduates in engineering and technology than, for example, France, Germany, Japan and the United States. Significantly, efforts by the Conservative government to overcome the heavy cultural prejudice against work in industry failed. Apart from the perennial lack of interest among the brightest pupils, industry itself failed in 1982 to provide funds for the engineering scholarships scheme run by the Department of Education and Science. Appeals for funds from members of the Engineering Employers Federation were unsuccessful. An even worse picture of cultural decadence emerged from a survey published in 1989 which showed that only 35 per cent of engineers graduating in that year intended to become professional engineers in industry; the rest planned to be general managers, financial consultants or academic researchers. This reflects their informed view of the status and rewards of engineers in Britain. Although leaders of the engineering profession persistently deny it, the comparatively low pay and social status of engineers in Britain are two major obstacles to recruitment. Even the shortage of graduate engineers, especially in manufacturing production, is not the greatest problem: the largest gap between Britain and its competitors is in the level of training and skills of the bulk of the workforce.

In Britain in 1985 the number of technicians qualified was of the order of 20 to 50 per cent lower than in France and Germany. The disparity in newly qualified craftsmen was even greater, ranging from 25 per cent fewer than in Japan to nearly 75 per cent fewer than in Germany. Even when faced with such evidence, industrialists were immune to requests to support government proposals for city technology colleges.[33]

The foundations of industrial success are inevitably the skills of the industrial workforce. There has been a failure to develop these skills through education and training. The reasons for this are rooted in British culture. Twelve years of New Right government have not changed things.

The Case of Rolls-Royce

The bankruptcy of Rolls-Royce in 1971 was discussed earlier, as an exemplary case of the need for British industry to be competitive. It is salutary in a different way to discuss this case further to show how a simplistic view of economics and market competitiveness can lead to unfortunate and unnecessary results. Some light is thrown on the nature of free markets, also.

The bid for the Lockheed Tri-Star engine contract was successful in 1968 at a price of $485,000 per RB211 engine. The prices of the American competitor engines were $600,000 for the General Electrical engine and $700,000 for Pratt and Whitney's. The British price substantially undercut the Americans, so there was no question of the British price being uncompetitive. (Unfortunately price-cutting is not the same thing as cost-cutting.) The free market drove Rolls-Royce's prices below the level of their costs. A market result of this sort is welcomed by strict-observance free-marketeers as evidence that, in the real world, there was no need for Rolls-Royce aero-engines. Evidently American companies could supply similar products more efficiently.

Reality was more complicated than this view allowed (as is frequently the case). The strategic military consequences have been mentioned. The political and economic effect of rendering unemployed 20,000 highly skilled Rolls-Royce employees, and many more who were indirectly employed in the industry, proved also to be unacceptable. But this is not the real problem with the simple market view of the Rolls-Royce case. There are three problems with the market demonstrated by this case. First, it cannot be assumed that a highly specialised, skilled workforce can be redeployed as simply and effectively as a bucolic workforce switching from glove-making to hat-making (as in Adam Smith's elemental vision). Secondly, Rolls-Royce was not operating in a perfect market. Its American competitors were highly advantaged, since both benefited from highly profitable orders for large numbers of military engines, and both received substantial financial subsidies from defence expenditure for development of their engines competing with the RB211. General Electric received about $400 million dollars in subsidies through defence contracts for the development of an engine that became, in one version, the rival to the RB211. There was not a free market in aero-engines; and the dice were loaded heavily against Rolls-Royce both financially and nationalistically.

The third problem with the simple market model is that it omits the role of government investment. Rolls-Royce was taken into public ownership in 1971 where it remained until May 1987, when it was privatised. The company made operating profits in every one of the 16 years it was in public ownership, ranging from just £1 million in 1979 to £273 million in 1986. There were profits before tax in eleven of the 16 years before privatisation, ranging from £5 million in 1975 to £120 million in 1986. By 1989, sales had reached nearly £3 billion, including £2.2 billion in exports; profits were a record £233 million; and shareholders' funds were £1.1 billion. RB211 sales accounted for at least 25 per cent of profits. The company's share of the world aero-engine market has risen from 5 per cent in 1971 to 20 per cent, and there are realistic plans to increase its share of this highly competitive, high value-added business to 30 per cent of the world market. Significantly, engineers continue to have substantial influence on the company. The Deputy Chairman in 1991 is Sir Ralph Robbins, an engineer with a lifetime's experience in the company.

The very considerable success of Roll-Royce between 1971 and 1989 was achieved by an extensive programme of investment. Investment in research and development was £1,540 million, compared to operating profits of £2,454 million – that is, 63 per cent. Capital spending was £737 million. Most of this investment occurred before privatisation in 1987. Advanced technology industries such as the aerospace industries frequently require step-changes in technology. There is considerable doubt whether private companies would ever embark on the huge investment involved without some long-term government support. The long-term view of investment in development has been taken in Japan by the government-sponsored agency MITI. The United States apparently approximates more closely to a free market, though in reality, defence expenditure serves in the United States the function of government investment in industrial production.

The Director General of the Engineering Industries said in 1988, 'Successful countries, including West Germany and Japan, provide resources (for industry) on an adequate scale, while the UK leaves the future to market forces. That means looking after oneself first. Who looks after UK Ltd?'

The case of Rolls-Royce demonstrates, first, that a short-term approach to investment and profitability may be economically imprudent, because a longer-term approach is more profitable and more effective. Secondly, judicious government investment in long-term projects may be vital to their success; not all government investment is wasted. Thirdly, it is not only mistaken but dangerous to suppose that perfect markets really exist. In the real world Britain's main industrial competitors benefit from long-term government investment, either directly or indirectly, and this must be reflected in British practice. It might be said that, in the long run, a government that invests in unprofitable business will ruin a country's economy. In the long run, in reality, we are all dead. In imperfectly competitive markets uneconomic but financially secured participants may kill off inadequately funded competitors before the long-term consequences of uneconomic practices prove ruinous.[34]

The City

It has already been noted that by 1990 the net contribution of the City to Britain's trade was zero as well as invisible. Other problems already mentioned include a short-term approach to investment and a reluctance to finance highly geared loans, both of which are obstacles to industrial development not experienced in other countries. The preoccupation of the City is with the paper transactions of company takeovers. This is one area in which Britain excels over its European counterparts, with three times the activity on mergers compared to Germany, France, Holland and other European countries. The amounts spent in the City on company takeovers in the 1980s were of the order of tenfold greater than all government spending on research and development (5 per cent of GDP and 0.62 per cent respectively). The real importance of this activity is reflected in the fact that Britain's largest corporate collapse, of the British and Commonwealth Merchant Bank in 1990, made no difference to anyone outside the City of London. Such companies exist only to make money by moving money: they do nothing else that would be noticed when they stop, and it makes no sensible difference to anything.[35]

The City underwent its greatest change ever when its traditional business was de-regulated in the 'Big Bang' of 1986. The idea was that free-market principles would generate more effective business. By

1989 it was reliably estimated that the market was losing £500 million a year, when it needed to make at least £450 million profit just to service loans for buy-outs before de-regulation occurred.[36]

By far the most significant feature of the City's business was the prevalence of malpractice and fraud in the 1980s. The City has traditionally been self-regulating. A succession of scandals showed that lying and illegality had become established as accepted norms in every branch of banking, insurance, stockbroking and company transactions. Lloyds of London was the most illustrious name involved. Other cases included the Johnson Matthey Bank which was rescued by the Bank of England after losing hundreds of millions in doubtful loans, the purchase of Harrods for £615 million by gentlemen who practised lies and deception about their financial status, and County National Westminster which was the subject of 'the most damning attack on a UK clearing bank ever written' after it promoted by complicated fraud a company takeover costing £837 million. Savings investors Barlow Clowes simply defrauded investors of £190 million. The Guinness Company engaged in 19 varieties of false accounting, conspiracy to defraud, theft and unlawful purchase in a takeover bid; and the purchase of Consolidated Goldfields in 1988 saw 'one of the biggest cases of mass insider dealings ever witnessed in the City'.[37]

Several features of these cases are relevant to the basic philosophy on which the markets in capital are based. It was necessary for the Bank of England to rescue Johnson Matthey, and it was thought fitting that investors in Barlow Clowes should be reimbursed by the government (because the Department of Trade and Industry had licensed the company to trade). Evidently, in the real world risk capital is expected by investors to be without risk, really: the government, that is the taxpayer, pays anyway for the 'risker's' security. In the Harrods case the government minister responsible refused to invoke the provisions of the Company Director's Disqualification Act (1980) to disbar from directorships persons 'not fit and proper', despite the fact that the official DTI report found that the individuals involved had 'practised lies and deception'. Nicholas Ridley said it would not be in the national interest to do so. In the County National Westminster case the report of the inquiry said that directors had shown 'a standard of conduct ... below that expected of responsible executives'. In this case it emerged that in the City it was regarded as routine to ignore stock exchange listing requirements and disclosure rules. The Guinness case was only discovered because it involved an American company, and the American regulatory body, the Securities and Exchange Commission, unearthed the illegal dealings (the major illicit American operations were orchestrated by Michael Milken who succeeded in inflating by illegal means his financial dealings so that by 1986 at $3 trillion they approximated to the gross domestic product of the United States). In Britain, after their failure to prevent another case of fraudulent practice, the 'self-regulating' body FIMBRA (Financial Investment Managers and Brokers Association) protested that it was unreasonable for the public to expect them to detect sophisticated fraud.[38]

No amount of evidence of fraud in financial markets can persuade New Right thinkers that the consideration of long-term self-interest alone is an inadequate market control of avarice. They are disposed to accept at face value the protestations of Michael Milken that his guilt reflects only on him personally, not the system and practices he exploits. Another view is that the philosophy of self-interested competition systematically produces such results. As one commentator remarked of Milken: 'Something in the process said that he always had to win, and he absolutely had to get the better of somebody whether or not it meant breaking the law.' No lesser an exponent of individualism than the Duke of Edinburgh was driven in 1990 to attack the City's failings, pointing out that: 'Nothing corrodes a community more quickly or more completely than lying, cheating, corruption and double dealing.' On the other hand Nicholas Ridley, the New Right Minister for Trade and Industry – 'a Thatcherite before Thatcher' – when called upon to act against such practices, judged that it wasn't in the public interest to do so.[39]

The evidence of corruption in the capital market of the 1980s should be sufficient to persuade an objective observer that such malpractice is innate to the system, not an aberration to be self-corrected.

Privatisation

The policy of selling off public assets to private owners was justified in three ways (apart from the general ideological commitment to private ownership, whatever the practical result). First, it was argued that private ownership would transform unprofitable public enterprises into profitable ones. Secondly, competition in the private sector would be more efficient than public ownership. Thirdly, the spread of popular share ownership would provide many more ordinary people with the benefits of private capital both financially and, most basically, morally, by way of self-reliance.

In the first case, some of the main concerns privatised were very effective and profitable under public ownership anyway. For example, British Oil, the telecommunications operations of the General Post Office and British Gas consistently earned annual profits of hundreds of millions before they were privatised. It is true that some others such as British Aerospace and British Airways reported improved profitability after privatisation, but they also had considerable debts written off prior to privatisation and achieved profitability by such easy short-term expedients as making masses of workers redundant, intensifying the labour of those remaining, increasing prices and charges, and disbursing earnings as maximal profits instead of investment.

Secondly, public utilities such as gas, water and electricity are natural monopolies and their transfer to private ownership does nothing to promote competition. It is in these cases that privatisation is seen most clearly as a purely doctrinal policy divorced from real utility. The vast majority of people do not want utilities to be privatised. For example, 79 per cent were opposed to water privatisation, and 84 per cent did not intend to buy shares.[40]

Thirdly, the New Right claim that privatisation promotes popular capitalism through share ownership does not bear examination. The greatest success of the policy was the employees' buy-out of the National Freight Corporation which was followed by a threefold increase in profitability. This result can as well be attributed to worker ownership and self-management – thoroughly left-wing principles – as to popular capitalism! Although many people did avail themselves of the opportunity to buy shares in privatised companies, very many did so merely to make quick killings from immediate resale – not to join in popular capitalism. For example, of 2.3 million people who bought shares in British Telecom only 1.3 million still had them in 1989. In 1986, 4.4 million people bought shares in British Gas, but only 2.7 million retained them in 1989. Although the proportion of individuals owning shares trebled during the 1980s, the balance of share ownership has not shifted from institutions and wealthy individuals. Stockbrokers regard the small investors' organisation as a 'farce' and no real provision is made for them by the Stock Exchange.[41]

The pickings to be had for speculative buyers were made easy by the gross undervaluation of shares in public enterprises. By one estimate, at least £1 billion was lost to the public purse in this way. Even though sales of public assets were sometimes of dubious legality, they generated large budget surpluses during the 1980s. It was an ex-Conservative Prime Minister, Harold Macmillan, who described this once and for all flogging off of public assets as 'selling the family silver'. It was clearly imprudent to treat the proceeds of such sales as current account income, in the way that the New Right chancellor did.[42]

In their doctrinaire enthusiasm 'privatisers' resorted to disreputable and illegal means. In their abortive attempt to privatise the nuclear power industry the government agreed at one stage to indemnify potential purchasers from the risks involved in taking on obsolete and dangerous plant, on the grounds that it would be unreasonable to expect a new owner to pay the cost of old workings and take risks. Nothing was heard of this doctrine during the 1984–5 miners' strike when the running costs of mines were calculated so as to include the cost of damage by old workings, retirement pensions and the like. Even this hooky-spooky was exceeded by the government's illegal bribes (euphemistically called 'sweeteners') to private companies buying public property. In the case of the British Aerospace purchase of Rover Cars, the European Commission headed by the ex-Conservative minister, Leon Brittan, ordered the company to repay £44 million in sweeteners and another £40 million in handouts for 'restructuring' that had not been carried out.[43]

Trade Unions and the Economy

Legislation was designed to curb the power of unions and specifically to curtail the use of strikes as a bargaining counter. This included acts to limit secondary picketing and action, curtail the closed shop, make unions financially liable to damages for strikes, and require secret ballots before strike action is taken. A reduction of strikes to the lowest level for fifty years was seen to be the result of these measures.

Another explanation is that trade unions were hobbled by massive unemployment of 3.7 million. Membership of unions dropped substantially, from over 13 million in 1979 to 10,387,238 in 1988. For example, employment in the coal industry fell from 125,000 in 1986 to 86,200 in 1988/89. British workers work the longest hours (39 hours per week average compared to 37–8 in Europe) and for the lowest pay. Taking the British average wage in 1989 as 100, that in

Japan was 121, in France 124, in the United States 133, and in Germany 172. Britain became the only major industrial nation in Europe without minimum wage legislation. The unions were restricted by legislation and their members constrained by the threat of unemployment from pursuing equitable wages and conditions. By 1990, however, it was evident that this was a stand-off position liable to change with economic circumstances. Evidently, in the absence of strikes, continuing wage settlements above the level of inflation were attributable to management policy and market forces in skills. The unions also learned something of rhetoric and tactics from the government. Strikes in 1988–9 by NHS workers, ambulancemen and, perhaps surprisingly, railwaymen received sympathetic support from a public which increasingly disbelieved government rhetoric that blamed unions for conditions when demonstrably the causes lay elsewhere, in government policy and external factors.[44]

Unemployment

Unemployment in 1979 was 5.3 per cent of the working population, 1.3 million. This level rose rapidly in the early years of Conservative administration, and official figures recorded an annual peak of 13.5 per cent, 3.27 million, in 1985. By December 1989 official figures were 5.8 per cent and 1.6 million unemployed.

There is no doubt that the New Right thinking was that in 1979 British industry and the public sector was over-staffed. Commensurate with this, government policy had the effect of shedding labour by means of high interest rates, increased national insurance contributions, increased VAT and severe public spending cuts. Margaret Thatcher denied that she wanted to send unemployment figures up. Her allies in the crusade for free markets, nevertheless, counted increased unemployment among the positive achievements of the New Right government. The use of a 'pool of unemployed' as a weapon against workers has long been a much favoured device of the Right.

The high levels of unemployment were dealt with by the government in various ways. First, the figures themselves were massaged downwards: 30 technical changes were made in the method of calculating unemployment figures between 1979 and 1990 and as a result of each of them fewer people seeking work were registered as unemployed. A salient example of the methods used was the removal from the register of people who were unemployed but on special 'schemes'; this change alone removed over half a million from the register in 1981. In 1990 the Minister for Employment told Parliament that the restart scheme for counselling the unemployed had dealt with 2,194,000 unemployed people, of whom only 11 per cent had found jobs. The Unemployment Unit records, based on the criteria used to show in 1979 that 'Labour isn't working', consistently show unemployment levels of half a million more than official estimates. Government ministers continue to deny that the statistics are manipulated, but there is no doubt that 'creative accounting' is the government's favoured method of 'reducing' unemployment. That is to say, the number *registered* as unemployed is reduced, not the number of unemployed.

Even on official estimates Britain's unemployment figures rank as the second highest in Europe. The real figures are substantially worse: at their peak in 1985 and 1986 there were 15.3 per cent, 3,772,900, unemployed, according to the Unemployment Unit.

As the figures for unemployment continued to be so bad, the government turned to showing that the number of people in employment was at record high levels (this has the rhetorical advantage exploited by the optimist who derives Panglossian satis-faction from the fact that his glass is half full, and his neighbour's is one-quarter empty). Thus Margaret Thatcher proudly announced in October 1989 that one of the massive achievements of her period in office was in jobs, with more people in work in Britain than ever before. In reality, real employment growth was virtually non-existent. The net *recorded* increase in employment between 1979 and 1989 was 978,000. Of these 440,000 were 'double-jobbers', that is people employed in two part-time jobs counted twice, and 470,000 were on training schemes; not, as Thatcher used to say when in opposition, in 'real jobs'. The net figure of real employment growth in ten years was exactly 68,000 for a population of 56 million.

Not least among the casualties of unemployment in Britain since 1979 has been the damage done to ordinary language, as the meaning of 'work', 'jobs', 'employment', 'training' and related words became lost as the government's redefinitions multiplied. The trustworthi-ness of official statistics and government pronouncements based on them was brought seriously into question, and with it the essential foundation of good government in its reputation for probity and the trust it enjoys with the population.[45]

ECONOMIC CONSEQUENCES

The economic results of ten years of New Right government have been proclaimed as a miracle by themselves. The picture is as follows, shown on the same comparative basis as that in Table 1.

TABLE 6 GNP PER CAPITA (UK = 100) 1970–88

	1970	1978	1988
United States	178	182	199
OECD	131	136	132
Japan	101	116	139
United Kingdom	100	100	100

Sources: as Table 1; OECD Main Economic Indicators February 1990

TABLE 7 COMPARISON OF KEY INDICATORS: 1988

	Unemployment (%)	Consumer prices (1985 = 100)	Interest rates (%)	Industrial production (1985=100)	GDP per capita ($)
Canada	7.8	113.1	11.17	113.4	15,139
Australia	7.2	126.9	15.2	109	10,634
United Kingdom	8.1	113.8	12.75	109.5	8,988
United States	5.5	109.4	6.5	110.9	17,965
Germany	8.7	98.8	3.5	106.1	10,935
Japan	2.5	101.4	2.5	112.9	12,208
Sweden	1.6	109.1	8.5	104.1	12,848

Source: OECD Main Economic Indicators February 1990

Table 6 shows that between 1978 and 1988 Britain made a small improvement in productivity compared to the OECD average. The outstanding fact, however, is the very much increased gap between the much more productive economies of the United States and Japan. Evidently, although a modest improvement in overall performance can be claimed by comparison with the least developed economies, comparison with our leading competitors shows that Britain's position has worsened, and this is the standard chosen by the New Right itself.

This conclusion is demonstrated in more detail in Table 7, which shows that, among the leading nations compared, Britain in 1988 had the second highest level of unemployment (really the highest when manipulation of the figures is accounted for), the second highest level of inflation, and the second highest interest rates. The much vaunted increase in productivity placed Britain only fourth, behind Canada, Japan and the United States. The most stark result is revealed by the comparison of gross domestic product per capita, which is a very good indicator of a nation's overall economic health. Britain has the lowest of the countries compared, and barely qualifies to be included among the most advanced industrial nations. Thus, after ten years and by their own chosen criteria, the New Right has failed to achieve the success they sought, first and foremost in the economic sphere.

These facts have not deterred Britain's New Right government from proclaiming their success in creating a miraculous transformation of Britain's economy. But their achievement lies only in the realms of rhetoric and the manipulation of figures, not in any real achievement. As Professor Wynn Godley has said:

> I regard the so-called Thatcher miracle as a gigantic con-trick ... The con has been achieved by ... the skilful but thoroughly dishonest presentation of the facts.[46]

People cannot, however, be fooled all of the time.

15   THE POLITICAL RECORD

SUMMARY RECORD: THE RHETORIC

In politics and government there are eight salient spheres of achievement claimed by the New Right. First is the claim that the autonomy of parliamentary government has been re-established because the trade unions have been excluded from participation. Secondly, the legitimacy of government is asserted on the basis of electoral results and the mandate they deliver. Thirdly, it is claimed that public spending was managed prudently by reducing borrowing, making economies and reducing the proportion of national income spent by government. Fourthly, as the only party to believe in lower taxation on moral grounds, the Conservative government reduced taxation, both the basic rate of income tax for everyone and the top rates as an incentive to enterprisers. Fifthly, the trade unions' political power has been curbed by effective legislation. Sixthly, government bureaucracy has been reduced to the point where the civil service is the smallest since the war. Seventhly, local government has been made accountable, especially through financial controls: first by rate-capping, then by the Poll Tax. Finally, eighth, over a range of foreign relations Britain's prestige has been restored: through strong nuclear defences, the Falklands War, in dealing with the European Economic Community, and through the sixth largest aid programme in the western world.[47]

SUMMARY RECORD: THE REALITY

The Courtier State

The practice in the 1970s of incorporating trade unions into government was among those most deplored by the New Right because, in their view, it compromised the authority of government. In 1977 John Hoskyns, who was later to be head of the Prime Minister's policy unit, prepared a secret paper entitled *Stepping Stones* in which it was proposed that there should be no question of 'getting on' with the unions. A programme of rhetorical denunciation was advised, 'digging every skeleton out of the union cupboard'. After that a Conservative government should sever all relations with union leaders. The paper advised that for the Tories to treat them as responsible figures, and thus give them more credibility, must in the end be a mistake. *Stepping Stones* provided the guide for the government's disincorporation of trade unions throughout the 1980s. Their survival on disempowered quangos was eventually terminated in 1988 by the unions themselves on the principle of non-cooperation with training policy.[48]

The result, however, was not government uncorrupted by the incorporation of external interests. What developed was more in keeping with Lord Hailsham's premonitions of elective dictatorship. Margaret Thatcher used the powers available to her under the constitution to develop a mode of personal government more akin to a feudal monarch's court than to the office of an elected head of state. Nicholas Kaldor had this in mind when he said paradoxically that Margaret Thatcher was the first Marxist (really Bolshevik!)

Prime Minister because of her expressed contempt for consensus politics. She had said in Australia:

> To me, consensus seems to be the process of abandoning all beliefs, principles, values, and policies ... It is the process of avoiding the very issues that have got to be solved merely to get people to come to an agreement on the way ahead.[49]

A less democratic view is hardly conceivable for the head of an elected government. Small wonder then that, instead of acting as the *primus inter pares* in a representative cabinet, and governing through an elected Parliament with the guidance of the permanent impartial civil service, Margaret Thatcher reigned over something like a personal court. This comprised in part civil servants picked for their ideological soundness, malleability and willingness to be economical with the truth under instructions from the Prime Minister. There were, in addition, personal assistants such as Bernard Ingham the Chief Press Secretary (called the 'Yorkshire Rasputin' by John Biffen), special advisors and consultants of no clear personal or constitutional status, such as the economist Professor Alan Walters, and a motley assortment of 'sound' carpet knights, drawn mainly from the more dubious corners of commerce and industry. Such were David Young (*Private Eye's* Lord Suit of property developments and illegal sweeteners), James Hanson (Lord Playboy – renowned for his shunning of high-technology, high-risk enterprises), and Jack Lyons, convicted in 1990 on five counts of false accounting, conspiracy and theft in the Guinness affair. John Hoskyns, author of *Stepping Stones*, was rewarded for his services to the nation with a knighthood.

The picture of the court is completed by peremptoriness, preferment and profligacy. Civil servants such as David Deux, with the temerity to challenge the convictions of the Prime Minister with mere contradictory facts, were debarred from advancement. Those like Clive Ponting, who disclosed malpractice by ministers, were prosecuted. Knighthoods and peerages were liberally distributed on a scale unknown since the Maundy Gregory scandals of the 1920s to persons such as Edwin McAlpine, Marcus Seiff, Victor Matthews, Arnold Weinstock, William Cayzer, Charles Forte, Frank Taylor, James Hanson, John King, Alistair McAlpine and Nigel Vinson, whose chief distinction is to have arranged for their companies to make handsome donations to Conservative Party funds. Industrial success was not sufficient recommendation for admission to the court. The outstandingly successful Chairman of ICI, John Harvey Jones, was not just the most noted excludee. He was the Prime Minister's least favourite businessman because he had told her in 1981 that she was ruining British industry (the fact that he was not a supporter of the Conservative Party was anyway sufficient reason for exclusion from the chairmanship of the University Grants Committee). Two other examples of *persona non grata* were the dancer Moira Shearer, who was excluded from the BBC Board, and Professor Richard Hoggart, excluded from the Arts Council, for similar reasons.[50]

One measure of the growth of the courtier state was the escalating cost of the Prime Minister's private office (when cuts in public spending were the order of the day). In 1981 it was just £35,762. The total cost of the Prime Minister's office in 1985–6 was £4.4 million and by 1989–90 was £7.9 million. By 1988 the cost of private advisors had increased sixfold since 1981 to £214,807 – that is in addition to the regular cost of civil servants in the Prime Minister's office.[51] Against the inclinations of industrialists themselves, the New Right government in the 1980s dissolved the elements of a corporate state, encompassing the elected representatives of over 13 million trade unionists, and established instead a court of preferred individuals, including cabinet ministers who were not elected by anybody, representing nobody as much as themselves, and nothing but the Prime Minister's own personal preference.

Legitimacy of Government

Ian Gilmour's principle of legitimacy has already been mentioned: that a clear majority not supporting a government constitutes a strong counter-mandate to its policies. Since 1979 Britain has endured a government which has the positive support of less than one third of the electorate (never more than 44 per cent of voters). Margaret Thatcher claimed that this level of support was sufficient to justify the presumption of approval of all policies pursued.

There is considerable evidence to show that, in fact, public support for many of the New Right's main policies was very limited, and in some cases almost negligible. Surveys of public opinion showed that clear majorities were opposed to privatisation of British Telecom and Electricity (both 56 per cent) and British Gas (57 per cent). An extraordinary majority opposed the privatisation of water (79 per cent) to no avail. The proportion of people disapproving of the abolition of the Greater London Council was 79 per cent; the Poll Tax 71 per cent; and the banning of trade unions at GCHQ 69 per cent.[52]

The New Right government was opposed in theory to the tyranny of the majority. In practice, it proved to be indifferent to the problem of the tyranny of a minority when the minority in question was itself. Health Minister Kenneth Clarke explained the new libertarian philosophy in practice in the case of health service reforms: most people, he said, may not be freely choosing what was happening, but they would learn to like it after the changes had been imposed. What Margaret Thatcher had enunciated as her principle of mandate in 1979 became the common (illegitimate) practice throughout the 1980s.

Public Spending and Borrowing

The government's aspiration to cut public spending was unfulfilled. An Adam Smith Institute man no less, MP John Redwood, pronounced it less than successful. In the last year of the Labour administration, 1977–8, total public spending was £55 billion. By 1987–8 it was £177 billion, 'a substantial increase in real terms, and a colossal increase in nominal terms'.[53]

Some extra government expenditure was by positive (and therefore contestable) choice, such as increased expenditure on policing (47 per cent) and defence (23 per cent). Some of it was, for demographic reasons, virtually inevitable, notably expenditure on the increased number of disabled and long-term sick. Another proportion was due to the (in New Right terms) 'unprincipled' decision to confirm post-arbitration pay increases for the nurses and other NHS staff (31 per cent). The greatest increase of all was due to the government's monetarist economic policies that led to a massive increase in unemployment and consequent increase in expenditure on training schemes (120 per cent), unemployment benefits and other related costs of social security.[54]

Reduction in public spending was achieved by cuts primarily in housing, schools, subsidies for food and to the nationalised industries. The public sector borrowing requirement was reduced to zero by 1986–7. At the same time the government was running record budget surpluses. The sources of the surpluses were the windfall proceeds from North Sea oil and once-for-all sales of public assets (always at substantial discounts to buyers) – 'selling off the family silver' *and* the nation's seed-corn. Remarkably the principles of accounting applied to privatisation did not reckon the income from assets continuing in public ownership as a credit. Also, a curious feature of the policy of selling council houses was the prohibition on the use of the proceeds of sales by councils.

In summary: the New Right government failed to reduce public spending between 1979 and 1990, and so failed by its own criterion. Had the real need for more public expenditure – in line with most other European countries – been accepted then British people would have been spared a great deal of hardship and the economy could have been in a much stronger position. Instead, the proceeds of North Sea oil sales were squandered on unemployment benefits and public assets were disposed of at heavy discounts to private owners.

Taxation and Incomes

The Conservatives say they are the only party that believes in lower taxation. If for 'lower taxation' we were to substitute 'lower rates of income tax on the highest earnings' then the evidence would support the claim. The greatest tax reductions in the 1980s were in the top rates of income tax: from 83 per cent in 1979 to 40 per cent in 1988. This was said to have the moral effect of promoting self-reliance (and honesty, since high taxation is an irresistible temptation to tax avoidance). Other practical effects intended were to increase the incentive to enterprise and hard work and thereby the 'honest' tax-take.

The evidence that tax cuts provide incentives to those with the highest incomes is inconclusive. Higher incomes generate higher tax revenues even at the lower rates, and the tax revenues were certainly higher after cuts. (It is worth reflecting on the view that if taxes aren't as high as 85 per cent there is more revenue because people with the highest incomes would have less desire to avoid paying tax. Another view is that if, contrarywise, such people paid their taxes like everybody else [on a PAYE basis perhaps] the rates would not *need* to be so high!)

Incomes of the highest earners certainly increased dramatically. This may be for several reasons. Market rates for special skills may warrant higher payments. The explanation favoured by enthusiasts of the New Right was that top pay was related to performance, and performance is related to the incentives provided by lower taxation.[55]

There is no evidence to support these views. First of all, work by the Institute for Fiscal Studies showed that the entire growth of aggregated tax revenues can easily be accounted for without reference to incentive effects. Higher income may be unrelated to harder work.[56] One factor is higher expectations of top executives who compare their incomes with American or European counterparts (this discounts lower living costs in Britain, and the fact that incomes of British workers at all levels compare unfavourably on the same basis). It is significant that many top executives had very substantial increases when their companies' profits were very modest. In 1989, for example, Bob Bowman of Beecham received a salary increase of 88 per cent when his company's profitability rose only 15 per cent. J. Craven, a director of Morgan Grenfell, received a 71 per cent increase although profits fell by 44 per cent. Banks were particularly indifferent to performance when deciding on salary increases. In 1989–90 Lloyds awarded their top executive an increase of 61.6 per cent although earnings per share fell by 100 per cent. The Midland Bank paid its chairman a salary increase of 25 per cent (£329,616) although the bank reported a loss of £261 million. A spokesman for the bank explained that senior boardroom salaries were not performance-related. The director general of the CBI said: 'There is no virtue in low pay at all.' A few chairmen simply award themselves higher salaries.[57] Most awards are made by 'remuneration committees' of non-executive directors; chairmen stand down when their own salaries are discussed. There is very little impartiality in this. As Dominic Lawson explained, the non-executive directors are usually the friends of senior executives. Moreover, by awarding large increases to others they increase the likelihood that they, in their own turn, will receive the (higher) 'going rate'. This cartel of top executive salary-fixers ensures that the market forces and performance indicators that determine employees' salaries do not intrude into their estimations of their own worth, which invariably reflect their high opinion of their own superior talents and energy, whatever company profits in the market may objectively be signalling.[58]

In smaller businesses and at the middle-management level of larger ones, there is sound evidence to show that potentially increased income from lower taxes does not provide a significant incentive to risk and work. Indeed the start-up of small business may be encouraged by higher levels of taxation: as enterprises strive to overcome financial stringencies, their efforts generate business. The growth of established small businesses is constrained far more by problems of management training and lack of skilled personnel than by inadequate tax incentives. In larger firms managers typically prefer less pressure to higher rewards through greater effort. The presumption that lower tax rates provide essential incentives to business enterprise is not clearly borne out. People's motivations are far more complex.[59]

The effect on morale and motivation of large differentials between top incomes and average incomes is a different matter. Workers are routinely compelled or exhorted to restrict wage claims to the performance of the company or even the nation, regardless of their own efforts or of inflation. It is highly likely that they will be demotivated or incensed by the huge increases in salary, unrelated to performance, awarded to directors. The director general of the CBI significantly did not acknowledge this. As evidence he cited the fact that when he, as head of the Audit Commission, had forgone a higher-than-inflation salary increase, the morale of the people in local government had not noticeably increased. This is to misunderstand the problem. People's morale is affected by many things, and local government workers had many other reasons to be demoralised besides the salary of the chairman of the Audit Commission. Whatever effect his wage restraint had clearly did not compensate. But in so far as relative income was a factor it is very likely that the acceptance of a higher salary by someone employed mainly to cut everyone else's would have had a very adverse effect on morale. What his restraint did, no doubt, was to avoid making morale worse. It was too much to expect a non-event to make it better. The failure of the director general of the CBI to recognise the negative impact on morale of the large salaries to top directors, unrelated to performance and inflation, is politically damaging. However, there is another significant feature of the relationship between executive salaries and taxation. When the top rate of tax was 83 per cent companies provided very substantial perquisites in kind: cars, medical insurance, holidays, even clothes. This was justified because commensurate increases in salaries would be taken in tax. What happened during the 1980s was that taxation was dramatically reduced and salaries were dramatically increased but perquisites continued to be dispensed as well. Greed is the only word suitable to describe the motivation for these developments.[60]

The effects of endemic greed at the top were anything but negligible to the population as a whole. The New Right government boasted of cuts in income tax rates. This rhetoric exploited the equation in the popular consciousness of tax with income tax. But the burden of indirect taxation in other forms (especially national insurance contributions and VAT) is greater than income tax. Income tax accounted for 34.6 per cent of all revenue in 1978–9, and was reduced to 28.1 per cent by 1988–9. But during the same period VAT rose from 8.3 to 15.1 per cent of all revenue (after a near doubling of the rate in 1979). National insurance, the forgotten tax, accounted for 18 per cent of revenue in 1989. As a consequence of these shifts in the pattern of taxation, most people were in fact more heavily taxed in 1988–9 than they were in 1978–9. The total tax burden on the average family (a husband on average earnings with wife and two children) increased from 35.1 per cent in 1978–9 to 37.3 in 1988–9.[61]

The shift in taxation has greatly advantaged the top earners, at the expense of people on lower incomes. In 1988–9 taxpayers paid £20 billion less income tax than they would have paid at 1978–9 rates. But 47 per cent of the savings went to the richest 10 per cent. Only 17 per cent went to the bottom 50 per cent of taxpayers. The poorest families, those on 50 per cent of average income, who only paid 2.5 per cent of earnings in income tax and national insurance in 1978–9, were paying 7.1 per cent by 1988–9. For those on 20 times average earnings the proportion fell from 74.3 per cent to just 38.5 per cent in 1988–9. VAT affected the worst off disproportionately in the same way. The poorest 20 per cent of the population paid 29.5 per cent of their income in indirect taxation, compared to the richest 20 per cent who paid just 21.1. per cent in this way. When various changes (meaning reductions) in state benefits are taken into account, as Graham Hills explained: 'Between 1978 and 1979 and 1988 and 1989, the bottom half of the population has lost £6.6 billion of which £5.6 billion has gone to the top 10 per cent; indeed £4.8 billion has gone to the top 5 per cent.' The cuts in direct taxes had been paid for by cuts in the generosity of benefits. There has been a major redistribution from those on lower incomes to the better off.[62]

For years the real situation was hidden by (perhaps) genuine statistical errors. In June 1987 the Prime Minister told Parliament that official figures for 1981, 1983 and 1985 showed that those on lower incomes had done much better than the population in general. This was proof that high incomes at the top 'trickled down' to the bottom, in the favoured metaphor. The statistics showing this were based on the (false) assumption that for 1981 and 1982 housing costs were net of housing rebates whereas they were gross. This error artificially depressed incomes estimated for 1981 and 1982 and so exaggerated the later increases in incomes. In reality the increase in income of the poorest 10 per cent was not twice the national average, but less than half. Not only were the worst off badly off, the gap between them and their compatriots widened more rapidly.[63]

Civil Service

The effect of market ideas on the civil service has been notably successful in some (marginal) ways. Between 1979 and 1986 the number of civil servants was reduced from 732,000 to 600,000, the lowest level since the war; the saving was £1 billion. A measure of the reduced bureaucracy was that by 1987 27,000 forms had been scrapped and 41,000 redesigned, at a saving of £14 million. The service was reorientated towards management and cost accounting instead of the administrative tradition.

Even these changes are not necessarily unqualified goods. For instance, reduction of staff employed by the Department of Trade and Industry by 26 per cent (12,513) was not obviously prudent with 3.7 million unemployed. Likewise, with the problem of tax evasion a hundredfold greater than dole fraud, the wisdom of reductions in Inland Revenue staff of 22 per cent (66,611) is not obvious either. The simple fact of reduced numbers of civil servants, without regard to their function or effect, is not cause for satisfaction. The New Right, of course, presumes quite baselessly that public employees are, by definition, unproductive and employees in private industry productive.

The practical consequence of this presumption has been to demoralise civil servants. An erosion in pay by 30 per cent relative to obviously comparable workers in the private sector lead to an exodus by many of the most able public servants, and to difficulties in recruiting the best qualified candidates because they declined to embark on careers that government ministers clearly believed were parasitic and contemptible; which attitude was reflected in levels of pay. The most basic consequence of the doctrine that civil servants are 'lean kine' was a destruction of the dignified ideal of public service. Lip-service only was paid to this, while policy and practices showed the truth. Even the man from Marks and Spencers, Derek Rayner, whose values transformed civil service practice, saw that, although government employees 'delivered the goods' to private sector standards, their employers failed to reciprocate with commensurate rewards.

Even those who were encouraged by new practices found fault with the new ethos. The service has been politicised more than ever before in modern times, if not by overtly political appointments then by the way it became necessary that Whitehall advice be attuned to ensure that 'it fell with a joyous note upon the ministerial ear'. A parallel development was the distinctive tendency to strengthen the grip of the state through obsessive secrecy: in 1987 the Cabinet Office issued advice to civil servants on how to evade scrutiny of their decisions by judicial review. The Adam Smith Institute, no less, found this indicative of the government's real intention to strengthen the power of state bureaucracy, not curtail it. The same intent was evident in some notorious special cases. In 1984 Clive Ponting, a senior civil servant, and in 1986–7 Peter Wright, an ex-MI5 officer, were prosecuted obsessively, supposedly in the interests of national security, but really to secure secretive government. In the Wright case, the head of the civil service was ignominiously obliged to confess to an Australian court that he was 'economical with the truth' when prosecuting the Wright case under instructions from the Prime Minister. In 1984 'national security' overrode freedom to join a union at Government Communications Headquarters – despite the unions giving a 'no-strike' undertaking. These nefarious happenings were indicative of a deep-rooted propensity to misrule that will be discussed presently.

The civil service was made smaller and cheaper by financial scrutiny during the 1980s. In almost every other way it suffered basic harm, and was diminished by New Right policies.[64]

Local Government

As with the civil service so local government was required to implement effective cost controls. Substantial cost reductions were enforced through legislation introducing compulsory competitive tendering for services, instead of established provision by the direct labour force. These measures eventually succeeded where previous attempts by governments of both colours had failed, by establishing systematic controls on costs. Even so, stringent controls of expenditure were not enforceable until rate levels were 'capped'; then eventually rates, as the primary source of local revenue, were replaced by the community charge or Poll Tax. Reducing costs, introducing effective cost control and limits, and reforming the basis of local government revenues are all changes that were seen as desirable by everybody, though reasons and motives varied (the Labour Party had itself announced that the party was over for local government, and cut the support grant substantially in 1976). These changes are unlikely to be reversed completely by any future government.

Poll Tax. The reform of local government finance by the introduction of the community charge had especially far-reaching effects, and warrants closer attention. The question of how best to raise money to pay for local services had greatly exercised Gladstone in Victorian times. The main problems are of fairness (how to distribute the tax burden equitably) and practicality (how to collect taxes effectively). Major reviews of the established local authority rating system, which was a property tax, had been carried out in 1976, 1981, 1982 and a White Paper produced in 1983. They all led to the conclusion that, despite the difficulties with the rating system, there was no clear alternative that was fairer or more practicable.

New Right thinking, especially that emanating from the Adam Smith Institute, requires that everybody who benefits from services should contribute to their cost and that local authorities should be accountable for their expenditure on services. In this view the problem was that local authorities, especially Labour-controlled ones, were raising too much money from individuals and businesses through the rates in order to provide services for other individuals who paid little or nothing in rates. The beneficiaries had every incentive to maintain in office councils who benefited them in this way, whereas individuals and businesses were penally taxed without redress. Some individuals had low incomes and made little use of public services, but lived in property with high rates. Other households had several wage-earners and made considerable use of local services, but paid little or nothing in rates. Businesses located in areas run by 'high-spending' councils were at a disadvantage compared to those in other areas. Moreover, businesses did not even have representation in the councils which imposed the taxation.

The solution derived from New Right principles was in three parts. First, a Unified Business Rate was introduced that was fixed and applied uniformly throughout the country. Councils were no longer to be able, at their own discretion, to raise extra money from businesses. Second, a basic charge was to be made to every member of the community for the provision of community services. This revived the ancient practice of taxing 'heads' indiscriminately, hence the pejorative label 'Poll Tax' which the Conservative government sought unsuccessfully to avoid. The basic charge was to be reduced for some people on low incomes, including students, but still in conformity with the principle that every beneficiary of services should pay. This was intended to encourage the interest of citizens in the conduct of local government and thereby make councils more accountable, thus enhancing local democracy. Third, councils were to be free to set the level of the community charge. This, however, was subject to rewards and penalties in the form of extra grants or cuts in central funding, depending upon whether the level set was below or above the level established by the government's own assessment of need. The Conservative manifesto of 1987 had contained a commitment to a reform of local government finances of the sort now proposed. In the event, Margaret Thatcher had to deploy all the resources available to her as Prime Minister to overcome opposition to the Poll Tax even from New-Right-thinking members of her own cabinet. Legislation was enacted first for Scotland through the Abolition of Domestic Rates (Scotland) Act (1987), then for England and Wales in 1988.

The Poll Tax had the fiscal effects it was intended to have. Many individuals who had paid high rates benefited from a reduced community charge. Typically, Grace Griffiths from Tynemouth aged 67 who lived alone and didn't use many services paid £400 in rates in 1989 and just £200 for the community charge in 1990. Many businesses benefited from the Unified Rate but, inevitably, others did not. By far the most conspicuous effect of the implementation of the Poll Tax, however, was to impose intolerable financial burdens on large numbers of people who, quite simply, could not afford to pay. Many people on the lowest incomes and those depending on Social Security benefits were required to find money to pay the basic community charge which in 1990 was an average of £363 (£7 per week). The requirement on local authorities to collect the charge and confiscate the property of or to prosecute non-payers further exacerbated the problem. Problems of fairness were compounded further still by provisions requiring charges on payers to be increased annually to compensate for shortfalls due to non-payment in previous years. Protests against the tax escalated from lobbying and petitioning to demonstrations organised by the Anti-Poll Tax Union, and culminated in violent scenes in council chambers and on the streets throughout the country.

The government defended the Poll Tax against these widespread protests and attacks. They blamed 'high spending' councils for the high level of the community charges set, despite strong disincentives to do so in the form of the standard services assessment and the disproportionate financial penalties imposed for 'overspending'. They pointed to local councils which they regarded as exemplary, such as Wandsworth where the community charge in 1990 was just £136, and compared them to 'high spending' Labour councils, such as Wandsworth's neighbour Haringey where the charge in the same year was £560.

Attempts to defend the Poll Tax proved ineffective. Significantly, some Conservative councils protested, and lifelong supporters of the Conservative Party joined the public demonstrations that the government tried to dismiss as merely the work of left-wing militants. A few councils like Wandsworth were able to set very low community charges, not only because they were relatively well off and had considerable reserves to draw on, but most significantly because they were the beneficiaries of special discretionary grants from the government such as the area protection grant. Most people regarded such special treatment as political gerrymandering.

Some leading Conservatives had had the foresight to anticipate the problems encountered by the introduction of what was almost universally regarded as an unfair tax. Nigel Lawson had predicted in 1986 that it would be 'completely unworkable and politically catastrophic'. Michael Heseltine, referring to the assumption of powers to enforce the capping of local government expenditure, called it 'an act of centralised power outside our experience'. The Conservative Bow Group of MPs pronounced the Poll Tax 'a financial and political disaster'. Political journalist Hugo Young summarised the Conservative reforms of local government finance as 'six years of political blundering on a scale unequalled in the postwar era'.

Even the most enthusiastic of Margaret Thatcher's supporters on the Poll Tax issue, Nicholas Ridley, recognised, with hindsight, that 'the community charge was much too high, particularly for those on low incomes'. The basic principle as expounded by spokesmen of the Adam Smith Institute was supposed still to be sound: that 'everyone should pay the same', as for TV licences or car tax. It is significant that in this matter proponents of Smith's free-market doctrine are holier than the Pope. For in the *Wealth of Nations* Smith wrote: 'It is not very unreasonable that the rich should contribute to the public expense, not only in proportion to their revenue, but something more than in that proportion.' Margaret Thatcher's equity-blindness in the matter of the Poll Tax contributed greatly to the public's perception of her ability to govern.

Some other practical developments in local government were commensurate with alternative theories. Housing had not always and everywhere flourished under local authority control. Schools, likewise, did not always benefit from the effective exclusion of parents and clients from participation in control. Together these activities account for most local government expenditure, and many others besides the New Right thinkers would wish to see local communities being given more control of such expenditure. The general shift in the function of local government from provider to enabler is in accordance with not only social democracy but with even the Trotskyist doctrine of the Fourth International: namely, self-management.

Although the New Right rhetoric promoted the virtues of a life unburdened by local government bureaucracy, the reality once again was different. By imposing limits to local government expenditure (based on inevitably arbitrary norms) the New Right Conservatives effectively removed from elected local government the power to decide, on behalf of the community it represented, what expenditure would be acceptable and which services to provide. In defence of this decisive move it was argued that central government has a more valid mandate than local government (presumably because it represents a wider constituency and the national interest). This argument fails at precisely the point where it needs to be effective: at the level of decision-making apposite to local government. By pursuing a vendetta against local government the New Right Conservatives have severely compromised the role and status of local democracy.

There are, of course, very good reasons for having quasi-autonomous local government, most of which chime with the central doctrines of the New Right. The power of local government, in its proper sphere, balances the tendency to overwhelming power at the centre. This is the flourishing of small platoons that Edmund Burke lauded as the foundation (on an intelligible scale) of good citizenship. Autonomous local government fosters diversity in policies and society that both Liberals and Conservatives offer reasons to value. Not least, local government provides an alternative means of political education where policies and politicians can prove their worth, as they did in the Victorian heyday, outside of the epicentre of Westminster.

The undermining of local government, making it wholly subservient to the centre, is among the most retrograde results of New Right policy since 1979.[65]

Trade Unions and Politics

The record of the New Right vendetta against trade unions has been referred to earlier, in connection with economic policy and the legitimacy of government. There are a number of other issues of a political nature concerning the trade unions which deserve further consideration. First is the matter of the power of union leaders, especially the power to call strikes without necessarily first holding a ballot of members. The Trade Unions Act (1984) required secret ballots before strikes were called. This measure extended democracy in unions and it would have been more to their credit had they made the change to mandatory ballots themselves (the historic miners' strike of 1974 was called after a pit-head ballot showed over-whelming support). That being so, it is interesting to reflect on the logic by which delegate conference decisions by unions are undemo-cratic without secret ballots on particular issues, whereas the decisions of a parliament of elected representatives (a delegate conference by another name) are democratic without the need for a referendum on particular tendentious issues.

Concern is regularly expressed in New Right quarters about the trade unions' links with the Labour Party and, in particular, the con-tributions to the political funds that are levied automatically unless members expressly opt out. By another provision of the 1984 Trade Unions Act, unions were required to ballot their members on the subject of the political fund. The final result of the ballots was that 38 out of 38 unions voted to retain their political funds; the average 'yes' vote was 83 per cent. Two unions (Hosiery and Knitwear workers and Inland Revenue staff) voted heavily in favour of estab-lishing a political fund for the first time.[66] This result strongly refuted the New Right propaganda to the effect that many (perhaps most) trade unionists did not support the unions' political activities, and their support for the Labour Party in particular. Significantly, the New Right rises to full song and dance about trade union contributions to the Labour Party but has nothing to say about the routine transfer of company funds to the Conservative Party (£1,751,898 was admitted to in 1986) and other right-wing organisations (another £541,164): there is no secret ballot of the shareholders of British and Commonwealth Shipping, United Biscuits, Trust House Forte, Hanson Trust et al before these transactions take place.[67]

Liberty has been routinely invoked to challenge the power of trade unions and their legal privileges especially the 'closed shop'. Some closed-shop arrangements, most notably among newspaper printworkers' unions, were indefensible and it was in almost everyone's interest to alter such arrangements, but this was by no means generally true. In fact, closed-shop arrangements were always much less widespread than the New Right demonology suggested.

Usually there are good reasons for a closed shop, to do with the special circumstances of a particular industry. Employers themselves often prefer closed-shop arrangements because they are conducive to more effective and efficient management, reducing as they do the complexity of management and the fragmentation of organisation. This explains why, even after a succession of government measures to break down the closed shop, there were still in 1989 2.6 million employees (including 10 per cent of the male workforce) working under closed-shop arrangements. The issue of individual liberty being compromised by the closed shop has been exaggerated, because unions have always recognised authentic dissent in principle as grounds for exemption.[68]

Defenders of liberty in trade union affairs have had other things to exercise them since 1979. First there is the licence to 'free-load' by those whose conscience forbids them to join a union but does not require them commensurately to forgo the benefits of the unions' collective action, in pay and other conditions of employment. This should not be merely a matter of conscience for people in their capacity as employees, any more than it is in their capacity as citizens and taxpayers. Secondly, New Right libertarians have been unconcerned about the denial of the right of people to be members of a trade union when they positively want to be. The refusal in 1986 to allow, against their wishes, employees at GCHQ to be members of a union violates principles of liberty every bit as much as requiring them to be members against their wish. Similarly, the removal in 1987 of schoolteachers' salary-negotiating rights, and the imposition by the state on them, and later on ambulancemen, of wage settlements without agreement is a denial of basic liberties to trade unionists. Unsurprisingly, by 1989 the United Nations' International Labour Organisation condemned the British government's increasingly illiberal labour laws.[69]

The Miners' Strike 1984–5

The event of outstanding significance for the politics of trade unions was undoubtedly the miners' strike of 1984–5. The strike put on public display most of the elements of New Right doctrine and practice. Ever since their successful strikes of 1972 and 1974 the National Union of Mineworkers was regarded by the Right as the embodiment of everything retrogressive about Britain. Had not Margaret Thatcher's iron soul been forged by those events? Of all the objectives to be achieved in realising the central aim of rolling back the frontiers of socialism, subordinating the NUM to state authority was the main one.

The dispute was ostensibly about matters of direct pertinence to the coal industry but really it was about the power of trade unionism in Britain. The NUM had agreed with the National Coal Board and the government a 'Plan for Coal' which secured the future of the industry in the context of a wider energy policy for the country. What was ostensibly in dispute was the NCB's decision to close pits and reduce the labour force, which the NUM argued was contrary to the agreements set out in the Plan for Coal. The real dispute was about the government's determination to crush the NUM, and so set an example to the rest of the trade union movement.

The conclusion that the strike was first provoked then orchestrated for this purpose is virtually impossible to evade. Faced in 1982 with confrontation by the miners over pit closures, the government made a tactical retreat until its preparations for the final confrontation were in place: these included legislation to prohibit secondary picketing and action (of a sort that had proved decisive in the 1974 dispute), giving employers legal remedies against political strikes, providing for the sequestration of union funds, and the curtailment of state benefits to strikers. Secondly, the government appointed as chairman of the NCB someone the Bishop of Durham described as 'an imported elderly American', Ian McGregor, who had already 'sorted out' the steel industry and taken on the American miners' unions with success. McGregor proceeded to concentrate control in his own hands and to dispose of senior NCB officials who might be sympathetic to the miners' case.[70] Thirdly, the government mobilised a national police force to use colonial policing methods against the mineworkers. The Association of Chief Police Officers (ACPO) was an organisation with no statutory status, originally set up to provide a forum for chief constables but without an extensive operational function. For the purpose of crushing the miners ACPO became in effect the High Command of the British State Police. Through the agency of ACPO's central intelligence unit, police from anywhere in the country can be deployed anywhere else. The methods in which the police had been trained since 1982 were derived from the experience of Hong Kong police dealing with 'colonial' riots. As set out in the *Public Order Manual*, tactics to be used escalate from 'information management' through 'controlled sound levels', 'baton charges', the use of plastic bullets and CS gas, to the use of firearms.

Controlled sound levels involve the use by the police of battle cries, chanting, shouting and rhythmic beating on protective shields. Although the tactics were designed to boost police morale, they proved more in practice to be provocative to miners (at least one policeman remained human in all of this, proposing instead a banner with the threatening emblem 'Disperse Or We Will Play Barry Manilow'). The Prime Minister assured ACPO that the army would be deployed, if necessary, to secure their objectives.[71]

To complete the preparations for the final conflict the government embarked on a propaganda war. One part of this was rationalisation: by insisting that many pits were uneconomic and must close for that reason. (Interestingly, the minister responsible, Mr Peter Walker, was a farmer who benefited considerably from the subsidised production of an uneconomic food mountain that nobody wanted to buy, all the while proclaiming that the country could not afford to go on producing mountains of uneconomic coal that nobody wanted to buy. Nobody noticed the difference!) Detailed analysis of the NCB's accounts by the Oxford economist Andrew Glyn showed that pits were only 'uneconomic' because the government sums were highly irregular. By counting 'transfer' costs of mining subsidence and pensions as running costs, real operational profits were turned into paper losses. Also, the government was charging the NCB interest rates over twice the rate of profit of private manufacturing industry. Something else lost in the popular rhetoric about 'uneconomic pits' was the fact that the government is itself virtually a monopoly buyer of the NCB's coal, so that it sets the price for coal used by the Central Electricity Generating Board. The CEGB makes a profit largely for the same reason that the NCB makes a loss, because the government sets the selling price of their own products: high for the CEGB, low for the NCB.[72] A second part of the propaganda war against the NUM involved the unions being denounced as 'the enemy within', subverting the British way of life as surely as the Argentines in the Falklands War had attempted to subvert it from without. The implication was clear: this was not an industrial dispute, but, according to the Conservative manifesto of 1983, a battle to show that Britain stands up for its own interests and for the cause of freedom against unprovoked aggression.

With preparations for confrontation completed, a strike was duly provoked on the 1 March 1984 by announcing without notice or consultation the closure of Cortonwood Colliery. It was not the least economic pit in the district, its immediate future had only just been confirmed, and miners had been transferred there from other pits marked for closure. Cortonwood is in the Yorkshire backyard of the NUM president, which fact, given the other circumstances, might have been considered sufficient provocation. The NUM's decision to call an all-out strike on the basis of a large majority of a delegate conference in favour, but without holding a ballot of all members, was as democratic as the British Parliament, but undoubtedly less democratic than it could have been and anyway unwise. It is unlikely, however, that a strike would have been averted for long, given the government's plans. Since the strike started at the end of the winter and coal stocks were high at power stations, the mineworkers were without two advantages they had had in 1974. Even so, the strike lasted for a year until the miners voted to return to work without achieving any of their original aims.[73]

In the course of the strike, what the New Right government meant by the rule of law and state authority became evident. The chairman of the NCB pursued overtly a policy of antagonising the union as well as defeating it. Of himself and his role he remarked: 'I am not one of your local characters. I don't vote here – I vote in Florida.' His intransigence was matched by that of the NUM president Arthur Scargill, so that conciliators in the NCB, the TUC and the government were without influence on events. These included the activities of *agents provocateurs*, notably David Hart who had become a libertarian at Eton (because he was, he said, unhappy with the anti-semitic prejudices there). He acted as unofficial advisor to Ian McGregor during the strike and at the same time had personal access to 10 Downing Street. From a room in Claridges hotel in London his activities ranged from sabotaging the Energy Secretary Peter Walker's efforts to reach a settlement, to giving financial backing and advice to the National Working Miners Committee, that became the breakaway Union of Democratic Mineworkers. Undoubtedly Hart promoted the influential New Right view that the strike was a political showdown with the forces of Marxism; divide and rule was the policy successfully pursued. The police were systematically deployed to intimidate strikers by a variety of means that were, to say the least, of dubious legality. For example, miners were stopped by the police and turned back at roadblocks hundreds of miles from the sites of potential picket lines, so suffering loss of their liberty of movement. Police provoked strikers to retaliation by the use of 'controlled sound levels' and feinting charges. At the Orgreave Coke Works on 18 June 1984 massed ranks of police charged with horses; the police's own video recording showed that their charges provoked violence from a previously peaceful crowd. Pickets were then arrested. A 'doctored' television news video showed the real order of events reversed, as if the miners had provoked the police. When these facts emerged in court, together with the revelation of the existence of the *Public Order Manual*, the fact that many police statements carried identical wording, and evidence that thousands of miners had been directed, even escorted, by police to Orgreave, the police dropped all charges. A study of the record of court decisions showed that most miners brought to trial were not convicted; either the cases against them were dismissed or they were merely bound over. Defence lawyer, Gareth Pierce, said the Orgreave incident was intended to be a military exercise by the police, to try out new illegal tactics, to make mass arrests, hurt people and break the strike. There was clear evidence that the police had set up the clash dubbed the Battle of Orgreave. In resisting the idea that the problem had arisen from defects in the public order law another defence lawyer said: 'No amendment to the law would prevent the police fabrication of evidence which formed the basis of the prosecution at the Orgreave trial.'[74]

The final upshot of the strike was a rapid contraction of the coal industry and of the NUM's membership. By 1989, 90 pits had been closed and 100,000 miners had lost their jobs. By the end of 1990 the workforce was down to about 60,000. The economics of the coal mines are more complex than is usually reckoned with. Alternative sources to British coal are not stable. Nuclear energy turned out to be far more expensive than the most expensive coal when proper cost-accounting was done – quite apart from the safety and environmental factors. Oil prices are volatile and Britain's own oil resources are limited. Imported coal is subject to fluctuating currency exchange rates and transport costs. Even by the criteria of free markets it is in these circumstances highly imprudent to pursue a policy of short-term economy. The policy of concentrating the remaining coal production in high-productivity mines is also problematic. The cost benefits of high-technology extraction methods seem spectacular until the cost of servicing the capital investment in the machines is taken into account. In Selby, for example, British Coal's own calculations on the economics of four superpits showed that an operating profit was turned into a financial loss after interest payments of £440 million had been paid.[75] There is an another factor that was never considered by Ian McGregor and his New Right paymasters, but was central to the thinking of the NCB's accounts advisor from 1950 to 1970, E.F.

Shumacher: the responsibility for future generations. In 1965 he wrote: 'It is a policy of doubtful wisdom and questionable morality for this generation to take the best resources and leave for its children only the worst. But it is surely criminal policy if, in addition, we wilfully sterilise, abandon, and thereby ruin such relatively inferior resources as we ourselves have opened up, but do not care to utilise. This is like the spiteful burglar who does not merely pinch the valuables, but in addition destroys everything he can't take.'[76] New right thinking did not extend beyond the simplistic economics of short-term profitability (though even these calculations, as we have seen, were politically loaded against coal).

The wider political significance of the miners' strike of 1984–5 is now clear. For ideological reasons the government pursued a vendetta against the trade unions by singling out the mineworkers. The confrontation suppressed union power as intended (and settled old scores in the bargain), but in the process real economics, the integrity of the law, established communities and social cohesion were all sacrificed at the altar of the authoritarian state. The government spent £3,000 million or more on the strike to save, by its own account, £250 million a year: this was said to be a worthwhile investment for the nation. Certainly the incidence of strikes was reduced, because the workforce was smaller. Productivity increased but economic production did not. The police succeeded in asserting the power of the state but the law and its agents were brought into disrepute, and whole sections of the population were profoundly alienated. In fact the government's victory over the miners was contrived by Pyrrhus. The crowning irony was that in 1989 the Nottinghamshire miners who comprised the bulk of the membership of the breakaway Union of Democratic Mineworkers found themselves redundant. The freeplay of market forces they had fought so hard for resulted in the NCB importing coal cheaper than they could produce it. In 1984 they had sung: 'I'm glad I'm British. I'm glad I'm free. I wish I were a dog and Arthur Scargill a tree.' In 1990 they were singing a different tune: the song of freeborn British unemployed and with a government which denied that this was any of its business.

Foreign Affairs

Nuclear Weapons. Central to New Right thinking in Britain is the conviction that Britain is and must remain a major power with a strong voice in the councils of the world. This was always important and always linked to military strength. In 1979 strengthening Britain's defences was included among the Conservatives five main tasks, but only as the fifth. By 1983 Margaret Thatcher counted defence as the first of the challenges facing the country: before unemployment and economic prosperity. This changed emphasis reflected the fact that in 1981 the Labour Party's annual conference had passed a resolution to commit a future Labour government to unilateral nuclear disarmament. Labour's policy was based primarily on moral considerations that were advanced by the Campaign for Nuclear Disarmament (led by Monsignor Bruce Kent) and eventually endorsed by a Church of England Synod report. The moral case for unilateral nuclear disarmament did not strike everybody as clear cut (there is arguably a moral obligation to deter and resist aggression). Whatever the moral case, Labour's adoption of a unilateralist policy was politically unpopular with the majority of the voters. Since in 1983 voters considered defence to be second only to unemployment in importance, Labour's policy was far from electors' views. There is sound evidence, both statistical and anecdotal, to suggest that Labour lost the general elections in 1983 and 1987 through its unilateral nuclear defence policy alone, apart from anything else.[77] The New Right Conservatives represented the country's view of nuclear defence policy, though the popular view of Britain's high standing as a world power is more complex and uncertain. What is beyond question is that the cost of nuclear weapons is extremely high, both directly, on the Exchequer, and indirectly in its effect on the country's research and development effort. The independence of Britain's nuclear deterrent, and so the weight it carries in international affairs (if any), can only be slight. Both Germany and Japan, freed of the financial burden of nuclear weapons, came through economic strength to exercise more real influence on affairs than Britain, for all the prestige nuclear weapons supposedly lent to her reputation.

The Falklands Campaign. There is no doubt that British people continued strongly to cherish the national pride that memories of Empire and victories in two world wars fostered. This is enough to explain the popular support for the government's response to the invasion by Argentine forces of the Falkland Islands in 1982. It isn't necessary to rehearse here the whole story of this episode. Relevant factors include the following. Geographically the Falklands have the same proximity to Argentina as the Shetland Islands do to Britain. Legally even the Duke of Wellington could not discern the legitimacy of Britain's claim to sovereignty in 1829, and Foreign Office reports continued to recognise the same difficulties in recent times. British diplomats and politicians were aware of Argentine ambitions to secure the sovereignty of the islands. At the time of the invasion serious thought was being given to ways of transferring sovereignty to Argentina, without jeopardising the essential interests of British Falklanders. Politically the British government had signalled its view of the importance of the Falklands in 1981 by deciding to withdraw the only naval presence there, an ice-patrol ship, to save the £3 million it cost. Diplomatically the Argentine government itself, as well as other Anglophile sources, had indicated its plans to act on its claim to sovereignty of the islands. In the event nothing was done by the British government until Argentine forces landed in the Falklands on 2 April 1982.[78] The Foreign Secretary, Lord Carrington, called this 'a national humiliation'. The Prime Minister authorised the Defence Minister, John Nott, to say to Parliament, on 3 April:

> We intend to solve the problem and we shall try to solve it continuingly by diplomatic means, but if that fails, *and it probably will do so*, we shall have no choice but to press forward with our plans retaining secrecy where necessary and flexibility to act as circumstances demand.[79] (Emphasis added.)

The British dispatched a naval task force to the Falklands by 5 April. The improbability of a diplomatic solution was settled on 2 May 1982 when (at 19.01 GMT) the Argentine battleship *Belgrano* was sunk by torpedoes from the British nuclear submarine *Conqueror*. At the time, the leader of the ruling Argentine junta, General Galtieri, had accepted in principle a peace proposal by the Peruvian President Terry Belaunde and the American Secretary of State Alexander Haig. Ratification by the junta was expected that evening at 22.00 GMT. The (new) British Foreign Minister, Francis Pym, decided not to take Haig's call about this development; it has been said that this was because he knew by then the decision had already been taken by the British government to sink the *Belgrano*.[80] On 21 May British troops established a beach head on the Falklands and the Argentine forces surrendered on 14 June 1982. The whole episode lasted six weeks.

Some other aspects of the Falklands War will be discussed later. There is no doubt that the Conservative government and many British people regarded the episode as a test of Britain's national character, a test of resolve to use military force when necessary to uphold Britain's interests, especially against unprovoked aggression. Leaving aside for the time being the question of misrule, the Conservative government's handling of the Falklands episode raises serious doubts about its competence. It must be held responsible for failure to recognise the dubiety of Britain's claims to sovereignty. It failed correspondingly to acknowledge the strength of the Argentines' case and the seriousness of their intention to press it. It allowed its obsession with economies to blind it to the Argentines' likely interpretation of cuts in expenditure on defence of the Falklands (the end result was that hundreds of lives were lost or ruined and billions of pounds expended unnecessarily). After diplomatic relations and trade with Argentina were restored in 1989, the country might well ponder what, really, all the sacrifice had been for. Tony Benn was not alone in imputing to the government less glorious motives for attacking 'the enemy without' than the official ones of British sovereignty, the right of Falklands colonists to self-determination (at any cost to the British taxpayer) and resistance to the aggression of military dictators.[81] British sovereignty, we know, is dubious. Colonists cannot have an open-ended claim on their compatriots. Some of the New Right's best friends are South American military dictators. One of the first acts of the New Right government was to remove the Labour government's embargo on the sale of arms to the military dictatorship of General Pinochet in Chile. Even more preposterous, the New Right minister, Cecil Parkinson, had as early as August 1980 said, on behalf of all his compatriots: 'The British admire the efforts made by Argentina to reduce inflation and their achievements so far.'[82] It was only *after* the invasion of the Falklands that New Right ministers talked about widespread violation of human rights by the 'strongman' they had only recently admired. To the New Right, the junta's methods were unremarkable so long as they were directed to bringing down inflation. Encroaching on to British possessions was evidently a different matter. The Falklands War was in a way a test of British character. The test showed various things. Between 1982 and 1987 the total costs of the 'campaign' amounted to over £3 billion, or more than £1.5 million for every man, woman and child in the Falklands. This shows, first, that rational considerations such as costs count for little against the emotive pull of national pride. Even in 1987–8 the cost of maintaining 'Fortress Falklands' was approximately £100,000 per islander per annum.[83] Secondly, the British are inclined to be indifferent to the legitimate claims of others. Thirdly, the line between warranted national pride and chauvinism is readily blurred by jingoistic politicians who exploit British people's pride and sense of nation. Fourthly, there is a very unadmirable tendency to be high-minded and bellicose when an enemy is comparatively weak (like Argentina) and Britain has strong allies (like the United States). When the enemy is comparatively strong (like China) and Britain has no strong allies in the cause (like Suez and Hong Kong), humility and pragmatism replace the rhetoric of glory and honour. Since 1979, Britain would have benefited both economically and diplomatically from a great deal less of Kipling-inspired dreams of glory, and a little more of humility and pragmatism.

Europe. Britain's relations with the European Economic Community have been strongly coloured by a presumption of Britain's special standing and importance in the world. Faced with an excessive financial contribution to the EEC budget, the Conservative government, following the strong lead of Margaret Thatcher, secured substantial refunds totalling, for example, £4.5 billion between 1984 and 1987. Britain has pressed to promote free trade as the overriding purpose of the Community. The results have so far not been very successful, with Britain running a deficit in trade with the Community of £11.7 billion by 1987. Except for this (so far) misplaced enthusiasm for free markets in Europe, the dominant New Right view, specifically the view of Margaret Thatcher, her 'family friend' Professor Alan Walters and a few close allies, notably Nicholas Ridley, was suspicion. They resist the development of the EEC into anything other than a convenient free-market area. The EEC's social charter, the provisions of which include minimum wages, workers' participation in management and guaranteed social welfare provision, has been strongly resisted and all but rejected by the New Right government. In other matters of the environment and health and safety the government preferred to uphold the freeborn right of every Briton to polluted drinking water and beaches, and carcinogenic cigarettes, rather than adopt alien EEC clean water, environment and health-warning legislation. Also, Britain was frequently found wanting by European courts in matters of equal opportunities, civil liberties and human rights. Economic and related constitutional factors proved to be the main bugbear in the New Right thinking about Europe. The single market was welcomed by them as a natural development of the main aims of the Community, while every other member saw the development of economic union, a single Euro-Bank and eventually a common currency to be inevitable, if not positively desirable, outcomes of the joint measures already agreed to. The dominant faction in the New Right resisted economic union and the common currency because, as Margaret Thatcher maintained, such measures were tantamount to surrendering the economic sovereignty of the country (and so the power of the British Parliament to govern Britain). For some New Right thinkers such ideas are anathema. The Secretary of State for Industry, Nicholas Ridley, confided to the *Spectator* in July 1990 his view of proposals for a joint EEC monetary policy, saying:

> This is all a German racket designed to take over the whole of Europe. It has to be thwarted. This rushed take-over by the Germans, on the worst possible basis, with the French behaving like poodles to the Germans, is absolutely intolerable.[84]

Propriety demanded that Ridley resign, albeit after some delay on both his part and the Prime Minister's. He was, nevertheless, voicing opinions shared by the Prime Minister. Any doubt on the matter was removed in October 1990 when Margaret Thatcher pronounced the other eleven leaders of the Community to be 'living in cloud cuckoo land' when they agreed to proceed with a joint monetary policy. Soon after, her deputy, Geoffrey Howe, resigned over the issue (thus did depart the last of the New Right Mohicans to survive in the government from the start in 1979).

An impolitic way of dealing with EEC leaders was habitual for Margaret Thatcher. Her regular harangues about what they regarded as piffling housekeeping sums of money earned her among them the appellation 'grocer's daughter'. Her invincible chauvinism is such that one commentator opines: 'It never enters her head that any proposal for change from outside is not necessarily unwelcome simply because it is un-British.'[85] Fundamentally she believes that there is no such thing as Europe. There are individual nations and those they have 'special relations' with who 'speak the same language'. Her chauvinism is so gross that she chose the occasion of the bicentennial celebrations of the French Revolution in Paris in July 1989 to lecture the French on liberty, and on how Britain by far preceded and excelled the French in these matters. In support she cited the Magna Carta, a document that expressly excludes almost the whole population from whatever rights it secures since they were not counted 'free men'.[86] It would be too extravagant to hope that much in the way of vision for the future of Europe could emerge out of chauvinism of this order. The positive prospects of developing a 'common European home' without insurmountable ideological differences and of an elected European Parliament with legislative powers; and the corresponding challenge of securing national identity within a wider federal European framework and of avoiding narrow nationalistic prejudices and conflicts – these seemed beyond the range of vision of the British Prime Minister in the autumn of 1990.

Third World Debt and Foreign Aid. After 1982, world bankers decided that long-term loans to the governments of developing countries were not as commercially attractive as they had been during the 1970s, and they began to demand repayment from debtors' export revenues. As a result, by 1990 Third World debt was an overwhelming problem that threatened to ruin the debtor countries. The solvency of many western banks was threatened as losses on defaulted Third World loans wiped out profits on other business. One concise measure of the order of the problem was the decision by two British banks, Lloyds and National Westminster, to write off between them debts totalling £1.7 billion, their estimate of the unrepayable debts owed by developing countries such as Brazil and Mexico. Developing countries are paying so much in interest on loans to banks of wealthy developed nations that their own economies are retrogressing. National income per head of the 15 most heavily indebted countries was in 1989 more than 7 per cent below its 1980 level.[87]

The effect on the lives of citizens of debtor countries is virtually catastrophic, with unemployment, industrial decay, and the collapse of housing, health, education and social welfare provision. Countries which export food have millions of underfed children, and health deteriorates as a result. Attempts have been made to expand the economies of debtor countries by creating Free Trade Zones, where taxes, duties and exchange controls are waived, wages, health and safety, and labour are de-regulated and civil liberties curtailed. Against these developments, unionised workers in Europe and the United States are warned that if they become too militant, production will be shifted to lower-cost, less troublesome labourforces in other countries. This is 'the free market in labour'.[88]

Against this background the New Right government in Britain systematically reduced its aid to developing countries. The ideal goal for such aid from developed countries suggested by the Brandt Commission in 1982 was 1 per cent of gross domestic product. If administered through the United Nations Educational, Scientific and Cultural Organisation (UNESCO), such sums would make a substantial impact on the welfare of developing nations. In 1987, for example, Britain would have granted aid of £4.92 billion. The Conservative manifesto of 1987 proudly boasted that Britain had provided £1.3 billion, that was 0.26 per cent of GDP. But in 1979 Britain had devoted proportionately twice as much, 0.52 per cent of its GDP, to aid for developing countries.[89] Thus, under the New Right administration, during a period in which an economic miracle had supposedly been wrought, aid to developing countries was halved. Nor was this all. In December 1985 Britain withdrew its financial support and membership of UNESCO. Aid was subsequently decided, not according to the educational, scientific and cultural needs of the nations as they themselves conceived them, but linked instead to trade with Britain. The Conservatives were proud to proclaim that their 'Aid and Trade Provision' had helped win good development contracts for British firms worth £2 billion between 1979 and 1987. In 1989 the Labour spokeswoman on aid, Joan Lestor, forced the Prime Minister reluctantly and tacitly to admit that British aid had been linked to arms sales. This explains why Malaysia, by no means a poor country, was receiving substantial British aid.

Before leaving the topic of aid it will be instructive to consider the manner in which the New Right government and the Prime Minister in particular dealt with attempts through formal questions in Parliament to establish the truth of allegations that, contrary to the legal provisions of the Overseas Aid Act (1966), British aid to Malaysia was being linked to defence sales (as an inducement). The question was pursued by Joan Lestor in Parliament as follows:[90]

Question 1 (17 May 1989):
Was there any reference to overseas aid in the correspondence which led to last year's arms agreement with Malaysia?
Reply by a minister:
All dealings between the two governments on the proposed sale of arms were formalised in the Memorandum of Understanding signed in September 1981. No mention is made in that document of overseas aid to Malaysia.
(Note: this reply evades the question about correspondence, and provides information only about a Memorandum of Understanding.)

Question 2 (13 June 1989):
Was there any reference to overseas aid in the correspondence which led to last year's arms agreement with Malaysia?

Reply by a minister:
Following the exchanges of Malaysian interest in UK overseas aid in early exchanges, my Right Honourable friend the Secretary of State for Defence made it clear to the Malaysian Finance Minister that it would not be acceptable to Her Majesty's Government to link aid with defence sales packages.

(Note: This reply establishes that it was said by the Secretary of State for Defence that a formal linking of aid to defence sales would not be acceptable, but continues to evade the question of whether aid was referred to by someone else in some other correspondence perhaps to be 'informally' linked with defence sales.)

Question 3 (23 June 1989):
Who indicated to the Malaysians that Britain would consider a request for overseas aid in the correspondence concerning the arms deal between the two governments?
Reply by Margaret Thatcher:
The government made clear to the Malaysian government on a number of occasions in 1988 that we were most willing to consider Malaysian requests for aid but not as an 'integral part' of a negotiated agreement on defence sales.

(Note: This reply indicated that aid and defence sales were both discussed but that the letter of the law had been observed by not linking the two formally.)

Question 4 (29 June 1989):
Have references to aid been made in correspondence between the British and Malaysian governments on the subject of defence sales?
Reply by Margaret Thatcher:
The contents of government to government correspondence are confidential.

Joan Lestor was entitled to draw from this the obvious conclusion that although British aid had not been openly pledged to secure the arms sale (since that was illegal), the two had been clearly linked in the actual (secret) negotiations. We will recall here 'the first and best lesson' that Margaret Thatcher learned as a barrister: 'Never admit more than you have to.' Evasion, giving misleading information, disingenuousness and breaking the substance and spirit of the law while seeming to observe the letter – these were the stock-in-trade of the New Right government under her leadership. At this point it is appropriate to turn to the general subject of misrule under the New Right.

Misrule

There is a common view that all politicians are devious and 'economical' with the truth; also, that British society and political institutions are so manifestly superior to totalitarian regimes that it is fatuous to compare even the worst problems and abuses here with those in undemocratic countries. Indeed (it is said), it is an insult to those who have resisted full-blown tyrannies.

The relevant institutional framework and conventions are British and contemporary. By these standards there is not the slightest doubt that government in Britain under the New Right leadership of Margaret Thatcher descended to depths that will not easily be fathomed. Neither will the reputation of government for integrity be easily salvaged. Already instances have been cited where the government was guilty of disingenuousness bordering on misrule: during the miners' strike of 1984–5, and on the question of overseas aid. Other cases illustrate even more clearly the unique unscrupulousness of Margaret Thatcher's administration.

Mrs Thatcher is a qualified lawyer. She is also extraordinarily combative and litigious. Her incessant (failed) efforts legally to suppress publication in Britain of the book *Spycatcher* were plainly obsessive. That being the case it is surely astonishing that she did not challenge the Labour MP Tam Dalyell who in Parliament denounced her as '... a sustained brazen deceiver', '... a bounder, a liar, a deceiver, a cheat and a crook'. Moreover, he has subsequently in public and in print said she was 'guilty of calculated murder ... for her own political ends'. It is understandable why Tam Dalyell, who continues undisturbed his duties as Member of Parliament for West Lothian, believes that Margaret Thatcher's silence in the face of such serious allegations is the silence of those who know they have no grounds whatsoever for protest.[91]

The Sinking of the Belgrano and the Falklands War. According to MP Tam Dalyell Margaret Thatcher was not notably different from her immediate predecessors in the manner of her exercise of prime ministerial power until the spring of 1982 when a 'sea change' occurred that resulted in her exercising an unprecedented personal grip on government. This coincided with the (undeclared) Falklands War. Dalyell's well documented allegation is that given the knowledge of a likely attack on the Falklands the Prime Minister was quite content to let the situation run, and by seeming inaction, to lure the Argentines on to the punch. A little war, deemed to be righteous by public opinion, might restore the domestic political fortunes of a Prime Minister who sat lower in the opinion polls than any Prime Minister since political polling began.[92]

This account of events coincides persuasively with most of the relevant evidence. In December 1981 a Gallup Poll showed that only 25 per cent of people approved of the Prime Minister's performance. The Conservative government was held in even lower regard: just 18 per cent of people approved of its record. Worst of all for the Conservatives was the result showing that only 12 per cent of people thought the party would be likely to win a general election. By the summer of 1982, after the Falklands episode in May and June, the Prime Minister's personal approval rating was 52 per cent; the government's 48 per cent, and, most significantly, the Conservatives' election prospects miraculously transformed with 66 per cent expecting them to win an election. If someone had plotted, for the advantage of the Conservative government and Prime Minister, to exploit the patriotism, loyalty and pride of the British people then they had certainly achieved their objective. According to Tam Dalyell and others, such a plot was perpetrated by Margaret Thatcher. Afterwards, as evidence that the official account of events was untrue in vital particulars the Prime Minster characteristically sought refuge in equivocation, prevarication and, finally, in official secrecy.

The nature of the plot that led to the sinking by British torpedoes of the Argentine cruiser *Belgrano* and culminated in war can be outlined briefly.[93] The British government knew that the Argentines were planning to invade the Falkland Islands long before they did in April. Far from taking action to discourage this, the government designated the only British naval vessel in the area for recall. After the Argentines had invaded the islands the British Parliament was told that the invasion was an act of aggression that came 'out of the blue'. Lord Carrington, the Foreign Secretary, called it a 'national humiliation' and Enoch Powell encouraged the Prime Minister to regard it as a test of her mettle as the so-called 'Iron Lady'. Diplomatic solutions were pursued at the same time as a task force was sent to the South Atlantic. By 2 May a proposal by the Peruvian President, Terry Belaunde, with the endorsement of the United States Secretary of State, had been provisionally agreed by the Argentine President Galtieri after consultation with members of his junta, and was due to be formally agreed by the junta later in the day (2 May). Before that happened the British nuclear submarine *Conqueror*, acting under instructions from the British War Cabinet at Chequers, sank the Argentine cruiser *Belgrano* which had a crew of 1,000, of whom 368 lost their lives. It is now clear that at the time the sinking was ordered, (1) the government knew of the Peruvian peace plan, (2) the Argentine ship was 59 miles outside of the 200 miles exclusion zone imposed by the British around the Falkland Islands, (3) the *Belgrano* was under orders to return to base, which fact was known to the British government, (4) the British submarine had been tracking the *Belgrano* for 30 hours, knew its position, its orders and destination, and knew, therefore, that it was not a threat to the British task force (which, as the Argentine Captain Bonzo later explained, was at a distance of 14 hours' top-speed sailing: provided the British fleet remained stationary!). By sinking the *Belgrano* with great loss of life, the British government ensured a military solution was necessary, the successful outcome of which would reflect favourably on the New Right government. Not, however, if the British public knew of the circumstances.

In order to mislead (and so misgovern) the British people Mrs Thatcher and her associates systematically misrepresented the facts. Prior knowledge of Argentine intentions was denied. Peaceful solutions were not pursued with the same zeal as military ones. Knowledge was denied of the successful, concrete, Peruvian peace proposal at the crucial time. The direct responsibility of the cabinet for the sinking was first evaded in a statement that the submarine commander had himself made the decision. Knowledge of the *Belgrano*'s orders to return to base was denied. It was officially stated that the *Belgrano* was an immediate threat to the task force that had been suddenly encountered shortly before it was sunk. In attempting to sustain their false account of events the government extended a labyrinth of contradictory implausible claims, the chief result of which was to undermine the credibility of those who made them.

William Whitelaw, who was Deputy Prime Minister at the time, responded to the allegation that the *Belgrano* was sunk in order to scupper the chances of peace (and ultimately to promote the interests of the Conservatives) by saying it was a wicked lie. He also said (in the space of six column-inches) that the charge 'is not true', 'is completely false,' is 'blackening (the) country', 'is sheer, unadulterated, 100 per cent piffle', and 'nonsense'.[94] Others may be forgiven for thinking that the (usually amiable) noble lord doth protest too much. The only substance to his response is the repetition of the claim that the *Belgrano* could have become a threat to the task force. There was (he was assured by Admiral Lewin) no way that a submarine could know what it was up to. But of course 1980s submarines equipped with sonar, radar, radio and satellite intelligence systems can tell where a decrepit, cadet-training, cruiser commissioned in 1939 (and shortly to be turned into a floating museum) is going. Whether or not Whitelaw knew, it is virtually certain that his leader knew it to be sailing under orders back to port when the order to sink it was given. Whitelaw asks what the outcome would have been if the *Belgrano* had attacked the British task force. The whole point of the criticism is that there was no good reason to suppose that it would, or even that it could, attack the task force. Finally, he wonders what people like Tam Dalyell think they are doing 'blackening their own country'. For this question the essence of the answer was provided by Margaret Thatcher herself when she was reproached in 1975 by British Embassy officials in Washington for criticising Britain while speaking in the USA as leader of the opposition. She replied: 'I'm not knocking Britain. I'm knocking Socialism.'[95] Tam Dalyell and others are not 'blackening their own country' when they question the highly dubious official view of events. They are challenging the propensity to disingenuousness, misinformation, deception and plain lying to Parliament and nation that have come to characterise the New Right government in Britain. Questioning the government, in case William Whitelaw has forgotten, is the role of Parliament, opposition and a free press in a democracy.

It is neither necessary nor possible in the space available to pursue here the other cases in the same detail as the *Belgrano* and the Falklands war. It was by no means an isolated case, and Tam Dalyell is undoubtedly correct to draw the conclusion that the sinking of the *Belgrano* provides the key to explaining numerous other cases. Among other cases of misrule and misconduct, the following are some of the best documented and most disturbing.

Clive Ponting and the Totalitarian Tendency. In connection with the *Belgrano* episode, a high-flying official at the Ministry of Defence, Clive Ponting, was prosecuted in 1984 under the provisions of Section Two of the Official Secrets Act for passing to a Member of Parliament

(Tam Dalyell) evidence that government ministers themselves had lied to Parliament.[96] The Act was being used, not to protect genuine military and diplomatic secrets, but to prevent proper scrutiny of the government's dubious actions. Two features of this case are especially significant. First, the judge in directing the jury construed the Act to mean that 'the policies of the State were the policies of the government then [July 1984] in power'. This goes against the well-established recognition that governments can act against the interests of the state. Secondly, the jury, against the judge's direction, acquitted Ponting, thus showing that people do not equate the best interest and policies of the state with that of the government of the day – which may be acting against the public interest.[97]

Westland Helicopters and Prime Ministerial Stonewalling. In the course of negotiations of the sale of the strategically important Westlands Helicopter Company, the Prime Minister was widely believed to be implicated in the illegal use of a letter from the Solicitor General, Sir Patrick Mayhew, to the Secretary of State for Defence, Michael Heseltine. The Prime Minister – who favoured selling to the American company Sikorsky – was unable to persuade the cabinet to her view against that of the Defence Secretary – who favoured a European consortium. The Solicitor General was persuaded by 10 Downing street (supposedly) to write confidentially to the Defence Secretary setting out his view that an important, pertinent, letter of his had contained certain material inaccuracies. The Solicitor General's letter was then leaked to the Press Association selectively so as to emphasise the material inaccuracies. This in turn had the effect of bypassing due process of government, discrediting the Defence Secretary and, the basic point, causing the Prime Minister's view to prevail. The order to leak illegally the confidential letter was traced to 10 Downing Street, but the Prime Minister denied any prior knowledge of it, let alone implication in the events. Instead another minister (of Trade and Industry), Leon Brittan, and a civil servant who acted under instructions, Collette Bowe, were scapegoated. Significantly Brittan was lauded even though he resigned and Collette Bowe was given immunity from prosecution. Although the sale of a helicopter company worth £50 million is in itself of little political significance, Michael Heseltine's claim that constitutional government had broken down shows the true significance of the episode. The really significant question was: 'Was the head of government involved in acts of dishonesty, and were those acts covered up?' The report of the

inquiry by the (Conservative-dominated) Commons Defence
Committee accused her of everything but a straight lie to the
Commons. Told by the committee that her explanations of the leak
were 'flimsy to say the least', the Prime Minister stonewalled. One
commentator observed: 'When you say you have told the truth what
is there left to say?' It is an astonishing feature of British government
that if a dissembling Prime Minister declines to speak, evidently
there is no recourse.[98]

Zircon and Intimidation of the BBC. The BBC produced a television
series, 'The Secret Society', for transmission in 1987. This included a
programme on the history of a spy satellite Zircon, the construction
of which (costing £500 million) had been authorised by the
government without Parliament being informed. Such secrecy was
not new, although it was contrary to an undertaking given in 1982.
Previous governments of all persuasions have done similar things.
What gave new cause for concern was the response to the programme
being made, which was to 'shoot the messenger', instead of
responding to the message. The BBC office in Glasgow was required
in January 1987 to hand over to the police the films and research
material for all of the programmes before they were transmitted. The
authority to impound the BBC's material proved to be difficult to
locate. Although the events took place in Scotland and required the
authority of Scottish officials, the Scottish police who carried out the
operation pressed to know ultimately on whose authority they were
acting. They were assured by the Metropolitan Police representative
who supervised the actions that it was on the authority of 10 Downing
Street. This was evidently an attempt to intimidate the BBC, to
discourage it from broadcasting material that might be detrimental
to the government in what was an election year. Eventually, after MPs
had seen the Zircon programme in Westminster, it was broadcast with
others in the series; although another, on cabinet secrecy, was not
transmitted. The wider issues raised include accountability to
Parliament, the freedom of the press, and the use of the police to
suppress information embarrassing to the government. As in the
Westland affair, the Prime Minister took pains (as did Henry II when
he rid himself of a turbulent priest) not to know the details of the
operation so that she could mislead everyone about her role as censor
without having actually to lie. Even admirers of Margaret Thatcher
might be able to see the parallels with Eastern Europe in this blatant
case of misrule.[99]

Executive Assassination in Gibraltar. In March 1988 three members of
the Irish Republican Army were shot dead in Gibraltar by British
security forces. At the time they were unarmed. This and other circumstances raised fundamental questions about the authority for and
legality of the killings. Further inquiry into the matter raised other
questions about the British government's systematic cover-up of
illicit activities. There is no doubt that the three persons killed were
members of the IRA and on 'active service', planning to explode a car
bomb on Gibraltar. The official account of the events was that Spanish
police assigned to tracking their progress and monitoring the presence
of a bomb had 'lost' them before they entered Gibraltar. British
security forces had come across them by surprise. Not knowing
whether they were armed or whether they might detonate a car
bomb the security men shot the three out of hand. As it happened,
the three were unarmed, had not been given an opportunity to
surrender, and had been shot repeatedly even after they were
wounded or already dead.

Eyewitnesses soon established that the events did not take place
as reported officially. No car bomb was found. The first reports of the
British and Spanish officials gave the same account: that Spanish police
had in fact tracked the three into Gibraltar. Their movements were
known (the fact that the British Prime Minister and intelligence
services sent messages of congratulations to the Spanish police for
their part in the operation would be otherwise inexplicable). Only later
did British officials change the story. The sworn testimony of the
senior Spanish police officer (like the log-book of the submarine
Conqueror that sank the *Belgrano*) was 'lost', by the British Embassy
in Madrid, and not available at the inquest. Attempts to establish the
facts, by newspaper journalists, the official inquest and television
reporters were systematically frustrated. One key eyewitness, a court
clerk, was subjected to character assassination in the *Daily Mail*,
which was edited by one of Margaret Thatcher's greatest admirers,
David English. The Prime Minister declined to require the SAS
officers involved to testify at the inquest. Then they were permitted
to testify incognito. Thames Television was subjected to extreme
pressure by the government to prevent them transmitting their own
findings in a programme, 'Death on the Rock'.

Undoubtedly the most plausible explanation of the events is that
10 Downing Street gave instructions to intelligence services and the
SAS to assassinate the three IRA operatives. This was done to order,
even though it was known that they were unarmed and there was no

car bomb at the time of the killings. Subsequent false statements were alibis that eyewitnesses, Spanish police and objective observers found to be totally implausible. One sort of view of the affair was the *Sun* newspaper's: 'They deserved to die like dogs.' The British government, however, is required to set and maintain higher standards than 'tabloid justice'. Section three of the Criminal Justice Act 1967 states: 'A person may use such force as is reasonable in the circumstances in preventing crime. Or in ... effecting the arrest of offenders.' This requirement had been violated with impunity by British security services. They were even commended. When the state itself violates the law then it provides no better example than terrorists themselves. Efforts to cover up the illegality merely compound the felony. Since 1979 under the New Right Party of Law and Order the pursuit of executive goals by secret and illegal means has grown significantly, and the Gibraltar shootings merely displayed this fact conspicuously.[100]

The Secret Services and the New Right. Evidence has piled up from innumerable sources that the British secret services have been subverting the democratic process, and in particular have been used to discredit politicians and even elected government ministers considered by Right thinkers to be undesirable influences on the social and political status quo. The most celebrated case in point was provided by a retired and disaffected MI5 officer, Peter Wright. Finding himself without a full pension after a lifetime of faithful devotion to the business of secretly undermining (mostly left-wing) 'enemies of the state', Wright elected to make money from his memoirs.[101] His recollections included efforts by the secret services to discredit ministers in Labour governments by digging dirt or, if necessary, inventing lies about them and leaking them to respectable journalists. Such efforts did not stop short of aspirations to destabilise and topple the elected Labour government of Harold Wilson. The attempts at enormous cost by Margaret Thatcher to suppress publication of Wright's book, initially worldwide then only in Britain, became one of the great *causes célèbres* of the 1980s. Publication in America was followed by publication everywhere else on the planet except Britain. The attempts to enforce the ban on the grounds of national security under the provisions of the Official Secrets Act descended into low farce by the time anyone who might wish to know what Wright said could do so. A preposterous affair was eventually ended by a British judge but not before the Cabinet Secretary, Sir

Robert Armstrong, had been obliged to confess to an Australian court that he had been 'economical with the truth' in the testimony he had given to it.[102]

Margaret Thatcher's excessive zeal to enforce public servants' duty of confidentiality in matters everybody already knew about becomes understandable when the substance of the matter is addressed: the subversive illegal activities of the secret services directed against left-wing groups and individuals.[103] Nobody doubts the need for secret security services. Heads of government in a democracy ought to be concerned that such services are subject to proper control by elected representatives of the people. During the 1960s and 1970s, evidently, necessary safeguards had failed. Secret service agents routinely used such tactics as 'surfacing' to discredit their targets: surfacing involves the planting of false information in some usually obscure but respectable publication gullible enough to publish it or anyway prepared to accept official briefings with unattributable information. The 'respectable' publication is then used as an authentic source of the discrediting information that official agencies can 'responsibly' use.[104] One exponent of such official but illegal legerdemain was Captain Colin Wallace of Military Intelligence. He explained how 'A senior officer would ask you to do a particular job and then he would say: "I don't want to know how you do it." So if it comes up at the Secretary of State's meeting and he is asked what he knows about it, he can say, "Absolutely nothing, Sir!"' Such low doings occasionally ascended to high farce. Wallace tells how false information planted by him was reported back to him by a very excited operative of another intelligence agency as evidence of a new political trend.[105] When necessary the same techniques of smears and dirty tricks are deployed by the secret state to discredit and harm even members of its own service if they stray too far on to the straight and narrow, as Wallace himself discovered. Another case became a *cause célèbre* when the Deputy Chief Constable of Manchester, John Stalker, was given the treatment after his investigation into an illegal 'shoot to kill' policy in Northern Ireland proved to be too fruitful and embarrassing.[106] Colin Wallace says that the process has degenerated to new depths during recent years to the point where government ministers have given false information to Parliament. As he recognised, this undermines democratic government, and so brings about the very thing that such tactics are supposedly seeking to prevent ('supposedly' is used here advisedly, since we have already seen that democracy is not held in high esteem by New Right thinkers).

Margaret Thatcher's personal connections with the secret services could hardly be closer. Among her friends were Chapman Pincher, the military and secrets journalist, and Maurice Oldfield, former head of MI6. Above all there was her friend and ally, Airey Neave, who had led her campaign for the leadership of the party. His connections with the secret services began in the Second World War and had been maintained ever since. Neave had in 1979 raised with former secret service operatives the possibility of 'stopping' Tony Benn if Labour came to power. His murder by Irish terrorists in 1979 was no doubt carefully targeted by them. It is said that had he lived he would have been minister without portfolio in the New Right cabinet – with special responsibility for coordinating the secret services activities.[107] Another figure with an imponderable role was David Sterling, the founder of the SAS, who shared with Airey Neave the distinction of having escaped from the famous Colditz Castle during the Second World War. During the 1970s he moved deeper into right-wing politics. As well as associating with organisations such as Aims of Industry he formed GB75, a private army recruited to counter industrial unrest and to act in the event of a general strike. He was knighted, on Margaret Thatcher's recommendation, in 1990.

The secret services exist legitimately to ensure the security of the state in so far as it represents the real interests of society. The tendency of officers to pursue during the 1960s their own political ends against elected governments, however, was criminal. The use since 1979 of the state's secret services to achieve by covert and illegal means what could not be sanctioned by any responsible authority is indefensible in a democracy, and must be counted among the most sinister and retrograde results of New Right government.

Miscellaneous Misdemeanours. The catalogue of misrule under the New Right is already too long to add to in detail. Other documented misdemeanours include burying inconvenient facts by releasing official reports at politically convenient times (like parliamentary recesses), restricting availability of copies and failing to report the whole truth; grossly exaggerating the extent of social welfare fraud; ministers refusing to act in the public interest against big business, by turning a blind eye to illegalities; the Prime Minister encouraging British companies to evade and undermine Commonwealth and EEC sanctions against South African apartheid; New Right ministers

(such as David Young) leaving government for very lucrative directorships in private companies they were recently dealing with
officially; the exploitation of opportunities for massive tax evasion by
leading Conservatives (such as Lady Porter) and Conservative Party
sponsors (such as Richard Branson) – and the reluctance of the
government to offend these supporters by changing the tax laws to
stop it.[108]

Summary Misrule. Two simple trends are discernible in all the cases
of misrule cited here. Even at the cost of acting at the limits of the law
and beyond, the New Right, under Margaret Thatcher, first deployed
the very considerable powers of the state to consolidate its hold on
the central state apparatus and to exercise it, not in the national
interest, but in the interest of a small group of wealthy individuals
at the expense of the rest of the population. Secondly, it pursued a
policy of destroying opposition both within and without the Conservative Party, and with its particular intention clearly expressed
throughout the 1970s – annihilating the very ideals of socialism in
Britain. Margaret Thatcher publicly declared her purpose: to 'stop the
onward march of socialism once and for all', 'to roll back the frontiers
of socialism', 'to bring about an irreversible shift ... of power'. She
pronounced James Callaghan 'the last Labour Prime Minister – and
I do mean the last Labour Prime Minister'. Evidently she was prepared
almost to stop at nothing to achieve these particular ends.[109]

16   THE SOCIAL RECORD

SUMMARY RECORD: THE RHETORIC

According to the official account, a Conservative dream was realised
during the New Right administration. This was the building of 'one
nation of free, prosperous and responsible families and people', the
giving of expression to 'the British instinct of choice and independence', and enabling many more families to enjoy the pride of
ownership – of homes, of shares and of pensions. Freedom was
secured by a strong framework of law and wholehearted commitment
to enforcing it. New Right policy ensured that the strength of the
police force reached record levels, and that police were much better
paid and equipped than ever before. Public confidence in policing was
improved by returning policemen to the beat. Sentencing was made

more severe; the biggest prison building programme this century was undertaken; and more prison staff recruited to deal with the increased numbers of prisoners. The health of British people steadily improved with life expectancy increasing and infant mortality decreasing. The government spent more on the health service than had any previous government. The health service was treating more patients than ever. The number of doctors, dentists and nurses was increased substantially and nurses' basic working hours reduced (from 40 to 37.5), with a substantial increase in pay as well. Home ownership was the great success story of housing policy: over one million council tenants became home owners and two million more families became home owners for the first time; two out of three homes were owned by the people who lived in them. Living standards became higher than ever before in history. Expenditure on social security benefits rose substantially (by £13 billion between 1979 and 1987) above the level of inflation. Help was targeted more effectively at people in real need: the elderly, the disabled, and those suffering long-term illness. In education the government provided more resources for schools than ever before: there were more teachers in proportion to pupils than ever; and British schools became world leaders in the use of computers in the classroom. Numerous major reforms were introduced with the implementation of a national core curriculum (which guarantees that all pupils study basic subjects); schools were enabled to control their own budgets (free of local authorities); greater parental influence was ensured both in the choice of schools and in participation in the governing of schools; and schools were allowed to opt out of Local Education Authority control. In higher education, the number of students enrolled increased dramatically by over 200,000; public sector institutions were removed from LEA control, and student grants reduced and supplemented by top-up loans. This catalogue does not exhaust the achievements claimed by the New Right for its social policies but it includes the main ones.

SUMMARY RECORD: THE REALITY

Law and Order

Despite the government's 'throwing money' at crime 'prevention' (really detection and punishment), by 1990 the number of reported criminal offences had risen to the highest level since records were first kept in 1857, with theft of various sorts accounting for more than half the offences. The clear-up rate fell to an all-time low also. Confidence in the police fell dramatically, particularly among groups which used to be their strongest supporters (such as women and the elderly).[110] Characteristically, the government rejected findings of Home Office research that clearly linked crime, particularly theft, to economic conditions. Instead of facing up to the implications of these results the government's response was to blame offenders, their families and those victims whose carelessness put temptation in the offender's way. Lack of curiosity about, or blind refusal to address the question of, *explaining* crime is characteristic of 'the stupid party' (philosopher/MP John Stuart Mill's name for the party that traditionally has scorned cerebral activity on principle). The results of a more severe sentencing policy were overcrowded prisons, prison riots and eventually a change to 'soft' non-custodial sentencing. Among the most telling failures of New Right policy on crime was the 'short sharp shock' treatment given to young offenders. It failed completely to have the desired and expected effects and was dropped quietly, presumably to save New Right thinkers the embarrassment of admitting that their 'blind' instinctive flair for penology had (as usual) failed them. The consequences of such blindness proved to be most damaging when dealing with terrorism. The interminable problem of violence in Northern Ireland has always had political and sectarian roots. By refusing frankly and openly to consider these root causes of the problem, by insisting that Irish republican violence was simply criminal violence, and by refusing to allow the terrorist's political case to be heard, the New Right government avoided the real issues, and so failed to approach, let alone achieve, a solution to the problem of political violence in Northern Ireland, really the greatest political problem facing British society. Mrs Thatcher recited her dogma that political violence never succeeds: a dogma which is as ineffectual as it is dubitable – as the recent history of colonial struggles goes to show (in Algeria, for example, indeed in the Irish Republic itself).

Health

Two authoritative reports in 1980 and 1987 by the Health Education Council (later the Health Education Authority) established that the elimination of material deprivation and not just the organisation of more efficient health care services had to become a national objective if the unfavourable health record (including high mortality rate) of the poorer sections of the population was to be remedied. All the recommendations of these reports were rejected by the government as too expensive, costed (by the government) in 1981 at £2 billion[111] (by way of comparison the cost of the defence of Fortress Falklands was over £3 billion between 1982 and 1987). Government claims that more was being spent on the health service than ever before were misleading because, after allowing for inflation, the increase in expenditure was negligible.[112] Also, claims to increased provision were specious: a reduction of working hours for nurses from 40 to 37.5 in 1980 merely increased the number of 'full-time equivalent' nurses without an extra hour being worked or an extra nurse employed. At the same time the demands on the service were growing, owing to the demographic trend to a higher proportion of old people in the population. The government claimed simply that it was spending more than ever before. While that may have been true, evidently not *enough* was being spent to meet the need to provide the same service for more people. One estimate suggests that additional expenditure 2.8 per cent above the level of inflation would be necessary.[113]

The government's response to complaints about underfunding was based on economies, 'affordability' and private provision. It was said that savings of £900 million from 'cost-improvement programmes' could be spent on improved health care. These savings were merely assumed, however, not real. For example, increased costs of services from renegotiated competitive tender-contracts were not allowed for; neither were interest charges on the capital costs of cost-cutting investments. As a result, the savings quoted by the government 'do not reflect genuine additional sources of finance' – in the words of a Kings Fund Institute report.[114] Always the government argued for services that the community could afford, and the amount spent, as a proportion of the gross domestic product, fell by over 7 per cent between 1981 and 1990. This reduction was from a level already only half the norm for comparable industrial nations. While other countries such as Germany, France, Belgium and Holland spend 9–10 per cent of their GDP on health care, Britain was spending just 5.5 per cent on the health service; per head of population in 1988–9 Britain spent £377 compared to £650 in Germany and £620 in France.[115] It was said that spending only half as much as other countries did not explain the relatively poor health service, but it is difficult to imagine more fatuous reasoning than that; reasoning that would not be entertained for a second in the matter of defence or law enforcement.[116] Instead of expenditure on health, Britain's New Right government chose to spend money disproportionately on defence, and to reduce taxes dramatically for the better off, from 83 per cent to 40 per cent.

In theory, tax reductions enable people to provide their own health care. Leaving aside the moral case in favour of shared communal health provision, it was evident that private health provision was an option only for the better off. People on average earnings (most people) did not benefit enough from tax relief to make private health insurance a real option. The costs of private health care in the real market proved to be extortionate, simply because the pricing policy of these health companies is geared to maximising profit rather than minimising costs to patients. In any case, it is obvious that private medical companies will not be interested in caring for severe and or chronic illness unless the sufferer is extraordinarily wealthy, which by definition is rarely and not a matter for general community care.[117]

The aggregate effect of New Right policies on the health service has been closure of hospitals and hospital wings, fewer beds, larger waiting lists, and higher prescription charges (an increase of 1,000 per cent by 1987).[118] New Right rhetoric has failed to persuade people that the health service is safe in their hands: even in October 1983, 85 per cent of voters wanted more money spent on health. An important indicator of the government's record in health care and medical research has been the attacks on it mounted by all three of the premier Royal Colleges and the British Medical Association. (The government's commendable crusade against the vested interests of the professions, including the medical profession, is for most purposes a separate matter from the issue of public expenditure and the standard of health care, and should not cloud those issues.)

Housing

Increasing home ownership by three million (26 per cent) ostensibly realises the New Right's broad aims of enhancing family life, promoting property ownership and fostering freedom through independence. In reality, the general state of housing in Britain is possibly the New Right's greatest single failure. While the number and proportion of owner-occupiers has increased, the number and proportion of homeless has increased even more. Under legislation requiring local authorities to house the homeless, 53,100 families qualified in 1978. By 1989 the number had increased to 120,500 (150,000 including Wales and Scotland). Only families with children qualify: if childless couples and individuals are included, the number would be 820,000, including 70,000 living rough in squats and hostels. One specific indicator with obvious wider implications is the number of families housed in bed and breakfast accommodation: in 1983 there were 2,700; by 1989 there were 11,880. At 1988 rates the annual cost of such accommodation for individuals was £11,315 compared to the cost of £7,400 to build a council house.[119] Parsimony wasn't even economical.

One main cause of greatly increased homelessness was the government's policy of selling off council houses to sitting tenants at huge discounts of between 30 and 60 per cent; as a result, council housing stock was reduced by one million. Annual lettings fell correspondingly from 274,000 in 1980 to 243,000 in 1986 (a reduction of 11 per cent). The proportion allocated to the homeless went up from one in six to one in four. The situation was made worse by the government's prohibition on councils building more houses. As a result the annual number of council houses built – 140,000 in 1977 – fell from 94,000 in 1980 to just 25,000 in 1988. Central government housing subsidies fell from £2,200 million in 1979–80 to £470 million in 1987–8 (78 per cent). Nor was the shortfall made up by other sectors. Housing associations' annual new-builds fell from 20,600 in 1978 to 8,700 in 1989. The total number of new houses, including those in the private sector, fell from 250,000 each year in the 1970s to 176,000 by 1987. The explosion in property prices meant the amount of private rented accommodation did not increase because it was more profitable to sell than to rent. (Property prices exploded because the government cut income tax, de-regulated loan finance and during the 1980s reduced interest rates).[120]

Most of the worsening problems of homelessness derived from government policies, some of which have just been mentioned. There were other policies, too, that affected housing. Young people were presumed to have welcoming homes open to them, and to have available to them paid places on Youth Training Schemes. Consequently, income support was withdrawn in 1989 from large numbers of young people (90,000) who had no family home and no training placement. Even some Conservative MPs of a more humane sort – led by Robin Squire, MP for Hornchurch – joined in the protest to repeal this legislation. Care-in-the-Community legislation – ostensibly intended to return the mentally handicapped and mentally ill to the community from institutions – has the practical effect of increasing dramatically the number of homeless, which has risen faster among the disabled than among others. In England, between 1979 and 1986, the increase in homelessness among the mentally ill was 92 per cent, and among the physically handicapped 99 per cent; compared to 57 per cent in the nation overall.[121]

Not only did homes become much more scarce, they became much less affordable as well. For those dependent on state housing benefit, the impact of legislation in 1987 was dramatic and for the worse. A million families ceased to be entitled to housing benefit, and another five million had housing support reduced. As a consequence, the government's Audit Report showed an immediate increase in rent arrears of 350 per cent (from £100 million in 1987 to £450 million in 1988). Such problems were not confined to the worst off who depended on renting council houses. The great extension of home ownership proved not to be an unqualified good for house buyers. House prices escalated as mortgages were extended to ever-higher multiples of annual income: whereas in the late 1970s twice annual income was usual, in the 1980s five times was not unusual. The measure of the increased mortgage debt was the figure for average outstanding mortgages. In 1979 it was £42.1 billion, whereas in 1988 it was £204.4 billion – virtually a fivefold increase. Mortgage repayments proved to be difficult to maintain, and by 1989 it was estimated that 380,000 people were behind with mortgage payments. In 1979 2,530 homes had been repossessed by building societies; by 1987 it was 22,930 – virtually a tenfold increase. Repossession and recorded arrears are, of course, only the tip of an iceberg of crippling housing costs. Many house owners who were not in mortgage arrears were under excessive financial strain nonetheless.[122]

Not only was the number of houses inadequate; the quality of housing stock was hardly improved at all (a remarkable reflection on the reality behind the 'economic miracle'). A housing survey published in 1989 by the Department of the Environment showed that the proportion of stock classified as unfit had fallen only slightly (from 6.3 to 5.6 per cent) between 1981 and 1986; and the proportion in serious disrepair had stayed the same (6 per cent). The Association of Metropolitan Authorities estimated that £86.5 billion was required to repair and improve housing and to meet urgent needs. The government's response was to introduce tests for the allocation of grants, the effect of which, according to the Environment Minister, was to exclude two million people from qualifying, three-quarters of whom would be on relatively modest incomes (below £12,000 in 1989) and one quarter with lower incomes (below £9,000).[123]

The New Right policy was to promote home ownership, in keeping with their general aim of bringing about an irreversible shift of power in favour of ordinary people and their families. In practice their policies had the opposite effect. In 1979 the average house price was 5.9 times the average wage of the *lowest* paid ten per cent of *manual* workers. By 1989 house prices had risen to 7.9 times the average wage for the same group. In contrast, for the *highest* paid ten per cent of *non-manual* workers the ratio of average house price to income had actually fallen by 5 per cent, from 2.1 times to 2.0 times. Another powerful class-based difference in housing was in the relative subsidies given. Whereas central government's subsidies for local government house-building were cut between 1979 and 1987–8 by a dramatic 78 per cent, tax relief on owner-occupier's mortgages rose from £1.64 billion in 1979–80 to £5.5 billion in 1988–9 – an increase of 235 per cent.[124]

The partisan political reasons for these great disparities in housing provision that further disadvantage the already badly off are obvious. Other policies demonstrated the New Right's determination for ideological reasons to detach housing from local government control, because of its inevitable basis in the community, and collective provision. If these ideological reasons were ever in doubt, no doubt remained after the tenants were consulted. The National Consumer Council asked council house tenants who they preferred as new landlords (assuming the local councils would not be). Still, a majority, 51 per cent, nominated local councils before housing associations and others. A MORI poll of council tenants in London showed that 94 per cent chose a council as their ideal landlord. This result was borne out by a ballot of residents in Peterborough New Town. The result was that 93.4 per cent of tenants chose the council as landlord on an 83.5 per cent turnout. Faced with such evidence, the government simply ignored it. The Housing Bill of 1988 provides for the counting of all non-votes as positive agreement with the transfer of houses from councils to other owners. More brazen undemocratic gerrymandering it is difficult to imagine, and was inconceivable before ten years of New Right administration engendered new levels of low expectations of government.[125]

Housing problems are indicative of the effects of the New Right's broadest economic policies – and their ultimate failure. The old ideals of family and property ownership provided the steam to drive the movement to private home ownership. The new libertarian doctrine of the free market dictated that controls should be removed if they prevented individuals from borrowing and investing. If individuals freely borrowed beyond their means this was, according to the doctrine, no business of the government's, just of the individuals themselves and their creditors. In the absence of a massive building programme to match uncontrolled borrowing, and with a limited supply of land, house prices simply escalated, so that earnings and house values came to be related only distantly, compared to previous ratios. For a period after the 1988 budget the rate of increase in house values seemed to render working for a living altogether less economic than cultivating the value of your house![126] People were then encouraged by the usurers to borrow heavily against the new high value of their homes for any kind of inessential consumption including (mainly foreign) holidays and imported luxury goods. What concern is it of banks and finance companies in a free society that a nation's balance of payments and industrial base are disintegrating when they can show profits and pay dividends? Inevitably, when the government was eventually driven by inflation and astronomic balance of payments deficits to increase interest rates, people with highly geared mortgages were financially ruined. The parallels between the Heath–Barber gazumper in the early 1970s and the Thatcher–Ridley 'high-gearers' in the late 1980s would not have escaped the attention of any prime minister less self-contained than Margaret Thatcher. After all, had she not deposed Edward Heath for his financial reck-lessness?

The plight of the countless homeless, and the millions dependent on the help of others to provide decent homes, is the inevitable consequence of market monomania and blindness. The free market does not provide public goods which it is not profitable for individuals to provide. The provision of decent low-cost housing for those millions of the population who are on below-average incomes is, almost by definition, not a profitable enterprise. Certainly such housing was not provided by the market in the 1980s, because there is no profit in it. The New Right proved to be incapable of providing decent housing for compatriots on low incomes. Altogether the market in housing in the 1980s served the real interests of only a small minority of the well off, strained the financial resources of middle-income home owners, and deposited countless homeless people into the streets and doss houses. The massive sell-off of council houses proved not to be a way to bolster the family and spread property ownership. If that had been true the government would have implemented a policy of continuing to build council houses for discount sale to new owners, and it would not have prohibited the use by councils of the proceeds from house sales for similar purposes. In the event it did not build for sale; and it did prohibit use of proceeds. Council houses were sold for cynical, short-term, political purposes only. First, council house sales generally undermined local government and specifically the links between local government (especially Labour councils) and the people they housed (mainly Labour voters). Secondly, the New Right Conservatives virtually bribed voters with billions of pounds (about £4.5 billion) of rate-payers' capital assets in much the same way that Henry VIII disposed of the assets of the monasteries to his political cronies.

Education

Schools. Educational policy in the 1980s was driven by Black Paper views of the 1970s and New Right thinking on markets applied to education in particular. The main promise was of higher standards of attainment, better teaching and more parental involvement. The Black Paper agenda suffered from the fact that it was based on polemic and ideology rather than respectable evidence. As Nigel Wright after some respectable research had already pointed out in 1977, there was no clear evidence that progressive, that is, 'pupil-centred', primary schools produce worse results than more traditional schools, as the Black Papers suggested. Also, in terms of academic achievement (as measured by O and A level results), there had been, as intended, an enormous increase over 25 years in the number of pupils passing these examinations, and little evidence to suggest, as the Black Papers did, that comprehensive schools had hindered this advance. Again, there was little sound evidence that violence and indiscipline in schools had been increasing. Altogether sight had been lost of the fact that such innovations as progressive methods and comprehensive schools had been made because what had gone before had, by universal agreement, demonstrably failed to benefit most pupils. Overall the evidence from public examinations was that a higher proportion of pupils were achieving higher levels of academic attainment.

But, notoriously, nothing so mundane as contrary evidence is of interest to conviction politicians and their educational pot-carriers.

The propensity prejudicially to ignore contrary evidence, or to misconstrue it, continued throughout the 1980s to characterise the pronouncements of New Right spokespersons such as Ray Honeyford and Steven Sexton. When authors of a research report on comprehensive schools concluded that: 'Schools failed because they *weren't* comprehensive rather than because they *were*', it was necessary for them to correct New Right commentators who perversely insisted that the research 'inescapably' proved the very opposite! The whole record of education in the 1980s is shot through with ideological disputes of this kind.[127]

Educational standards were to be pursued by changing not only the curriculum, but also delivery and assessment. The quality of teaching was to be improved by attacking sub-standard teaching and by changes to teacher training. Parental involvement was to be pursued by removing control from local government and giving parents greater involvement both in their choice of schools and in governance. In practice these inherently laudable, or anyway unexceptionable, objectives were subverted. Apart from other problems (to be discussed presently) the curriculum proposed became so inflated that only a Victorian cottonmill timetable and calendar could accommodate it. (The Centre for Policy Studies duly proposed in November 1990 such gradgrind measures.) The demands for assessment proposed at ages seven, eleven, 14 and 16, proved so impractical, onerous and counterproductive that even the New Right Minister for Education eventually saw the need to drop many of them. Attacks on incompetent teachers were a regular feature of New Right rhetoric about educational standards, although no criteria of competence were specified, other than those already in use, no practical means of applying them suggested, other than those already applicable, and no evidence of the extent of the problem, anyway, ever adduced. There was no evidence that parents with children in state schools were any more inclined to involve themselves with school management and curriculum matters than were parents with children in private schools. In the matter of *choice* of schools, this so evidently depends on financial resources and geography that a policy of promoting choice without the provision of commensurate resources is mere rhetoric.

Policies were pursued to change the organisation and management of schools along market lines. First schools were offered the opportunity to manage their own budgets, free of local authority control, though in practice schools lacked either the trained personnel or the resources properly to assume the greater autonomy this prospect offered. After 1988 schools were also free to opt out of local authority control altogether if a majority of parents so wished. Again, this shift to a market in education proved highly problematic in practice for lack of funds and expertise, even assuming that it was desirable in principle, which was far from clear. Generally, schools were moved towards greater management autonomy without the necessary preparation and resources.

The curriculum was subject to three major changes. First was the exercise of greater central control and influence. Schools were liberated from local authority influence only to be subject to the constraints of a national curriculum, and to the financial constraints inherent in funding from the Manpower Services Commission (MSC) as well as from the Department of Education and Science. The idea of a national curriculum had been strongly promoted by James Callaghan, the Labour Prime Minister, in 1975, as had the need to make education more relevant to the 'world of work'. The idea of a national curriculum has certain undeniable merits, mainly as a basis for ensuring basic knowledge, skills and standards. In practice, however, the central planners of the curriculum sought to promote approved but tendentious views through the required syllabus, notably in history, education for citizenship and science. The science curriculum was to reflect the second influence, the imperative to orient education to practical, profit-making studies, typically, electronics was to be studied in preference to 'pure' physics. Both of these developments could readily be seen as moves to deploy school curricula to promote a preferred, conservative and capitalist, view of the world in a way incompatible with the liberal view of the aims of education subscribed to by most teachers. The thrust to more vocationally orientated education was given great impetus by the involvement for the first time in schools of the MSC. By making funds available to schools through the MSC rather than the usual channels, the government intended to ensure that developments linked to work, particularly in manufacturing industry, would be given priority, and be properly accounted for. The government was most proud that British schools as part of this development were world leaders in the use of computers in the classroom. The third influence on the curriculum was the introduction of the General Certificate of Secondary Education (GCSE). This provided a curriculum far better suited to the needs of most pupils than the 'gold standard' of the General Certificate of Education by comprising broader studies with obvious application by practical teaching, and by introducing modes of continuous assessment. The implementation almost simultaneously of all three major innovations placed extraordinary burdens on teachers that were not reflected either in their salaries or in the regard shown them by the government.

Teaching resources were, in secondary schools at any rate, ostensibly at something of a record high. The government's way of expressing it in July 1986 was to announce that there were two million 'surplus' school places. In fact the overall national pupil teacher ratio in state schools came down from 20:1 in 1975–6 to 17:1 in 1988 due to the demographic trend that saw far fewer pupils of school age before the number of teachers was reduced commensurately. It is significant that even with this reduced ratio, class sizes were still substantially larger then those in 'good' private schools where classes of 14 are normal. New Right ministers thus made sure that their own children sat in private-school classes substantially smaller than those they deemed to be uneconomic in state schools, here were Britain's double standards at work in schools. By translating the reduced ratios into 'surplus' school places the government lost the opportunity to improve the standard of education for pupils without recruiting more teachers. Nevertheless the New Right manifesto of 1987 proclaimed that there were more teachers in proportion to pupils than ever before, implying that more teachers had been hired. In fact a paradox developed where there were – by the stipulated ratios – surplus teachers, yet teacher shortages as well. There was no real paradox, however, because teachers were employed in schools that could not be closed even though they had relatively few pupils, and there were shortages in specific subjects that other teachers were not qualified to teach (even so, the situation became so desperate that many teachers were conducting classes they were not qualified to teach). Mathematics, science, technology and foreign languages were the main shortage subjects. In 1988 alone, 2,100 graduate scientists and mathematicians left the teaching profession before retirement age, along with 970 linguists; in all a total of 14,490 teachers left the profession before retirement. Teachers left schools in such large numbers because of the excessive stress they were experiencing, largely due to the low status and low pay. Maths, science and language teachers, in particular, found it easy to multiply their salaries by moving to employment in industry and commerce. Financial resources were inadequate both for educational materials and for building work. The *Mail On Sunday*, a newspaper well known for its support of the New Right, published in May 1990 the results of a survey of educational resources in schools that it commissioned from the National Foundation for Educational Research. Under the banner headline 'Scandal of our Schools' it was reported that parents were providing primary schools with almost £40 million in funds per year without which many could not keep going; one third of all money spent in schools on books and equipment came from parents; and one third of the schools used parents to teach both arithmetic and computer studies. Out of 19,228 schools, 2,572 were receiving more from parents than they were from the state. Capital investment in schools in 1988–9 was £192 million compared to £258 million in 1979–80, a decrease of 26 per cent. All this, and yet the government was claiming that it was providing more resources for pupils than ever before. John Tomlinson explained: 'The broad picture that most of those working in the service might accept would be that though resources increased in real terms it was not sufficient to maintain the former (pre-1979) level of service.'[128]

Educational developments in the 1980s cannot be adequately discussed without mention of the government's political agenda. For general ideological reasons the government was opposed to trade unions and public sector employment. Members of teaching unions were, therefore, anathematised twice-over. For good measure teachers have pretensions to professional status and the government was engaged in a jihad against vested interests of professionals as well. Thus teachers, as trade unionists, were excluded from participation in educational policy-making through quangos (such as the Schools Council) which were eventually disbanded. As public sector employees they were routinely lectured to on their parasitical status and subjected to the indignity not only of having pay settlements imposed on them, but of having their pay-negotiating rights formally withdrawn altogether. As professional teachers they were subjected to a campaign calculated to undermine their pride and collective resistance to the incursion of New Right policies into their professional domain.

Reflection on the salient developments in state school education under the New Right leads to several insights into its thinking and suggests some conclusions of more general relevance. Some developments, such as the stronger orientation towards vocationalism and the GCSE, were largely unproblematic in themselves and would have been pursued by most other governments. The manner of their introduction – precipitately, autocratically and with inadequate funding – was probably peculiar to the New Right's way of doing things. The programme to 'marketise' the organisational management of schools was largely irrelevant to the real and central tasks of most schools, improved teaching and learning, and merely diverted energies and resources from these tasks. There is a serious problem about the rationale for regarding all institutions, especially schools, as competitors in a market place. When money is spent on a swimming pool (because it will look good in a marketing brochure and attract pupils), rather than on a substantial (but unspectacular) library, something is going wrong with the essential educational process. The government's professed aims, of promoting greater parental choice, is in practice highly suspect. If members of the government really believed that parental choice was the best guarantee of a child's education, then why did it not provide *cash redeemable* education vouchers (thereby de-regulating the lives of its citizens)? Of course these options are unacceptable for a good reason: the need to ensure an adequate education for children, whatever parents would opt for. But that is precisely the point of compulsory state education by professionals in the first place, and also the reason why parents entrust pupils to the process of education in private schools.

Government control of the content of the national curriculum in practice proved that worries were justified. Keith Joseph, when Minister of Education, prohibited examination of the social responsibility of scientists in the science curriculum. The bias of the science curriculum towards industrial applications and the introduction of computers to schools were problematic for a similar reason: they ignored or took for granted values that were strongly contested in society at large. The policy of promoting vocational education in general and computing in particular was problematic from a purely utilitarian viewpoint, also. Japanese industrial success was built on a broad school curriculum with little or no specifically vocational content. The Japanese success in microelectronics and computing had been achieved although there were virtually no computers in their schools. In Japan industry itself and higher technical education provided most vocational training, including computing. In practice, much use of computers in British schools was at a very low level of skill and in reality, where information technology is concerned, employers often preferred beginners because they did not have to unlearn imperfectly acquired and irrelevant computing skills. The thrust to vocationalism in schools also proved to be problematic as the impact of economic recession and new technology together made the future of work and the pattern of employment more uncertain than ever before. Schooling was blamed for most of the ills of society, including supposed industrial failure. Consequently, schoolteachers were scapegoats. In reality, schools inevitably reflect society. This problem also highlighted the failure of the New Right to address the fundamental question of what school education is *for*. If it is to serve the development of free citizens in a democracy, then the uncritical presumption of the partial values of industrial capitalism is unjustifiable. If education is to serve to promote community, civil society and a cohesive nation, then the fragmentation and ghettoisation of schooling (by institution, region, class, religion and eventually, perhaps, race as well) cannot serve that purpose. And if all schools are to be as autonomous as private schools, there could be no justification for the imposition of central control of the curriculum and other matters. Educational policy in the 1980s exemplified very clearly the irreconcilable contradictions at the root of New Right thinking, as well as other faults of fact and value.[129]

Further and Higher Education. Education after compulsory schooling in Britain falls into distinct categories. The further education of the 16–18-year-old group has been referred to already in connection with Britain's failure to provide vocational training of technical trades and crafts in numbers to match industrial competitors (see 'Industry', p87). By the late 1980s only 32 per cent of this age group were in fulltime study, compared, for example, to 58 per cent in France, 69 per cent in Japan and 79 per cent in the United States. In the age group 20 to 24 Britain, again, lags behind other developed nations. World Bank data for students in this age group shows Britain at 22 per cent, Italy 26 per cent, West Germany and France 30 per cent, South Korea 32 per cent, Sweden 38 per cent, Canada 55 per cent and the United States 57 per cent. These figures reflect the resources devoted to education in different countries, with Britain spending substantially less than others. Moreover, the situation has deteriorated in the 1980s both relative to other countries and in terms of GDP, as Table 8 shows.[130]

TABLE 8 COMPARISON OF EXPENDITURE ON EDUCATION

| Country | Per cent of GDP spent | | Country |
	1975	1983	
Netherlands	8.2	8.5	Israel
Denmark	7.8	8.4	Sweden
Norway	7.1	7.4	Netherlands
Sweden	7.1	7.0	Denmark
Israel	6.7	7.0	Norway
United Kingdom	6.7	6.8	Ireland
United States	6.5	6.8	United States
Ireland	6.2	5.8	France
Japan	5.5	5.7	Italy
France	5.2	5.6	Japan
West Germany	5.1	5.3	*United Kingdom*
Italy	4.1	4.8	West Germany

Source: United Nations Educational Social and Cultural Organisation Statistical Yearbook 1987[131]

As these data show, whereas in 1975 only four of the twelve leading nations compared spent a higher proportion of gross domestic product on education than Britain, by 1983 only one spent a lower proportion per capita (and that was West Germany which had an 18 per cent higher GDP). Another fact worth recording is that at 1983 rates there would have been an extra £7 billion available if Britain's defence expenditure had been at the German level, and £16.55 billion if at the Japanese level.[132] When discussing 'what the nation can afford' to pay for education and academic research these New Right policies should be borne in mind.

New Right policy on higher education (again) reflected the imperatives of the strong state and free-market principles. It is convenient to consider the intention and impact of this under five headings: aims and rationale, organisation and management, curriculum, access and resourcing.

First, the purpose of higher education was called into question. The traditional mission of universities – to pursue disinterestedly learning for its own sake – was challenged. Universities were 'steered' by government directives and financial controls towards meeting the needs of the economy, primarily through research and teaching geared directly to industry and the market. In the spirit of the times the Prime Minister in 1987 informed a history undergraduate that his course was a luxury.[133] Keith Joseph so disvalued the social sciences that he insisted on changing the name of the Social Science Research Council to the Economic and Social Research Council; thereby indicating where the new priority lay as well as enforcing his epistemological prejudices. In the public sector, polytechnics and colleges, the shift was even more explicit as academic institutions were restyled as educational 'corporations'. Some of this change was uncontentious and thought to be long overdue by other political parties. As early as 1958 the Cambridge philosopher, Professor C. D. Broad, had criticised an avowedly useless but fashionable brand of ordinary-language philosophy saying, '[I will not] speculate how long an impoverished community, such as contemporary England, will continue to pay salaries of individuals whose only function, on their own showing, is to treat a disease which they catch from each other and impart to their pupils.'[134] Formerly enthusiastic proponents of polytechnics worried about the 'academic drift' of these institutions towards ineffectual university norms and away from their practical function.[135] Even so the New Right efforts to dissolve the traditional aims and rationale of higher education and replace them with utilitarian market values is best described as philistine. There is some truth also in the charge that the government conducted a special vendetta against the humanities and social sciences because they are critical disciplines disposed to question presumptions, including the dogmatics of New Right thinking, and, in the case of the social sciences, to conduct inquiries into the origins of wealth, power and misrule likely to be unconducive to the view of the world portrayed in government propaganda. These policies were in their effect destructive of the foundations of democracy and true liberty of scholarly opinion. Ominously, under the pretext of enhancing efficiency, tenure was removed from university appointments so that troublesome academics could be dismissed on whatever pretexts authoritarian administrators might care to concoct (preferably economic ones). In short, the New Right government had little or no interest in, or commitment to, the perennial values of academic learning and teaching; indeed it had a positive antipathy that was reciprocated when, for the first time, Oxford University decided not to distinguish an Oxonian Prime Minister by conferring on her an honorary doctorate.[136]

The organisation and management of the universities was radically transformed in various ways, the effects of which were to render them less autonomous, more subservient to the state and more accommodating to the needs of industry and commerce. The power of the purse and financial accounting was the main method, and this will be discussed presently. One undoubted benefit of the new values was that, for the first time, proper accounting procedures were forced on a system which had previously had no clear idea of costs or even the number of students following different courses nationally. The University Grants Committee was first transformed into a management tool for quality control, then replaced by the Universities Funding Council that abandoned altogether the UGC's role of distancing government from the universities. The UFC's role, under the supervision of its first chairman, Lord Chilver (ex-United Biscuits), was to ensure that the government's intentions were realised by securing value for money and the relevance (to commerce) of academic courses. Similar measures were taken in the public sector, first through the National Advisory Body and later through the Polytechnics and Colleges Funding Council. In addition, public sector institutions were formally divorced from local government control by the 1988 Education Act, ostensibly to free them from local political control. In reality what happened was that the accountability of institutions to local communities was lost and the new governing bodies had no elected representatives but were dominated by centrally appointed members from industry and business. Finally, the broad effect was to make all such institutions dependent on a monopoly provider and auditor, the state. All of this was promoted in the name of accountability and efficiency, yet in practice there was no real accounting of the management of such institutions. Some polytechnics and colleges were managed by individuals who had no managerial training, no commercial experience, and who demonstrated real incompetence by industrial performance criteria; yet they remained 'in post' after vesting and even awarded themselves substantially increased salaries in line with their alleged new 'commercial' responsibilities.[137]

The curriculum of higher education received the attention of ministers whose values embraced high Tory elitism and free-market ideas of efficiency and affordability. Elitists had never been convinced of the desirability of higher-education-for-all anyway. The most vocal elitists, such as Peregrine Worsthorne, Maurice Cowling, Roger Scruton, C. B. Cox, A. E. Dyson, Kingsley Amis, Keith Joseph and

Robert Jackson, were basically word-men and common-room ironists but technological ignoramuses, themselves unable to set any sort of example in marketable scientific or technological competence. The Prime Minister herself had shown her fierce dedication to science and business by opting for law and then politics almost as soon as she graduated in chemistry. Science and technology were strictly for lower orders in this view. The real elite (people like themselves) could be amply provided for by Oxbridge and a few distinguished older establishments with a traditional curriculum in conventional disciplines. As a result, pressure was put on universities to close small departments of 'Gothic' (in reality often low-cost philosophy departments) and focus on 'marketable' courses. Public sector institutions were encouraged by financial disincentives, and by the operation of a centrally planned quota system, to consolidate on vocationally oriented courses.

The new control by state bodies (NAB and PCFC) of numbers of students entering specific higher education courses was a remarkably Stalinist outcome of the New Right market philosophy for higher education.

Student numbers and choice were other main variables affecting curriculum and, through funding, other factors particularly in the public sector. Conservative governments were eager to point to the fact that the number of school-leavers entering further and higher education had increased by 200,000 between 1979 and 1990. This had been achieved not as a result of Conservative government policy but because of demographic trends and the comprehensive school system which enabled far more pupils to qualify with A levels than ever before. In other debates, however, comprehensives were denigrated for lowering standards. For elitists more inevitably means worse, anyway. The universities insisted on maintaining the 'unit of resource' – funding per student – so at first they refused to accept more students. Students went instead to public-sector institutions, which were paid less for each student, although the standard of academic work and degrees awarded were officially the same, and were maintained through the system of external examination, peer review and government inspection. New Right elitism was confounded by this expansion of the numbers of students pursuing higher education, but its free-market instincts were satisfied so long as 'more' didn't mean 'costs more'. Public sector institutions were encouraged through financial threats to accept more students without commensurate increases in funds. The imperatives of staff job-security achieved what simple arithmetic and considerations of plain equity could not: the provision of the same higher education for much larger numbers of students at half the cost, with (supposedly) no loss of quality. The government also declared its resolve to expand the provision for part-time students in higher education. This objective was not accompanied by a commensurate increase in funding. As a result large numbers of potential students who could not afford fees and other costs and who were not grant-funded on a pro-rata basis were effectively excluded from higher education. The government's 'solution' was to replace grants with loans despite the fact that studies showed it would take one hundred years to recuperate the loans, and that the success of loan systems elsewhere depended on very low interest rates that Britain doesn't have. Banks naturally refused to cooperate with this unprofitable proposal.[138]

Resources for higher education fell along with reduced expenditure on all education, from 6.7 per cent of GDP in 1975 to 5.3 per cent in 1983. University funding was reduced by 15 per cent in 1981 – but not by the principle of equal misery. Some universities were unaffected while others had UFC funds cut by 40 per cent. Predictably, Oxbridge and the home universities of UFC members were least affected. Ironically, the universities most affected were the new technological universities such as Salford, Aston and Bradford, which had done more than most others to satisfy the New Right's market criteria but had failed to satisfy New Right elitism. This result exemplified, again, the philosophical contradictions at the root of New Right thinking and policy. The government's intention was that institutions should seek funding from other sources: students and industry, as well as private benefactors. Overseas students were charged 'economic' fees for the first time. This proved to be so obviously of short-term benefit only (because students and their future allegiance tended to go elsewhere) that the policy was later quietly modified. Industry proved to be largely immune to the blandishments of academia, despite some highly publicised developments. The University of Salford, for example, widely publicised projects developed with industry after the cuts of 1981. But by 1983 funding from industry was only of the order of £30,000 whereas the government had quietly compensated the university for the loss of UFC grants by allocating £1 million in public funds from the budget of the Department of Trade and Industry. (The fact that Salford's Vice-Chancellor, Professor John Ashworth, had been a recent member of the Downing Street think tank was surely relevant to this courtesy service to the University of Salford.) Unlike the United States, Britain has no well-established conventions of private munificence, and many universities started from scratch in a hopeless race for life to replace cuts in public funding with charitable donations from alumni and other philanthropes. Keith Joseph, predictably, could see all the difficulties attendant on attempts to change traditional methods of British banks financing industry, but was (selectively) blind to the difficulties of changing the traditional methods of financing higher education. Public-sector institutions had a stronger tradition of working with industry and commerce, but even they could not effectively compensate for substantial government underfunding.

The various *ad hoc* measures adopted by institutions throughout the 1980s did not resolve resourcing problems, which were greatly exacerbated by the substantial increase in student numbers. With an eye to their all-important criterion of value for money, New Right enthusiasts pointed out the larger numbers of students enrolled in higher education in other countries which did not necessarily spend more on higher education than Britain. This is doubtful, but even if it were true no account was taken of three crucial factors in assessing value for money: the average time taken to graduate, completion rates, and the standard of final awards. Students following degree courses in other countries, such as the United States and Germany, typically take four, five or more years of study to complete, whereas in Britain three years is the norm. Also, the non-completion rate in other countries is very much higher than in Britain. Moreover, the academic standard attained by British graduates after a three-year fulltime course is very often higher than graduates in other countries at the same stage. The American bachelor's degree, in particular, generally compares unfavourably to the British first degree. If student/staff ratio's in Britain are lower than in other countries that would explain the higher completion rates, the shorter time taken and the higher standards reached. By these criteria British academics do provide value for money that any competent businessman would be pleased to acknowledge. Instead, the New Right governments have proceeded to fund higher education on the presumption that there is a need for more value for money, based on the most crass criteria of numbers of students and staff and without regard to other relevant factors. Not the least result has been a serious decline in the pay and conditions of service of academic staff. As financial constraints have eroded pay, their workload has increased with increased numbers of students as well as the proliferation of other demands on time and energy. Pay has been eroded in the public sector by 40 per cent since 1974 when the Houghton Committee compared pay of academics in the public sector with others, based on qualifications, experience and responsibilities. Free-marketeers such as Keith Joseph say 1974 was a merely arbitrary date for comparison. This ignores the essential fact that the comparison was made not just at a given time, but on the basis of numerous relevant criteria and after careful, informed deliberation by impartial assessors. The fact is that the New Right government exploited for eleven years the dedication of staff to students and their vocation as well as their weak bargaining position in order to systematically erode educational provision and academics' pay and conditions of service. Typically, the government's rhetoric shifted from the unchallengeable (because unspecific) allegation that some academics were not earning their keep to the (implicit) allegation that all academics were 'lean kine' in need of reality therapy. This reflected three things: first, the refusal of the government to recognise that public services are not merely parasitic on the country's economic life but are a necessary adjunct to it; secondly, the firm resolve to exercise the sort of parsimony in academic pay awards that was conspicuously absent in the generous self-assessment of the pay of business executives; thirdly, a deep and indiscriminate dislike of intellectuals (people who think), especially those who live in ivory towers. Even after ten years of financial cuts, restructuring and securing alternative sources of funding, at the end of 1990 at least 44 of 74 universities were running at a loss, and an unknown number of others were under severe financial strain.[139]

At the root of the problems in higher education since 1979 is the New Right's ambivalence about it. In its Tory mood it recognises that society needs an educated population and workforce (though it evades the resource implications of this). In its libertarian mood it denies altogether that there is such a thing as society and supposes that higher education benefits mainly those who have it and who, therefore, should themselves pay for it. The result is an underfunded, overstressed and demoralised system which appoints hardly any young academics to steady employment and loses, by emigration, the best that it has to other countries. This decay and demoralisation at the core of a modern, information-based society is a legacy of the New Right that will not be easily or quickly remedied.

Social Welfare

Many of the effects of New Right policies on welfare have already been discussed in connection with industry and unemployment, taxation, health, housing and education. Other effects have been discussed extensively elsewhere and it will be sufficient to summarise just some of the most salient ones here.[140] The main criticism of New Right policy is that it generally increased poverty in the country, as the price for increasing the wealth of the best off. The rhetoric of the New Right depended on a philosophical distinction between relative and absolute poverty. Evidence of increased poverty was dismissed on the grounds that increased inequalities due to greatly increased wealth did not entail that the worst off were worse off than before, merely less well off than others. In her final speech as Prime Minister, Margaret Thatcher accused critics of preferring equal deprivation to better welfare for the worst off if that meant others were even better off. In reality, so far as incomes were concerned, the worst off 20 per cent were absolutely worse off as a result of New Right policies: 6 per cent worse off in 1988 than in 1979.[141] Two other indicators of poverty show different aspects of the same general picture. By the minimal criterion of income at the supplementary benefit level or below, the number of poor persons increased by 55 per cent between 1979 (6,070,000) and 1985 (9,380,000). The number of poor children increased (from 1,180,000 to 2,250,000).[142] Even among people in work the position deteriorated dramatically for the lowest paid. By the Council of Europe's criterion of decency (two-thirds of median earnings or less) the numbers in Britain not receiving a 'decent' income reached 45.8 per cent of the working population (9,430,000) by 1987; an increase of 20 per cent since 1979.[143] Pharisees (like Keith Joseph) were apt to recite the truism that a person's worth and quality of life isn't measured by wealth and income. They would say that money is not enough for a happy life. But they neglect another truism, that it is necessary for a happy life to have enough money.

Between 1979 and 1987 the number of households depending on supplementary benefit increased from 2.9 million to 4.9 million (69 per cent), with a trebling of the number of unemployed receiving benefit.[144]

The Social Security Act (1986) was designed to ensure that welfare expenditure was targeted so as to meet the most pressing real needs rather than indiscriminately to dispense benefits (such as child benefit) whether the recipients needed them or not. The system of income support, which had previously provided special ex-gratia payments for immediate needs, was replaced by the social fund. This made loans available on a means-tested basis and only when all other alternative means, including charity, had been exhausted. The qualifying standards for distributing these funds were initially so stringent that it was necessary for the DHSS to instruct its officers to relax their application so that funds could be dispensed at all. One example of the system at work will suffice to illustrate its nature and effect. In Crewe, Cheshire, with the assistance and support of a member of the Crewe Area Health Authority, an 82-year-old pensioner whose electric stove had worn out applied to the DHSS for money from the Social Fund to replace it. After assessing the application the officer concerned decided that no payment would be made. When it was pointed out that without a stove the old woman would have no hot food, and winter was approaching, the officer ventured the opinion that hot food was not a necessity. New Right policy, as embodied in the Social Security Act, created a climate in which callousness of this sort became routine.

The general trend towards hardship from reduced welfare provision is exemplified in a variety of ways by different categories of the badly off. Pensioners have suffered in absolute terms because pensions were after 1980 linked to the average of selected prices (excluding gas and electricity) instead of to average earnings (for example, gas and electricity prices increased more than the rate of inflation). Also, cuts in health service funding affected old people disproportionately because there were more of them with relatively less provision. Disabled people were far more disadvantaged than other groups, with two-thirds of them living at or below the poverty line. Characteristically, the government contrived to ensure that the publication of the official report of the true facts was first delayed, then released without publicity in 1988. Mentally ill people were supposed to benefit from a care-in-the-community policy, by returning them from psychiatric hospitals to the community. In practice, although between 1979 and 1986 28,500 longstay mental patients were released into the community, only 2,230 extra places were provided in care centres. The rest were either deposited without care into unsuitable accommodation or ended up living on the streets. There was nothing to prevent them taking their own lives, and some did. Even a Right-wing Conservative, Nicholas Winterton, told Parliament it was a tragedy that for purely economic reasons psychiatric hospitals were being closed and the sites sold off for redevelopment. Families with young children suffered significant loss of income after a family credit system replaced family income supplement and other benefits. Despite 'targeting' benefits to the most needy cases they were still worse off because other government policies imposed extra charges, for water rates and Poll Tax (at least 20 per cent had to be paid), and the special-needs grants were discontinued. Ian Gilmour, the former Conservative minister, castigated the government in 1988, accusing it of hypocrisy and lack of compassion: 'The same people who welcome tax cuts which give £100 a week or more to the very rich, very solemnly announce that it is utterly wrong that the same very rich should receive £2.25 per child per week in child benefit. If the rich don't need child benefit, they don't need tax cuts either.' Women were systematically disadvantaged by the 1980 Employment Act which seriously weakened rights to paid maternity leave and to protection from dismissal when pregnant. The many women who care for elderly and disabled relatives suffered cuts in local authority support services, and were vigorously denied financial support of the kind that was mandatory in Europe. Although many more mothers of young children wish to work (including 41 per cent of single women parents), lack of creche facilities makes this impossible. Not only are there far fewer creche facilities in Britain; the government refuses to allow tax relief for the costs of paying for them. Margaret Thatcher, who employed nannies to bring up her children while she pursued a career in politics, in November 1990 said she did not like the idea of a whole generation of creche children growing up: it was cant of this sort that resulted eventually in her political assassination by her own party.[145]

Cant was systematic in the realm of social welfare. In 1988 the minister, Norman Fowler, distinguished between 'the honest taxpayer' and 'the welfare cheat'. The reality was that tax evasion was endemic (costing £5,000 million) but of little concern to the government (there were just 20 prosecutions), whereas the much lesser problem of dole fraud (costing £500 million) was prosecuted with fanatical zeal (14,000 prosecutions). There was little or no official concern about the low rate (50 per cent) of take-up of benefits to which people were entitled.[146]

There are various possible ways out of these problems. One way much preferred by the New Right is to treat those in need of welfare as suffering from simple misfortune, calling (morally) for voluntary care, especially from their families and neighbours, without the need for state intervention. Related to this is the doctrine of the individual moral duty of charity due to the worst off from the best off. This, also, is not a matter for the state. Charity is the chief theoretical vehicle for reconciling the free market and the minimal state with the need for decent levels of social welfare; in practice, however, it proved to have a broken down, obsolete and hopelessly underpowered engine. The economic 'miracle' took its course, and taxes on dividends and top incomes were reduced dramatically, but the blessed flower of charity failed to bloom from the predicted effects of wealth 'trickle down'. The opposite happened in fact. Thousands of voluntary and charity groups were forced to the brink of extinction as local authorities were forced by the government to cut back their support. Charities reported that after 1986 individual donations remained static against rising incomes and inflation, and company donations fell by 14 per cent as a proportion of pre-tax profits between 1984 and 1989. The number of people volunteering for charity work also fell substantially. Mrs Thatcher had boasted at her party conference in 1989 that 'for every Pharisee our country produces you will find at least three good Samaritans'. The evidence provided by the people who know something about the facts showed the opposite. It is true that personal donations to charity increased by 32 per cent between 1982 and 1986. But this largely reflected the charities' increased use of professional agencies for publicity and for collecting money. Even so, private charity did not compensate for the loss of funding due to government parsimony. Private charity is bound to be marginal to adequate welfare provision. For example, in 1986 personal donations to charities totalled £3.5 billion, compared to £60.64 billion spent by government in 1985–6 on social security, health, housing and overseas aid: that is, 5.7 per cent. Private charity proved to be unequal to the real need.[147] This is no more than even a childish acquaintance with the Victorian realities of the nineteenth century would lead us to expect. A society based exclusively on the values of individualism, competition, self-help and the survival of the (economically) fittest will obviously tend strongly to produce this result. A government led by Margaret Thatcher, who said there is no such thing as society, seems bound, inevitably, to produce it – disguised only by suppression of the facts and rhetoric that resolutely defies the evidence ('the resolute approach').

A third option was suggested even by Geoffrey Howe – that the government should concern itself with improving standards in the social services. That such a suggestion should have come to seem uncharacteristic of a New Right minister – to the point even of seeming outlandish from such a source – is a measure of the social climate of Britain in 1989.[148]

Class

The end of the class system in Britain has been announced more frequently than the phantom retirements of Gracie Fields and Frank Sinatra, and usually by people who would prefer not to have to acknowledge its existence. Others, like Keith Joseph, acknowledge the existence of the class system but persuade themselves that it was open to all talents even before 1979. As he said: 'In this blessed country there is almost infinite mobility between classes.' It has already been remarked that the researches he cited established in 1980 the opposite conclusion: in Britain there are inequalities of a gross kind, and there has been no change in relative life chances. By every relevant criterion class differences have been sharply increased since 1979.

Wealth is the single most significant indicator. Characteristically, the New Right disbanded the Royal Commission investigating the distribution of wealth and income shortly after taking office, and has done its best to avoid finding out about such things ever since. Under New Right government the top 10 per cent of the population had, by 1985, recovered the relative share they had lost through redistribution over the previous twenty years. The wealth of the top 1 per cent more than doubled between 1979 and 1989 to 17 per cent of the total. By 1989 the wealthiest 10 per cent owned more than 50 per cent of wealth compared to just 7 per cent by the poorest 50 per cent. These relative proportions must, of course, be related as well to absolute levels which for the poorest entail homelessness and such privations as inability to afford a stove for hot food. *The Times* 1990 survey of Britain's richest 200 people showed a remarkably high proportion of 'old' rich (106), including 54 aristocrats and 35 old Etonians. New wealth tends to be very volatile and evaporates quickly. After tax, the share of income of the top 5 per cent of the population increased by 50 per cent (from 10 to 15 per cent) between 1979 and 1989. That of the top 1 per cent increased by 100 per cent (from 3 to 6 per cent). As Gordon Brown pointed out, no other developed country saw such a growth of inequality of incomes, because Britain is the only country that has introduced regressive taxation and at the same time removed minimum-wage legislation and cut social security benefits.[149] By the end of 1990 the gap between high-paid and low-paid employees was the widest since records were first kept in 1886: the highest income increased 16 times more than the lowest.[150]

The effect of class differences in wealth and income is felt in every other aspect of life: mortality and health, education, employment, social welfare, even equality under the law.[151] Needless to say, the quality of cultural life deteriorates when facilities such as museums are no longer regarded as public goods but commercial services provided only at economic prices.

Nothing exemplifies Britain's class (and caste) system so much as the double standards that apply to pay. As we have noted, company directors are laws unto themselves and contrive through their salary-fixing cartels to pay one another astronomical sums regardless of company performance. Emoluments for the more dignified establishment employments, such as judging, politicking and soldiering, are based on the assumption that few people have the necessary abilities and the principle that such labourers are worthy of their hire. Even if the assumption were true there is no reason to withhold equitable pay from lesser mortals merely on the grounds that another could labour just as well. There is, however, no reason to suppose that the assumption is true. In any case there is no inclination to establish a true market for establishment people's pay. If the argument for exorbitant rewards from the scarcity of talent is plausible then why do engineers who are both talented and scarce, as well as vitally important to the economy, have such low pay and status in Britain when their opposite numbers in other countries are relatively much better off? There is no explanation, other than class-ridden cultural perversion, why a productive professional engineer's pay should be reckoned in thousands when a young upwardly mobile city gentleman is offered tens and even hundreds of thousands.[152] A leader in *The Times*, commenting on the government's policy, pointed out that

> Britain's industrial decline has been accompanied by a constant under-use and under-reward of practical engineers in business. If this is to be changed quickly then society, through its government and its academic bodies, must be seen to be giving new emphasis and according new prestige to this activity. By saying that it cannot afford to give such precedence to one discipline over others and concluding that any initiative must conform to the wishes of established institutions, the government has dropped a catch.[153]

At the end of the Thatcher Decade (in 1990), 'old money still predominated and paternalism appeared to be making a comeback. That trend (was) strengthened (in the following) year, suggesting that the new wealth is both fragile and vulnerable while old wealth is remarkably stable.' In November 1990 a remarkable court case demonstrated most vividly the failure of the New Right to make headway in changing the class system. The Duke of Westminster succeeded in preserving seven blocks of flats in Millbank, London, for the use of local inhabitants on low incomes. The flats had been leased to the local council by an earlier duke in 1937 on condition that they be used as dwellings for the working class. The leader of the council, the New Right ... Shirley Porter, had argued that the term 'working class' no longer had any meaning in housing law. The presiding judge, Justice Harman, deemed that the fact that Parliament no longer used the term did not determine the meaning of those words in ordinary English speech.[154] Old class, old money, old privilege survived to prevail over tax-avoiding, privatising, self-centred, free-market, profiteering, New-Right-thinking parvenues.

Some people of a credulous turn of mind thought that Margaret Thatcher was committed to subverting Britain's antediluvian caste system. Even after she revived hereditary peerages for Willie Whitelaw there was scope for belief in her meritocratic tendency since he was without posterity. Any doubt about the matter was removed when she ennobled her husband with an hereditary title in her retirement honours list. In this way she secured ennoblement for her son Mark, anyone less useful and distinguished than whom is inconceivable. Anyone else might have done the same thing in order to bring the honours system into terminal disrepute: no such radical motive was attributable to Lady Thatcher.

17   THE CULTURAL RECORD

SUMMARY RECORD: THE RHETORIC

The New Right congratulated itself on changing the country for the better, by discovering a new strength and a new pride, and by fostering a new spirit of enterprise. Britain, they said, has come right by her own efforts. By trusting the character and talents of the people, the government was gratified to discover that the British instinct for choice and independence flourished. Together the British people were building one nation of free, prosperous and responsible people. In particular the 1980s saw over a million more people self-employed, and a net increase in the number of registered small businesses of more than 500 per week. This was the secure economic basis on which all other progress could depend. Successful enterprise in its turn rests on individualism: the basic morality of responsibility and self-help.[155]

SUMMARY RECORD: THE REALITY

The Enterprise Culture

Previous discussion has already shown that the achievements claimed by the New Right, in the spheres of economics, politics and society, are mostly a triumph of rhetoric over reality, and many parts of the record in those spheres are closely related to the claims made to a radical transformation of British attitudes and welfare. Among the most striking are the economic facts of more self-employed people and more small businesses – as evidence of a new enterprising spirit. An enterprising spirit is highly desirable; but self-employment isn't the same thing. A great many people registered as self-employed under government schemes the main function of which was to reduce the number of registered unemployed. Similar considerations apply to the start-up rate of small businesses which proliferated when many redundant people were given business start-up grants and loans. By their very nature the majority of such efforts are unlikely to flourish and grow into large companies employing many workers. It should have surprised no one, therefore, that in 1990 the Confederation of British Industry reported that bankruptcies were running at their highest level for 50 years, with 15,000 companies failing annually, and jobs being lost at a rate of 10,000 a month in manufacturing industry alone.[156] High inflation and interest rates, together with general recession, have merely exacerbated the general trend. Keith Joseph (speaking from the double shelter provided by his family inheritance and a seat in the Lords) positively welcomes the avalanche of failing businesses as evidence that the pure market is in full spate: New Right theory vindicated. Those whose livelihoods are forfeit must take a more sober and less complacent view of the bracing rigours of the market.

Attitudes

The attitudes of British people are a matter of some interest, since this was the fundamental concern of Margaret Thatcher. It is not always clear from the available analysis whether the New Right is supposed to have profited from attitudes prevalent in 1979 by offering policies that gave expression to them, or whether, having secured power, Margaret Thatcher's governments then proceeded to change attitudes. Neo-Marxists are inclined to the former view, that a mood developed during the 1970s which was harvested by New Right rhetoric so as to achieve electoral success. The evidence for this is very fragile: first of all because electoral success was very flimsy, with only a third of electors supporting the Conservatives; secondly, because the evidence of opinion surveys shows that in 1979 only a minority subscribed to central New Right doctrines such as the need to reduce taxes (37 per cent) and to oppose trade unions (56 per cent thought they were a good thing – even after the winter of discontent). In the 1983 election the Conservatives won a landslide majority of parliamentary seats despite the fact that (on the strong evidence of a *Daily Telegraph* Gallup poll), the electorate by far preferred Labour policy on most key issues such as spending more on the NHS (85 per cent), tackling pollution (72 per cent), equal opportunities for women (68 per cent), prices and incomes control (66 per cent), and public spending to reduce unemployment (63 per cent). Other axioms of New Right thinking had little or only minority support, such as spending on the defence of the Falklands (58 per cent positively opposed), re-establishing grammar schools (26 per cent), and stricter laws regulating trade unions (33 per cent). The poll showed that unilateral nuclear disarmament (giving up Britain's nuclear weapons whatever other countries decide) was positively rejected by 45 per cent of the electorate, including 19 per cent of Labour voters (despite the party's unilateralist policy). This was by far the most unpopular policy on any issue, with 75 per cent of Conservative voters opposing it. It is likely that many people voted Conservative for this reason alone, and that Labour lost the election as a consequence.[157]

Evidently most people approved of some New Right policies, especially council house sales (72 per cent) and the requirement for trade unions' election ballots (70 per cent). However, the claim that attitudes were fundamentally changed over ten years in the approved New Right direction is disproved by numerous surveys and studies of public opinion.[158] It will suffice here to mention only some of the

most striking evidence. In the economic sphere, an increasing majority
(62 per cent in 1980 to 81 per cent in 1986) thought the government
should give priority to reducing unemployment before inflation. A
1989 poll showed that 64 per cent of people thought that the
government should guarantee every person a steady job and a decent
standard of living. Only 14 per cent were in favour of more privatisation. Almost as many wanted more nationalisation (38 per cent) as
were satisfied with the existing level (41 per cent). In the political
sphere (in Britain as a whole), a steadily increasing majority said that
trade unions are a good thing, from 56 per cent (in 1979–80) to 70 per
cent (in 1987–8). In the social sphere, people overwhelmingly preferred
a society in which caring for others is more highly rewarded (79 per
cent), and a majority preferred a society which emphasises social and
collective provisions of welfare (55 per cent to 40 per cent who
preferred self-help). A huge majority (83 per cent) disapproved of the
sharp reduction in council house building. On the question of general
social welfare benefits, only 17 per cent by 1987 thought that state
provision had gone too far. In the cultural sphere, one most substantial
claim made by Margaret Thatcher is that 'we have regained our
national self-respect'. Even after the Falklands War only 18 per cent
of people said in 1985 that they had more pride in Britain than five
years before; 42 per cent said they had less. More recently still, only
18 per cent were optimistic compared to 32 per cent who thought
Britain was deteriorating in status. Evidently, the new self-respect was
just another invention of interminable New Right rhetoric.[159]

New Right values were not predominant in Britain in 1979. In 1990
after eleven years of New Right government nothing much had
changed, as electoral support showed. More people continued to
prefer public control of the economy to private enterprise (47 per cent
versus 39 per cent), and collective welfare provision to self-help (54
per cent versus 40 per cent). At the end of the Thatcher decade
different researchers reached similar conclusions. Ivor Crewe said,
'The electorate is hardly suffused with Thatcherite values either on
the economic or moral plane.' John Rentoul concluded that 'there has
been no shift towards individualism in the 1980s'. Jacobs and
Worcester reported that Margaret Thatcher's crusade against socialism
had failed. This fact, of course, implies nothing as to whether it
would have succeeded given even more time, or whether it would
have been practically and morally better for Britain had it succeeded.
The New Right certainly had more opportunity to succeed than
almost any other government. The simple fact is that, despite con-

siderable orchestrated rhetoric to establish the opposite, New Right policies failed to alter fundamentally people's attitudes as intended. The evidence suggests there was, instead, a considerable reaction against New Right excesses which led to Margaret Thatcher's downfall. At the time of her political 'assassination' in November 1990, polls showed that only one in five of the electorate believed that she reflected ordinary people's views.[160]

Squalid Britain

Victorian England was distinguished by the coexistence of private affluence and public squalor. The New Right's admiration for Victorian values, appropriately, therefore, goes with a reappearance during the 1980s of Dickensian squalor as an accompaniment to an economic 'miracle'. Squalid political practice has already been mentioned: misrule, official evasion of facts and related evasion of government responsibility, barely legal vendettas (against persons, trade unions, and professions) and self-serving (ex) government ministers have all been characteristics of New Right government since 1979. The pervasiveness of public squalor is well enough exemplified with reference to just a few illustrations.

The environment, both built and natural, suffered massive deterioration during the 1980s. There was a failure to invest in the infrastructure of roads, sewers and water supply that was indicative of declining public standards. The government programme to regenerate inner cities through British Urban Development (BUD) was launched in 1988, as promised during the 1987 election campaign. By October 1990 it was being quietly wound down as a result of the withdrawal of government grants, and private developers deciding there was too much risk and not enough incentive. River pollution worsened relentlessly, and the number of prosecutions by water authorities escalated from 90 in 1981 to 254 in 1986–7, with most resulting in convictions. In September 1989 the European Commission undertook to prosecute the British government for refusing to clean up drinking water, and similar action was proposed over the quality of bathing water. Britain became the dirty man of Europe, as well as its most prominent economic invalid.[161]

Health and safety in Britain generally fell below normal European standards also. Eggs and beef were just two of the most conspicuous examples of substandard food. The Health Minister Edwina Currie felt obliged to resign because of the furore that followed her revelation that British eggs were infected with salmonella. The characteristically British response to the problem caused by ('economic') battery farming methods was, first, for government departments to hide the evidence, then to deny the risk, then, when that failed, to change the subject to the question of ministerial imprudence affecting the livelihood of egg producers. The logic was repeated in the case of cattle infected with bovine spongiform encephalitis. British cattle became infected from 'economic' feed made from diseased sheep offal of a sort that Europeans would deem unfit. EEC countries banned the import of the beef. British officials first of all denied there could be a disease at all, then tried to diminish its importance. This effort included one of the most squalid acts of political exploitation ever. The Minister for Agriculture, John Selwyn Gummer, publicly fed his young daughter a hamburger to show that doubting scientists know less than a Conservative cabinet minister about such things. One indicator of deteriorating standards of food safety was the dramatic increase in the number of cases of food poisoning recorded: from 10,380 in 1980 to 28,000 in 1988 (169 per cent)[162] (with the trend accelerating after that). This increase occurred during a time when the number of health and safety inspectors was reduced, from 1,424 in 1979 to 1,165 by 1987.

Safety deteriorated elsewhere until in the late 1980s spectacular disasters, each with much loss of life due to poor safety, became a regular feature of public life. A P&O cross-channel ferry sank outside Zeebrugge harbour after it had sailed with its bow doors open. The official inquiry found negligence including company management ignoring (even ridiculing) forewarnings of the disaster. In the North Sea oil fields one of the biggest rigs, Piper Alpha, collapsed after an uncontained fire. The report of the inquiry into that disaster concluded that the government's responsibility for safety had not been adequately discharged. In particular, the Department of Energy was not adequately equipped. The owners, Occidental Oil, were remiss in failing to implement adequate safety measures, which eventually were to cost at least £2 billion but came too late. Inadequate safety linked to poor equipment and procedures led to a Thames pleasure boat, the *Marchioness*, being sunk after a collision. Margaret Thatcher's preposterous explanation for this disaster was that greater affluence was bound to lead to greater exposure to such risks. Inadequate safety measures and practices due to cavalier attitudes to minimising costs: evidently to her mind these things didn't come into it. A fire at London Underground's King's Cross station (during a rush hour) was attributed to poor materials, poor safety practices and inadequate staffing levels after economies had been implemented. In this case, the executive responsible sought to blame a phantom arsonist rather than admit proven culpability. The incidence of rail collisions increased dramatically at the same time as cost-cutting increased; from 54 collisions in 1982 to 86 in 1988. The most salutary case occurred in December 1988 when crowded commuter trains crashed at Clapham Junction killing 35 people. The inquiry found the cause to be a signal fault due to inadequacies in the instruction of technicians and in the supervision and testing of previous repair work; also a rewiring programme was found to have been initiated with 'reckless haste'. The engineer involved told the inquiry that he and some colleagues had been working a 60-hour, seven-day week for a month before the rewiring work that caused the crash. Other individuals were doing the work of six men. As public service workers, British Rail's safety engineers are specifically what Keith Joseph calls 'lean kine' and are therefore paid less than those of equivalent skills in the private sector. Consequently, recruitment and retention of staff is difficult and leads to the gross overwork of staff who are employed. The operational need to overwork is exacerbated by financial need due to high living costs, especially housing costs in Greater London. What could be described as a mere wiring fault due to a technician's mistake turned out to be the inevitable final tragic outcome of overworking, undervaluing, underpaying the workforce in an underfunded, undervalued public service, against a background of a failing market economy with escalating living costs: a prism for viewing Britain's public squalor. The 'market' was signalling that insufficient resources were being spent on rail safety: the message, unfortunately, came via loss of life that could have been prevented by intelligent planning and spending. Such 'intervention' was ruled out, however, by the government's New Right doctrines which had led to a reduction by half of the government's subsidy to railways between 1979 and 1989 (from £1,024 million to £517 million), and indirectly to what the director general of the Confederation of British Industry described as the worst transport infrastructure in Europe. The chairman of British Rail articulated the doctrine clearly as follows: 'Our duty is not to run a service that is desirable – it is to run a service that will be profitable.'[163]

'Mrs Thatcher will be remembered only for this: that she brought the beggars back to the streets of London.' Neil Ascherson heard that 'voice in the air' saying what any visitor to the city (and other large cities) could confirm after years of New Right government. An estimated 2,000 people (at least) were said in 1990 to live on the streets of the capital, and another 35,000 estimated to be living in squats. The lives of these homeless and rootless compatriots are the final evidence, if that were needed, that the free market has failed masses of British people, even if it has benefited others. The wider significance of the thousands of homeless beggars on the streets of Britain's cities is that they prove indisputably that there is a lack of community in a population driven primarily by market forces – or none sufficient to provide stable accommodation, livelihoods and a place for all its members. Indeed one of the attractions of New Right doctrine for its leading adepts is its repudiation of collective guilt, bourgeois guilt. Margaret Thatcher defined this as 'that sense of guilt and self-criticism that affects those, not only the very rich, who cling to a relatively comfortable life while feeling a troublesome pang of conscience because there are others less well off'. On another account she was less emollient, dismissing expressions of concern for the badly off as 'drivelling and drooling'.[164]

The manifest environmental, social and human damage caused by New Right policies provoked the churches into open opposition to government policy. The Archbishop of Canterbury said there was a 'danger of Britain becoming a "pharisee" society based on self-interest and intolerance'. The Roman Catholic Archbishop of Glasgow said it was right for the church to criticise politicians for framing laws that caused poverty: 'You can't preach the gospel to people who are poor and starving.' The president of the Methodist Conference said that government policies were a perversion of Christianity; a 'sinister threat' to the building of community and did not uphold the common good.

The most notorious clerical critic, the Bishop of Durham, Dr David Jenkins, said government policies were wicked. In 1989 more than a dozen senior clergy from many denominations endorsed a declaration drawn up by Christian Action on Poverty which included a wide-ranging attack on government policy. The Church of England published two reports on the bad social effects of the government's policies: *Faith in the Cities* in 1985 and *Living Faith in the Cities* in 1990. The first report was denounced by government ministers as 'pure Marxist theology'. The second set out the evidence that Britain's urban underclass was suffering a grave and fundamental injustice, questioned the market economy and called for the church to be allowed to make a moral input into the government's decision-making.[165] Margaret Thatcher responded to these criticisms with an address to the General Assembly of the Church of Scotland. In it she argued that Christianity is about spiritual redemption, not social reform. Misinterpreting the parable of the talents she said we must work and use our talents to create wealth – 'If a man will not work he shall not eat' – and unless the incentive is there, there are undoubtedly those (unlike her) who would not work hard. She reminded the assembled dignitaries of the woman with the alabaster jar of ointment – an allusion to Jesus's reproach to his disciples who criticised the giving of an expensive gift before spending the money on charity. Possibly the most significant statement was her admission that she had always had difficulty interpreting the biblical precept to love our neighbour 'as ourselves'. This difficulty is resolved, she explained, when self-hatred is allowed for: we should hate our neighbours as we should ourselves, when we fall behind in the hard work and wealth-creation stakes. This view of the Prime Minister's, being self-righteous, censorious and hypocritical, satisfies amply the criteria for pharisaism. (Robert Runcie might well say: If the mitre fits, wear it.)[166]

Civil Liberties

The freedom of individuals is supposedly the most basic cultural value of the New Right, and the most persistent theme of its rhetoric. Freedom of choice in the economic sphere was promoted through the extension of the market at the expense of state provision. In other spheres the achievement of freedom, and even the aspiration to secure freedom, has been much less conspicuous. Sympathetic observers can point to legislation such as that which separates the taxation of women from their husband's, permits (for pension purposes) women to retire at the same age as men, and recognises rape within marriage; each of which in various ways extends in law individual choice and so freedom. Such measures, however, reflect general developments in western culture over twelve years rather than New Right philosophy, and in practice they have often been opposed by the New Right. In fact, the general tendency of New Right government in the sphere of personal liberties has been clearly and strongly retrogressive. The proliferation and flourishing since 1979 of organisations and campaigns to oppose the erosion of personal civil liberties in Britain is one powerful indicator of this general trend. The list includes the Campaign for Freedom of Information, the Constitutional Reform Centre, Samizdat – 'a popular front of the mind to secure the departure of this [New Right] government', and Charter 88, the main objectives of which include the securing of civil liberties, freedom of information and open government. Longer established movements such as the Campaign for Electoral Reform and the National Council for Civil Liberties gained fresh momentum, and international organisations such as Amnesty International and the Index on Censorship turned their attention for the first time to Britain.[167]

The causes for concern extend to all the spheres of personal liberty defended by John Stuart Mill. A selection from innumerable examples should suffice to show the general tendency. The basic right of citizens to information affecting their lives was denied even in matters of health and safety. In one typical case scientists consulted by the government about a potential cancer hazard in milk were forbidden by a minister, under the provisions of the Official Secrets Act, to publicise their cautionary view and recommendations. In the political sphere the public were, after 1988, denied the opportunity to hear views of official representatives of Sinn Fein, the IRA and other proscribed groups. The Protection of Privacy Bill (1988) seriously handicapped journalists' legitimate investigations in the public interest. Most significantly, the government's Official Secrets Bill (1989) excluded 'public interest' as a defence for public servants who disclose evidence of crimes, misdemeanours and malpractice in government and administration. Such a defence had secured the acquittal of Clive Ponting in 1984. Almost everybody can agree that secrecy is essential in some matters, but after 1979 secrecy increasingly became an end in itself for a government that (presumably) had more and more to hide. The most shocking and revealing effusion of that time was Lord Denning's opinion that it is better that the truth be suppressed, even if innocent people are hanged or gaoled for life, than that the law and its enforcers should be brought into general disrepute.[168]

Freedom of opinion and expression were undermined in a variety of ways, notably surveillance and censorship. Official surveillance by phonetapping increased substantially. In 1980 there had been 40 tappers at work with just 600 warrants. By 1986, 60 tappers were at work fulltime on 30,000 lines and the cost of such (secret) operations had escalated to £10 million. The tendency after 1972 for the British Secret Service to investigate then 'blacklist' fellow citizens rather than enemy agents was thus very greatly increased. To be subject to a surveillance order and blacklisted it was sufficient to be a trade unionist or engaged in open opposition to New Right policies (such as a nuclear defence strategy). The BBC and ITV were subjected to strong ministerial pressure to censor or withhold the broadcasting of programmes that were critical of or embarrassing to the government, or even (as in the case of 'Tumbledown', a programme on the Falklands Campaign) simply presenting a realistic view departing from the officially approved 'enhanced' one. Other examples, such as Zircon and 'Death on the Rock', have been mentioned earlier. It is to the credit of the broadcasting authorities that at the time most of these pressures were resisted; but the censorious official ethos was a creeping malaise that persisted through the manipulation of key appointments within the government's gift.[169]

Freedom of association was most conspicuously under attack through the government's vendetta against trade unions. Membership of trade unions was treated as tantamount to potential subversion of the state: this was never more evident than in the government's ban on trade unions at the Government Communications Headquarters (GCHQ) in 1984. There can be no reasonable doubt that this ban was precipitated by 'leaking' of scandalous facts surrounding the sinking of the *Belgrano* during the Falklands conflict: notably information about the *Belgrano*'s sailing orders and course that was known to the Prime Minister when the decision was taken to sink the Argentine cruiser. Margaret Thatcher, evidently, was (as usual) more inclined to shoot the messenger than heed the message. Neither, evidently, was she above personal vindictiveness. The revolution in the law and practice relating to trade unions is regarded by the New Right as successful on a splendid scale: the 'snake of intolerable union power has been scotched', though not (of course) to the complete satisfaction of strict observance free-marketeers. Dr Kevin Dowd (situated strategically in a safe place as a lecturer in economics at Nottingham University) even went so far as to advocate in 1990 the abolition of trade unions by reintroducing the Combination Acts of the early nineteenth century.[170]

Freedom of movement, assembly and demonstration have all been undermined by the strengthening of anti-union law and police powers under provisions for the preservation of public order, together with the propensity of the police to use these powers. Gypsies are now evicted from sites where local people find them distasteful. 'Hippy' convoys are deemed undesirable, waylaid by police columns on public highways and denied access to publicly owned places (such as Stonehenge). People can be stopped at police roadblocks under the provisions of the Police and Criminal Evidence Act and their journeys terminated hundreds of miles from their destination if it is deemed that an arrestable offence is 'likely' to occur (as when police in 1984–5 arrested Kent miners en route to Nottingham or on picket lines, only to drop charges later). Increasingly, persons of sorts not approved of by the government have had their freedom of movement curtailed, often for no better reason than that other persons of a sort commonly found in places like Finchley don't like them or their way of life.

Freedom under the law has been further undermined by the introduction of summary trials (trials without juries) in Northern Ireland, and also the termination of the historic 'right to silence' under police interrogation. The European Court of Human Rights found it necessary to condemn the former practice. The latter practice goes with the prescription to presume guilt in a matter on which a defendant is silent. In these ways time-honoured rights, not to be forced into self-incrimination on false confessions, and to be tried by a court of peers, have been sacrificed to the demands of administration. Shortly after she was elected to Parliament Margaret Thatcher said: 'The paramount function of this distinguished House is to safeguard civil liberties rather than to think that administrative convenience should take first place in law.' During more than eleven years of government led by her the opposite happened: administrative convenience took first place and civil liberties were very greatly neglected.[171]

Civil liberties have been eroded as central powers of the state have been grossly expanded and consolidated. Individuals employed in the public service have been debarred from candidacy for elected office. Representative local government has been made subservient to the state. The state has been made coextensive with the government of the day. The essence of government is notionally the cabinet, but in practice the cabinet is now subservient to a presidential style Prime Minister. Citizens are subject to coercive laws; the laws are enforced by the police; the police are subordinate to the secret services; the secret services are under the control of the Prime Minister (so long as the 'spirit of the constitution', that is the social status quo, is unchallenged). This is the elective dictatorship envisaged by Lord Hailsham.

The deteriorating state of civil liberties under New Right government, as has already been established, led by reaction to the growth of numerous reforming movements. Some of those, notably

Charter 88 and Samizdat, fashioned themselves after Eastern European dissident movements. Critics, including the journalists Bernard Levin and Hugo Young and the New Right philosopher-zealot Tony Flew, tended to dismiss their role-modelling as mere self-indulgence and affectation which could be construed as insulting to those other dissidents who opposed terminally repressive states. Such criticisms miss a crucial point. Soviet-state dissidents sought to secure civil liberties where few, if any, existed. Physical as well as intellectual courage was undoubtedly required of them. In Britain, civil liberties groups seek to preserve existing civil liberties before they are eroded irreparably. If they continue in the meantime to enjoy the protection of some of the customs and institutions that remain while others are eroded, this is hardly a cause for criticism. As the old saying has it: the price of freedom is eternal vigilance. It would be preposterous to wait until civil liberties had been eroded by Right-wing zealots (as in Chile) so far that only by acts of physical heroism could there be hope of retrieving them. As it is, civil liberties have deteriorated since 1979 to the point that not only neo-Marxists and traditional radicals dissent but also Law Lords (Scarman), peers (such as Lord Broxbourne and Lady Ewart-Biggs), senior civil servants (such as Permanent Secretaries Sir Frank Cooper, Defence, and Sir Douglas Wass, Treasury), even Conservative MPs (such as Richard Shepard and Jonathan Aitken) and ex-cabinet ministers (such as Ian Gilmour). When the point is reached where the law requires that the interests of the state are the interests of the government of the day, and where in the name of the national interest secrecy is required in whatever matter a minister may personally deem appropriate, it is time to recognise that civil liberties are exposed to unacceptable risks, especially from individuals of dubious personal integrity and whose *mentis* may not be as *compos* as it ought to be.[172]

The Constitution

Between 1979 and 1990 the celebrated phlegmatic disposition of British people in matters political was tested to the limit. It was clear that strong government was being exercised against the wishes of most people, that the society was descending into squalor even while unprecedented affluence was being celebrated, and that historic civil liberties were being eroded by a party proclaiming individual liberty as its primary value. New Right government has been returned three times against the wishes of a substantial majority of voters (58 per cent in 1987) and without the support of an even larger proportion of electors (68.5 per cent; over two-thirds). The 'first past the post' electoral system ensured that more votes were wasted, being cast for losing candidates (48 per cent), than were effectively used to elect candidates (30 per cent). Another 22 per cent of votes merely added to ('boosted') winning candidates' morale by increasing their majorities. The most striking effects of the electoral system were to enable the return of governments without a majority of votes (as in 1951 and February 1974) and to distort the representation of voters in Parliament. In the 1983 election, Labour and the Alliance (of Liberal and Social Democratic Parties) each received about one quarter of the votes cast but Labour won 32 per cent of parliamentary seats and the Alliance just 4 per cent. In the 1987 election, the Alliance parties received 22.6 per cent of the vote, and won just 3.4 per cent of seats. Evidently the electoral system was grossly inadequate for representative government. The New Right government increasingly pursued policies against the wishes and even with the active opposition of large to overwhelming majorities of the people. As we have seen people were not adequately informed on matters that affected them, and civil liberties were progressively eroded. Along with this, the power of the state was systematically increased at the expense of local and (in the case of Scotland, Wales and Northern Ireland) constituent national government. Many came to think that established power structures in Britain, including the unelected House of Lords, served no justifiable purpose in a democracy, but did perpetrate a system of power and privilege that was not responsive to most people's wishes and interests.[173]

By 1988, millions of British people were vaguely fed up with the state of affairs that was greatly exacerbated by the personality and style of the eleven-year head of the New Right government, Margaret Thatcher. She managed to make seem intolerable a political programme that was already conspicuously lacking in democratic scruples and concern for the common good. Many people came to recognise that without a written constitution to set limits to executive power, without a Freedom of Information Act to ensure open government, and without a Bill of Rights to preserve civil liberties, the British Prime Minister exercised untrammelled power to a degree unparalleled in the developed world and which, indeed, had not been exercised since the absolute divine-right monarchy of Charles I. Stripped by a grocer's daughter of its veneer of *noblesse oblige* and humbug, the United Kingdom was revealed for all to see as essentially a medieval monarchy that tolerates only a certain amount of democracy in one of the three parts of its unwritten constitution. A strong lead towards change was taken in Scotland where, in 1988, a constitutional convention promulgated a Claim of Right for Scotland. This pointed out that in 1979 the Scots had voted in a referendum on the question of a devolved Scottish Assembly. By the criteria used in Westminster they voted for such an assembly, but special rules resulted in them being refused it. In the 1980s Scotland's plight was a reduction-to-absurdity of the nation's as a whole. It was governed by a party that won only a seventh of the seats and a quarter of the vote there, and their elected representatives had no effective power to influence events. By 1990, such issues were firmly on the agenda of pressure groups and to an extent the political parties. Tens of thousands had been moved to sign Charter 88, and countless others sympathised with its particular aims, especially to secure electoral reform in order to rescue the nation forever from strong but wrong-headed government by unscrupulous 'conviction' politicians. Its other demands include a Bill of Rights; subjection of the executive and administration to the rule of law; a Freedom of Information Act; reform of the second chamber of Parliament; an independent judiciary; legal remedies for abuse of state power; equitable distribution of power between local, regional and national government; and ultimately a written constitution (conspicuously absent from the demands is any reference to the most archaic of all manifestations of arbitrary power, the monarchy).[174]

Experience of New Right rule in the 1980s demonstrated to many British people that political culture and institutions were not adequately linked to popular opinion, and could too easily be detached from it. The remedy evidently needed to be more secure than tacit conventions and the manners of well-bred chaps could provide. What was needed were formal and institutionalised safeguards, of the sort enjoyed in every other developed country. Traditionalists from across the political spectrum resisted what they saw as compromises to the sovereignty of Parliament, and spoke of the need for political culture to change by evolution rather than by designing Bills of Rights and written constitutions. What such conservatism overlooks is that Bills of Rights and written constitutions are well-tried and successful ways for political culture to evolve ('evolution' is not an abstract thing devoid of content, plans or intention). Also, the sovereignty of the British Parliament is not an unqualified benefit. Indeed, it is in practice a positive burden in so far as it is really the absolute power of a Prime Minister. In most other developed countries the people are sovereign, as they are in most European countries. Europe already provides a Bill of Rights and EEC laws supersede the British Parliament anyway. It is in Europe, most certainly, that constitutional reform and the political culture will be transformed in future. The New Right government of Margaret Thatcher not only did not welcome such a prospect; it positively rejected it.

18 MORE RIGHT TURNS

With more than eleven years experience of New Right government, converts whose 'Right turns' were publicised in 1978 (see Chapter 7) were in a strategically advantaged position to evaluate the record against their own expectations. First, a roll call is illuminating. The interlocutor, Conservative MP Patrick Cormack, took the view that desirable changes had been made but perhaps they had gone too far too quickly. (He was also prescient about Margaret Thatcher's leadership as we shall presently see.) Reg Prentice was satisfied that there had been radical improvements during the 1980s in all matters of principal concern to him. Max Beloff said he had never thought of himself in the context of the New Right. Edward Pearce 're-ratted'. He had in 1978 thought that the only totalitarian threat was on the left. By 1989 he was expressing incredulity at Margaret Thatcher's 'deep ignorance' of the history of human rights. Hugh Thomas was involved with the work of the government and was reluctant to express a view, as, for different reasons, were Kingsley Amis and Alun Gwynne-Jones. Graham Hough was indisposed. Paul Johnson was unresponsive on the subject of his turning right but his puerile and uncritical idol-worship of Margaret Thatcher continued even after her party had her put down, politically.[175]

On the whole the Right-turns subscribed to the official Conservative view that the New Right governments led by Margaret Thatcher had very real and remarkable achievements to their credit. The main ones include curtailing trade union power, fostering individual liberty and enterprise, maintaining sound defences, and restoring Britain's standing in the world, especially the EEC. None of this would have been possible, they believed, without the personal determination and dynamism of Margaret Thatcher. There is a pattern to the judgements which is striking, however. The New Right achievements are recognised in a general way, but not uncritically. What is striking is that criticism of the New Right government's record emerges in areas in which the Right-turns have special knowledge or interest. Patrick Cormack himself is an old-fashioned Conservative MP. Allowing for the discretion incumbent upon him, it is evident that it was the personality and leadership style of Margaret Thatcher that was found most wanting: she having outlived whatever use the country once had (if any) for a fearsome, impatient, undiplomatic, combative and impulsive Machiavellian plotter at the helm. Reg Prentice, a former Labour Minister for Overseas Development, acknowledged that our overseas aid performance, which was bad under Labour, was worse under the Conservatives. Max Beloff, the first Vice-Chancellor of the (free-market) University of Buckingham, fought fiercely in the House of Lords in 1989 against the government's radical proposals for the financing of higher education by replacing student grants with loans. Kingsley Amis, special advisor on excellence in education and the arts to the Adam Smith Institute and the Centre for Policy Studies, was 'rather disappointed with Conservative policy in Higher Education'. In a *Sunday Times* interview he said: 'The way they treat research is ridiculous. It's as if you said to Einstein, "Albert we want you to find out how the Universe works, but you've only got £10,000 and six months to do it in", and I'm against "vocational training". People need to be educated, not trained to work.' As a professional speculator in political stocks Edward Pearce said: 'When windy academics talked about the word I never understood it, but watching Mrs Thatcher and the British people I know exactly what is meant by alienation.' Taking 'Thatchers as gilts', he wrote in 1990, he had sold Thatchers heavily after 1984 [GCHQ], missing the very top of the market but was in solid profit. She was no longer bankable. Hugh Thomas, an historian, was exercised in 1978 by the prospect that a Labour government's programme to shift power to working people might, as intended, be impossible to go back on; that is be really irreversible. In 1990, he was, as chairman of the New Right board of directors of the Centre for Policy Studies, too closely involved himself with her programme to comment on Margaret Thatcher's objective 'to roll back the frontiers of socialism' and ensure that James Callaghan was the last ('I do mean the last') Labour Prime Minister.[176]

Apart from the reservations just mentioned, the Right-turns were also concerned about a variety of other developments, including the inequities of the Poll Tax; removal of school teachers' wage-bargaining rights, neglect of the less fortunate in society (including the unemployed), and too much transfer of power from local authorities to Whitehall.

Beyond a certain point there is a perhaps natural tendency for this group to evade in various ways the evidence that the New Right programme of eleven years has in reality failed. There are four distinguishable modes of evasion that would be of interest to political psychologists. First is the misperception and misunderstanding strategy. Thus, the government's acceptance of the doubling or trebling of unemployment is perceived by the public as a lack of concern for the jobless, though it isn't really. Similarly, the almost universal execration of health service reforms is attributed simply to the ineffectiveness of the way the need for reforms has been demonstrated, not the reforms themselves and their effects. Second is the resort to conundrum, whereby undeniable facts are left unaccounted for and without obvious implications being drawn for cherished beliefs incompatible with them. (In the spirit of conundrum Edward Pearce in 1978 had boldly cited Walt Whitman's words: 'Do I contradict myself? Very well, then, I contradict myself.') Thus, it is proclaimed that the rule of law (including tax law) is vital, and so law enforcement is vital. Then the contradicting fact is confronted and acknowledged that, despite clear evidence that tax evasion costs the Exchequer one hundred times more than dole fraud, the government increased the number of dole-fraud investigators but cut the number of Inland Revenue staff by a massive 14,500 between 1979 and 1986. Faced with the fact, and the question of how to reconcile the contradiction, the (professed) backer of law and order says only: 'I do not know the answer to that question.' Third is defence by flat rejection of the evidence. Thus it is said that 'we have no means of knowing whether a large majority of the electorate does not want these changes' (made by government policy). However, opinion polls, the results of elections (to the European and Westminster Parliaments and to local government), prominent media campaigns, mass demonstrations and even riots all provide very reliable means. Reliable enough anyway, evidently, to justify Margaret Thatcher's political execution by her own party when such evidence showed that she was an insurmountable electoral liability. Fourth, is the credulity strategy whereby any official explanation that is offered for dubious events is bought by true believers regardless of whether or not it is the best fit among the clear options on offer. Thus, when the European Commission declared illegal the government's payment of about £80 million in sweeteners to British Aerospace, the true believer will pass over the most plausible explanation, to do with ideological graft, preferring instead the official self-exculpation to the effect that the government could not otherwise have disposed of the Rover car company because it was not worth buying without the illegal blandishments (an honest try would have been a fine thing).

Before leaving this retrospective on prominent Right-turns there is one final *post hoc* development that is worthy of record. In 1978, of the eight who (as Churchill would have said) 'ratted', only Alun Gwynne Jones had already been ennobled (as Lord Chalfont, by a Labour government). During eleven years of New Right rule four out of the seven others were distinguished, a quite extraordinary proportion. Max Beloff and Hugh Thomas were made peers; Reg Prentice and Kingsley Amis were knighted for their distinguished services to the nation. Evidently a well-publicised conversion to Margaret Thatcher's way of thinking was not an obstacle to the attainment of the public honours at her disposal.

There is some cause for satisfaction for Right-turns, though much less than they claim as has been shown here. Some of the record, they admit, is disappointing. The case showing that a great deal more of the record is a failure has been, in a variety of ways, evaded. Patrick Cormack, however, did not evade the single most striking effect of eleven years of New Right government lead by Margaret Thatcher: her great unpopularity. With admirable prescience, in August 1989 he pointed to the strong advantages to the Conservative Party of her making way for others; otherwise another electoral victory could not be taken for granted.[177] By October 1990 this view was so widely shared in the parliamentary Conservative Party that her leadership was successfully challenged. The events merit no little attention.

19 THE QUEEN IS DEAD! LONG LIVE THE QUEEN?

In November 1990 Margaret Thatcher was replaced as leader of the Conservative Party and Prime Minister by John Major after due process had been observed for electing the leader of the parliamentary Conservative Party. According to the most widely held view few events in recent political history could equal this for surprise and potentially momentous consequences. She was the longest-serving Prime Minster of the century and one of the longest-serving ever. Under her leadership the party had won three parliamentary elections and lost none. Due to her, a widely acclaimed economic miracle had been wrought. The authority of Parliament in the country was unchallenged. The standing of Britain in the world was again high. A new spirit of enterprise prevailed in the land. The government was vigorous and determined, with a substantial programme of new measures to pursue during a fourth successive term of office. Margaret Thatcher was 'the greatest peacetime Prime Minister of the century'. All this and yet she was voted out of office, not by her official opponents or the electorate, but by colleagues in her own parliamentary party.

The explanation for this remarkable occurrence has various aspects. In the light of them her rejection is not surprising, and the nature of the New Right's supposed ascendency is greatly clarified. To begin with, the economic record after ten years was unimpressive and rhetoric could not talk away inflation, high interest rates, huge trade deficits and growing unemployment. In the political sphere, there were overwhelming difficulties both at home, because of the Poll Tax, and abroad, in the European Economic Community, to do with economic, monetary and political union. Socially, the divisions in the country could no longer be ignored because they spilled on to the streets and the vast majority of people were dissatisfied with social welfare provision. Fear for the NHS was especially widespread. Finally, concern about the blatantly authoritarian character of Thatcher government was widely shared and expressed.

These circumstances provide the background to the chain of events leading to the end of Margaret Thatcher's New Right government. In May 1989, when she celebrated the completion of ten consecutive years as Prime Minister, few observers could have foreseen her departure in such a way so soon. Yet the evidence was already abundantly to hand. The economic record since 1979 had been effectively exposed as a comprehensive failure by Gordon Brown from the opposition front bench in October 1988. All of the other factors had been at least latent throughout Margaret Thatcher's leadership of her party. There was nothing new about either inequitable taxation policies or her chauvinism. Social welfare, including the NHS, had been systematically starved of necessary funds from the start in 1979, as comparison with other countries showed. Authoritarianism had always been Margaret Thatcher's style; only people used once to call it 'conviction politics' before its cumulative effects became more widely known and felt. When these factors are borne in mind the unfolding of events after May 1989 is unsurprising.

Immediately after the tenth anniversary celebrations the Conservatives suffered their worst by-election defeat in 54 years when, in June 1989, they lost a very safe parliamentary seat in the Vale of Glamorgan. In June 1989 the Conservatives lost badly in the elections to the European Parliament fought on Margaret Thatcher's manifesto. In July 1989 she was booed in Paris during an insulting chauvinistic address on the subject of human rights at the celebration of the bicentennial of the French Revolution. At the EEC summer summit in Madrid in 1989 the two most senior cabinet ministers, the Foreign Secretary (Geoffrey Howe) and the Chancellor of the Exchequer (Nigel Lawson), both threatened to resign unless economic and monetary union were accepted in principle: so they were. Howe paid the price when he was demoted and humiliated in a cabinet reshuffle in August. In October 1989 Anthony Meyer challenged for the leadership of the party and won 67 votes, enough to signal substantial disaffection in the party. Government communiques were issued to reassure the world that the Prime Minister would in future be listening (more than ever!) to her colleagues. In 1990 the pattern of the previous year was repeated. Key cabinet ministers (for social services and for Wales) resigned 'to spend more time with their families'. A May by-election in North Staffordshire, fought mainly on the issue of the Poll Tax, was lost to Labour. The summer was punctuated by demonstrations and riots that expressed opposition to the Poll Tax even from traditional Conservative voters. Events moved very quickly in the autumn. The Conservatives suffered heavy defeats in by-elections. In Eastbourne a majority of over 15,000 was overturned. Another seat was lost in Bradford and the party was humiliated by coming third in Bootle. At the EEC economic summit in Rome Margaret Thatcher alone dissented from measures agreed for economic union and in a way that showed she really agreed with the xenophobic outbursts of former Secretary of State for Trade and Industry, Nicholas Ridley, who had been forced to resign in September. After an unrepentant speech to the Commons in which the Prime Minister prophesied there would be no economic union with Europe in her lifetime, the Foreign Secretary Geoffrey Howe resigned. His resignation speech in the Commons two weeks later surprised everybody because instead of the predicted call for party unity it proved to be an almost unprecedented act of political character assassination of the Prime Minister: attacking the policies she pursued (on Europe), the manner of her pursuing them, and her autocratic political persona. Howe's concluding enjoiner to his colleagues in the party, to consider taking action against her, finally precipitated an open challenge for the leadership from a serious opponent, Michael Heseltine.[178] The first ballot under the rules for leadership elections was held on 20 November, when the Prime Minister failed to secure enough votes to prevent a second ballot. In a typical tactical move that probably decisively lost her her most powerful support, she immediately (and without consultation with her cabinet colleagues and party officials) announced to television reporters that she would fight on in the second ballot. This tactic to 'bounce' members of the government into supporting her probably finally convinced them that she was incorrigibly determined to have power at any cost. In any event, support for her evaporated almost overnight after that episode and she withdrew from the second ballot, but endorsed the candidacy of the Chancellor of the Exchequer, John Major. Major was deemed to be elected when the two other candidates withdrew after the result of the second ballot was announced on 27 November 1990. The winner survived reports that Margaret Thatcher had reassured her supporters at Conservative Party Central Office that if Major was elected leader, she would be 'a good backseat driver'.[179]

The issues over which the greatest champion of New Right ideas lost her preeminent positions as leader of the Conservative Party and Prime Minister are confused enough to need examination. Ostensibly, the immediate cause of the challenge to her leadership was her position on economic union with the EEC. However, on this issue, opinion in the country was evenly divided, and support among Conservative MPs for her general position was overwhelming (75 per cent, according to a Gallup poll reported in the *Sunday Telegraph*). The most plausible political explanation for the collapse of support among MPs was the wide unpopularity among voters of the leader and policies associated with her. Among the popular views revealed by opinion polls at the time of the leadership election were these: 68 per cent of all electors thought she should resign before the next election; 40 per cent of Conservative voters thought that she was no longer a good Prime Minister. Most telling, 87 per cent of voters who had defected from the Conservatives did not like their policies; 91 per cent of former Conservative voters wanted to abolish or to greatly modify the Poll Tax. Only 20 per cent of voters thought that the Prime Minister reflected ordinary people's views. A Harris poll of 28 October showed the consequence of these views: the Labour Party would have overwhelming support in a general election, with 48 per cent for Labour and 32 per cent for the Conservatives. Other polls corroborated this picture. The *Mail on Sunday* on 4 November reported a Labour lead in the polls of 21 per cent. When the leadership contest was inaugurated, polls showed the extent of the electoral handicap Margaret Thatcher was to her party. Support for the party under her leadership would be only 36 per cent against 48 per cent for Labour. If Michael Heseltine were leader support for Conservatives would be 47 per cent against 40 per cent for Labour. One poll showed that only 13 per cent of voters believed that Margaret Thatcher should lead the Conservatives. The effect of such results was decisive among Conservative MPs, especially the 55 who with slim majorities were most vulnerable. As the *Sunday Times* leader writer pointed out: 'The Tories have a nose for survival in power unmatched by any other party in the democratic world. And politics is an unforgiving business.' Thus, one main immediate reason for Margaret Thatcher's downfall was her parliamentary party colleagues' wish to retain their seats when their constituents rejected her policies, particularly on the Poll Tax. It is worth stressing here that, although for some MPs the Poll Tax may have been inefficient, flat-rated, regressive and bad in principle, for most of them the worst thing about it was that it violated the paramount principle of staying in office.[180]

It is possible that a Prime Minister might survive the unpopularity of policies and even the instinct for survival of back-bench MPs provided she could command loyal and principled support. By October 1990, Margaret Thatcher's abrasive personality had disposed of every close supporter. One uncritical idolator celebrated the fact that most of the 372 Conservative MPs had at some time been insulted by her. This, he said, was a sensible thing for her to do when everybody in the world was either incompetent or foolish. This is the sort of unmitigated balderdash that softens the brains of absolute monarchs, like Margaret Thatcher. In 1977 she had sanctimoniously preached in Zurich on the theme of Lord Acton's famous remark that 'power corrupts and absolute power corrupts absolutely'. In November 1990 a *Sunday Times* writer, Robert Harris, described accurately how far she had forgotten the theme of her own sermon when he wrote:

The crisis is entirely the responsibility of the Prime Minister: of her addiction to power, of her arrogance, of the contempt with which she treats her colleagues ... For more than a decade, the Prime Minister has abused the power of her office to undermine and crush anyone who opposed her. She has now achieved what one presumes is her idea of state of grace; to be the only member of the 1979 cabinet still in government. No other leader in British political history has behaved in such a fashion. Her style *is* the substance of the crisis ... she will destroy any minister who crosses her ; ... she lacks the common sense and even, dare one say it, the common decency to preside over a talented cabinet; she has become a menace to our system of government and to our national interest; ... she is, in sum, unfit to rule.[181]

Margaret Thatcher was extruded from the leadership of her party because she persisted with policies that became electoral liabilities in a democracy, and because she was unable to conduct herself in a manner required of her: as *primus inter pares* in a cabinet of peers, in a Parliament of elected representatives of the people, a substantial majority of whom did not support her and a vast majority of whom positively opposed her policies. One legacy of her regime was exemplified by the confession of one MP during the leadership election that he proposed to lie. 'I shall vote for Michael then tell my constituents I voted for Maggie.' It is fitting that those who live by the lie should die by the lie.[182]

Two aspects of the Conservatives' leadership election of 1990 raise wider issues that warrant some comment. First, a drift to presidential-style government was evident in the way the Prime Minister's supporters and some others of a constitutional bent argued that electors had voted for Margaret Thatcher as Prime Minister, and so only the electors, at a general election, could legitimately remove her; not the parliamentary Conservative Party. This is a misrepresentation of the electoral system. First, electors in the British system only vote for a constituency MP. Parties who offer candidates select their leader, and the head of the government is the one who has the support of sufficient MPs. Secondly, the parallels between the Conservative leadership elections of 1975 and 1990 are striking. Margaret Thatcher succeeded in replacing an unpopular leader, despite being an unfancied outsider. Michael Heseltine succeeded in replacing an unpopular leader, albeit unintentionally, with an unfancied outsider, John Major. In both cases, the main attraction of the successful candidate was that they weren't the hated leader. Talk of political philosophy and ideology in these circumstances is almost as risible as fulminations by losers against treachery. If there is a moral to the story for leaders and led alike, it is that power does corrupt and absolute power really does corrupt absolutely. Constitutional reform in the mundane, republican direction is clearly what is required.

The immediate effect of the change of leadership of the Conservative Party was uncertain so far as New Right thinking and policies are concerned. Michael Heseltine had been anxious during the leadership campaign to stress his free-market credentials. He said: 'Wherever you look, you find that I have been at the leading edge of what is described as Thatcherism.' What he offered in addition to defending Thatcherism's project was the political ability to carry it out, including winning the next general election.[183] Pundits opined that the New Right think tanks, the Institute for Economic Affairs, the Centre for Policy Studies and the Adam Smith Institute, would be most likely to continue as before under John Major's leadership of the Party. There is no doubt that in November 1990 the Conservative Party acted on the belief that New Right policies had been pursued too far too fast, with excessive zeal and with too little regard to enlightened self-interest (if not too little compassion). So soon after a change of leadership it is difficult to predict what will happen. The New Right thinking could persist with the more amenable style necessary for political business to continue and for electoral success. Alternatively, the change of leadership could signal the end of 'conviction' politics of the New Right and a return to consensus. Whatever the future has in store, there was an irresistible feel of completion to the moment of departure of Margaret Thatcher from the vanguard of the New Right politics in Britain.

20   SUMMARY AND CONCLUSIONS

The record of eleven years of New Right government during the 1980s can be assessed in a variety of ways. The most obvious is according to the five practical tasks they set themselves in 1979. Then there is the criterion of the real creed. Finally there is the test of professed theoretical foundations. This leads to an appraisal of the theoretical foundations themselves. First, the tasks; these were as follows, with results:

1 To restore the health of our economic and social life by controlling inflation and striking a fair balance between the rights and duties of the trade union movement.

The economic record is of failure. In particular, inflation in 1990 was at the same level it was in 1979 and is still, after eleven and a half years, the government's declared number one priority. The criteria of interest rates, balance of trade (especially in manufactured goods) and unemployment show the same record of failure (see pp81–98). Trade unions have certainly been subordinated to government authority. The effects of mass unemployment explain a great deal of this. A great deal else is attributed to the government's dubious vendetta against the unions, the long-term effects of which are unlikely to be beneficial or lasting (see pp94–5 and pp112–19). Certainly, members of British trade unions work longer hours for less pay than workers in any other advanced industrial nation, after eleven and a half years of New Right rule.

2 To restore incentives so that hard work pays, success is rewarded and genuine new jobs are created in an expanding economy.

Massive cuts in income tax for the highest paid have provided financial incentives for the best off, though there is no evidence that cash incentives are the most important motivators. There were no such incentives anyway for most people, least of all for those on the lowest incomes. Employees in the public sector were excluded, on principle, from the award of incentives. Executives were as generous in the non-performance-related awards they made to themselves as they were stringent in restricting the incomes of their subordinates to the minimum possible (see pp103–6). Virtually no genuine new jobs were created because after a catastrophic collapse in 1979 the economy got back to the size it was in 1979 only by 1988 (see pp95–8). The most prolific growth of all was in the output of rhetoric and the massaging of data.

The related aims of reducing the role of the state in industry and spreading ownership of shares more widely were promoted through the privatisation of state-owned industries. Billions of pounds were lost to the public purse as shares were sold substantially below their market value. Many of the new owners sold immediately for a quick killing. At the end of it all only a small fraction of the population (about 15 per cent) owned shares privately, and only a negligible fraction of shares at that. The government had encouraged speculation more than thrift.

3 To uphold Parliament and the rule of law.

The authority of Parliament was certainly asserted over trade unions, although the methods resorted to went to the limits of legality and beyond. The state itself was not always seen to act within the law (see pp112–19 and pp128–31). The record on crime was one simply of unrelieved failure, with record rates of crime repeatedly reported, despite unprecedented expenditure on law and order (see pp139–40).

4 To support family life, by helping people to become house owners, raising the standards of their children's education, and concentrating welfare services on the effective support of the old, the sick, the disabled and those who are in real need.

House ownership was increased dramatically; by the expedients of flogging off local authority property at knock-down prices, and encouraging people to borrow heavily on house mortgages. It would be more accurate to say that home mortgaging increased dramatically. The nature of such 'ownership' was revealed by the unprecedented number of homes repossessed from mortgages by the real owners – the building societies and banks – as high interest rates made it impossible for the new 'owners' to make repayments (see pp142–7). Homelessness was a scandal by the late 1980s, with thousands sleeping on the streets of London alone. In education innumerable ideologically motivated schemes for testing and for school reorganisation so swamped the teaching profession that it has become virtually impossible for schools to cope. Low pay and a government vendetta reduced morale to the point where many schools were unable to provide regular teachers in front of classes. In key subjects such as science, mathematics and foreign languages the shortage of teachers reached crisis proportions. Compared to these problems, schemes for local management and opting out of local authority control were merely irritating distractions (see pp147–53). In the field of social welfare, pensioners lost the link between pensions and average earnings, and the gap between need and expenditure in the health service widened to the point where the system was on the verge of collapse. The government ignored the fact that every other developed nation spent a greater proportion of its income on health, and spoke only of increased expenditure (see pp161–5 and pp140–2). The various categories of disabled continued to suffer most of all, and the means-testing of benefits predictably led to the reduction or withdrawal of support from countless individuals in real need because the system operated by cash limits, rather than needs criteria (see pp161–5).

5 To strengthen Britain's defences and work with our allies to protect our interests in an increasingly hostile world.

Nuclear defences were maintained, though at uncalculated cost to the rest of the economy. Considerable political capital was gained through the Falklands War for the Conservative government. However, the necessity for the war and the course it took raised serious questions about both the competence and the probity of Margaret Thatcher's leadership (see pp119–28 and 128–32).

The most fundamental aim of all, to change the national attitude of mind, was not realised. In 1990 far more British people (47 per cent) preferred a mainly socialist society in which public interest and a more controlled economy are most important, to 'a mainly capitalist society in which private interest and free enterprise are most important' (39 per cent). What was most striking was that in 1989, after ten years of instruction in New Right living, even fewer people (32 per cent) thought it was the government's job to make certain that people could get ahead on their own (ie, encourage self-help) than had thought so in 1947 (40 per cent).[184]

On the day she was first elected Prime Minister in 1979 Margaret Thatcher recited some words of St Francis of Assisi: 'Where there is discord may we bring harmony, where there is error may we bring truth, where there is doubt may we bring faith and where there is despair may we bring hope.' These words rank with Neville Chamberlain's proclaiming of 'Peace in our time' as the least prophetic utterances ever made by a British Prime Minister. Confrontation was the chief *modus operandi*. By 1990 British society was much more divided by region, between the employed and the unemployed, and by wealth, income and life-chances (that is, class) than it had been for over 60 years. Disingenuousness became the normal mode of communication of a government infamous for being economical with the truth. Secrecy became an end in itself and national security an excuse to hide from the public, and even from Parliament, facts inconvenient to the government. For the millions of unemployed, homeless, old and ill people, despair was a common condition unrelieved by the fact that the best off had become very considerably better off. By the test of its own manifesto the New Right failed comprehensively.

Another way of assessing the record of the New Right is according to the creed that distinguishes it (as opposed to a shopping list of tasks set out in their official manifestoes). This turns out to be the simplest way of doing it, if Honderich is correct in concluding that it is not by its view of change, or of theory, or of human nature, or of society, or of government, or of equality that conservatism is distinguished, but by its uniquely exclusive regard for self: selfishness, or greed.[185] If greed is the test of the success of New Right policy then massive shifts in wealth, income and opportunity in favour of the best off at the expense of the worst off could be counted a success by the main beneficiaries themselves, by those who were impressed by the acquisition of even a modest council house, and by others who may not have won out in the 'casino economy', but had strong hopes of doing so. Given the iniquities of the British electoral system, less than one in three such people is enough to return a New Right government, if by this test they are greedy enough. Perhaps they were, and that is all there was to it.

A third and more penetrating way of assessing the record is with reference to the theoretical foundations of New Right thinking. For the present purpose a brief consideration of four distinguishable strands will suffice. First, there is the traditional high Toryism of the Peterhouse school. Among its traditional values, patriotism, state authority and inequality are salient. By these standards the record of the New Right is both impressive (and not). The Falklands War re-established Britain's status as a virile nation to be respected internationally. Our Daniel-daring-to-be-different in other areas (in Europe and the Commonwealth) served the same purpose. The authority of the state was asserted over trade unions and local government, and inequality flourished. Depending on the point of view, the record by these standards was either a success or not. True-blues might be impressed; but others using the same test might be sceptical about the glory in venturing near defeat by a non-league team; the merits of eroding the time-honoured freedom from central government of the small platoons in the shires and great municipalities; and the virtue in the growth of the 'loadsamoney' yuppie-yob culture. Teaching others how to live is an avocation of the Peterhouse school of old-Toryism that encouraged some of them to think that Britain (Margaret Thatcher really) had almost single-handedly undermined communism in Eastern Europe. This interpretation of events takes the prize for foolishness in the face of historical, economic and geopolitical realities, among which Britain's insignificance, and dependency on and sub-servience to the United States, are not the least relevant.

Secondly, there is the free-market philosophy of Lord North Street. By this standard the record is again both mixed and ambivalent. On the plus side: state monopolies were sold off, self-employment boomed, inflation was reduced and the unemployment caused in the process was not shirked, income taxes were reduced, and the trade unions were disciplined by market forces. Unfortunately, inflation was reduced only temporarily, and reached the 1979 levels again, only after ten years; but at double or treble the level of unemployment. Government spending was actually increased, largely as a result of massive unemployment. The prophet of monetarism and the free market himself, Keith Joseph, had said he would halve government subsidies to industry: when confronted with the realities he doubled them instead. A member of the Conservative Bow Group said of Joseph in 1981 that he was by universal consent the most dismal disappointment of the administration.[186] Failure of government to invest in industry at levels comparable to Britain's main competitors was a significant factor in the poor performance of manufacturing industry. Taxation as a whole was increased, including employers' National Insurance contributions. Cowing the trade unions with mass unemployment is not everybody's idea of successful economic policy.

Thirdly, the ideas of the Public Choice school illuminate the record. If government policy and spending are taken to be ways of buying votes or satisfying the vested interests of powerful lobbies against the general public interest, then it might be thought that certain abuses were stopped. The civil service, the trade unions, the CBI, the professions, the poverty lobby, among numerous others, no longer received special ministrations to their vested interests. By the same standards, however, the pork-barrelling continued unabated; only the beneficiaries were different. Council house sales at prices 30 to 60 per cent below market values bought enough working-class votes to secure election victory. Shares in privatised companies at a fraction of market value bribed even more to vote Conservative. State bribery on such a scale had not been known since the dissolution of the monasteries by Henry VIII. Other satisfied recipients of largesse from the pork-barrel included the City, those who were already the most wealthy, and the forces of law and order: in short, the friends and supporters of the government, and those it relied upon to keep order at the trough.

Fourthly, libertarian ideals of individualism and self-help provide different standards and different judgements. By these standards the Prime Minister's pronouncement that there is no such thing as society was encouraging evidence that the appropriate values were at work. The removal of economic controls, the reduction of bureaucracy, the erosion of collective provision and the growth of private provision in education, welfare and municipal services were all positive signs that they were working to good effect. But the manifest growth of homelessness, and decay in the health, education and social services reached levels that were intolerable to everyone except those in whom libertarianism amounted to monomania. Above all, the growth of the authoritarian powers of the central state violated the central value espoused by the libertarian right. Libertarians themselves most certainly regret greatly the loss of civil liberties and the growth of the authoritarian central state.

The rhetoric notwithstanding, by the New Right's own standards the record in the spheres of economics, politics, society and culture is one of comprehensive failure. By other standards it is even worse. It might be argued, of course, that the failures were merely contingent. They might not have occurred if policies had been closer to principles, or if ministers had been more competent or more resolute, or if circumstances had been different. We know that external circumstances were the same or similar for other, more successful, countries. Internal circumstances persist, but for other governments as well. Twelve years in office is more than almost any other government has been allowed to test its policies, whatever the qualities of its ministers. In any case Margaret Thatcher's uncompromising personality gives all the certainty possible that contingent incompetence and irresolution in implementing New Right policies would be at a minimum. What remains is the question of whether the failures were due to accidental failures in application which might have been remedied, or whether they were the inevitable result of a philosophy which is irredeemably flawed. That is another story.

NOTES AND REFERENCES: PART 1

1 Hudson Institute (1974); Tyrell (1977); Seldon (1978); Lawson (1980); Hall and Jacques (1983); Marquand (1988); Jessop et al. (1988); Gamble (1988); Haseler (1989).
2 Ministry of Labour (1966). Table A1 'Production, Incomes and Employment'.
3 Playfair (1885: 1970 p63); Siegfried (1931); Einzig (1969); Weiner (1981); Elbaum and Lazonick (1986).
4 Nevin (1983 p179 Table IIa).
5 OECD (December 1978 p136).
6 Fay and Young (14 May 1978 p33).
7 OECD (December 1978, June 1980).
8 Nevin (1983 p178 Table Ia); ILO (1978 p272).
9 Prais (1981).
10 Treasury Autumn Statement (HMSO 1988) cited in Brittan (1989 p14).
11 European Commission Annual Economic Report cited in Brown (1989 p37 Table I).
12 Gray (1971).
13 Labour Party (1982 p18 Table 2.4).
14 Clarke (1967).
15 Shonfield (1958 pp 153–9).
16 Labour Party (1982 p19).
17 Raw (1977).
18 Sampson (1977).
19 Wigham (1961); Pelling (1971).
20 Johnson (1978 p78).
21 Thomas (1985 pp147–53).
22 Heath et al. (1985 p132 Table 9.1).
23 Hailsham (1976); Benn (1979).
24 Cosgrave (1975 p193).
25 Gilmour (1978 p211).
26 Scruton (1980 p69).
27 Worsthorne (1979).
28 Cliff (1975 p178).
29 Revolutionary Communist Party of Britain (1981 p10).
30 Cited Johnson (1978 p79).
31 Haseler (1976 p104) and Gilmour (1978 p155).
32 Garner (1979).
33 Black (1980).
34 Marquand (1988 p172).
35 Man of Everest, Harrap, 1955, pp224–5; quoted in Crosland (1964 p102).
36 Wilson (1989 pp13–20).
37 Goldthorpe et al. (1980 p114); cf Halsey et al. (1980).
38 Harris (1966 p179).
39 Joseph (1979).
40 *The Times* (10 September 1980 p4).

41 Dahrendorf (1982 pp73–8).
42 Blackburn (1967).
43 Hudson Institute (1974 p124).
44 Nishiyama and Allen (1974 pp15–21).
45 Allen (1979 p69).
46 Dahrendorf (1982).
47 Reimer (1971); Illich (1973).
48 Edgeley (1978).
49 Weiner (1981).
50 Booker (1970).
51 Brittan (1988 p2).
52 Keynes (1936).
53 Tarling and Wilkinson (1977).
54 S. Williams (1981); Marquand (1988); see also Pym (1985).
55 Benn (1980).
56 Gilmour (1976, p21).
57 Bevan (1978 [1952] p62).
58 Kolakowski and Hampshire (1977); Oxford University Socialist Discussion Group (1989).
59 Cowling (1989).
60 Benton (1987), Cowling (1989).
61 Seldon in N. Barry et al. (1984 ppxv–xxxii).
62 Harris and Seldon (1977). This provides an excellent summary of the IEA's philosophy, aims and activities from its inception to 1977, a period during which the foundation of New Right thinking and policy was laid. Although the preoccupation is with economic analysis, political and philosophical elements are also addressed.
63 Friedman (1970 p24).
64 Hayek (1975, 1978).
65 Casey (1978), Scruton (1980).
66 Minogue (1978).
67 J. M. Buchanan (1968); Tullock (1976); Buchanan and Tullock in Seldon (1981 pp79–97); Mitchell (1988).
68 Joseph (1975 p6), Cosgrave (1975 p127). Citing National Income and Expenditure 1963–73 'Blue Book' HMSO 1974.
69 Culyer (1981).
70 Harris and Seldon (1977).
71 Haseler (1989 p35).
72 Hayek (1960 p388).
73 Scruton (1980 p157).
74 Hayek (1960 p383).
75 Thatcher (1977 p12).
76 Smith (1910 [1776] Vol I, p13).
77 Smith (1910 [1776] Vol I p400).
78 Letwin (1978).
79 Joseph (1975 pp8–9).
80 Cosgrave (1975).
81 Cosgrave (1975 p70).
82 Cosgrave (1975 p47).

83   Gilmour (1978 pp168, 167).
84   Cowling (1989 p11).
85   Cormack (1978).
86   Bevan (1978 [1952] p33).
87   Thatcher, speech to Conservative Party Conference, Blackpool 1979 (1989a p50).
88   Thatcher (1977 p96).
89   Wrong (1979 pp204–16).
90   D. King (1987 p131 Table 7.4).
91   Thatcher (1989a p50).
92   Quoted in Cosgrave (1975 p102).
93   Shenfield (1983 p20).
94   H. Wilson (1977 pp292–3).
95   Shonfield (1958 pp99–101).
96   Labour Party Defence Study Group (1977 p44); OECD Main Economic Indicators December 1978. Author's calculations.
97   Allen in Nishiyama and Allen (1974 p47).
98   Shonfield (1958 p127).
99   Quoted by Fay and Young (21 May 1978 p33).
100   Pratten (1990).
101   Rothstein (1950 pp12–15; pp129–31). Total industrial output in 1920 was not much more than 13 per cent of the level of 1913 (p131). In 1913 output was of the order 15 per cent that of the USA (eg 4 per cent of coal production; 9 per cent iron; 25 per cent railways; p13). *Welfare*, USSR Novosti Press Agency Moscow (1973 p5).
102   Jonathan Steele 'Soviet Splits Deepen' *Guardian* (3 July 1990 p6); Stockholm International Peace Research Institute (SIPRI) Yearbook (1989 Table 5A.3).
103   Estimate of USSR GDP in IISS (1990 p32); for USA GDP ref OECD *Main Economic Indicators* February (1990 p172).
104   Thomas (1979 p13).
105   Nossiter (1978 p48) citing, for 1855–1945, *National Income Expenditure and Output of the United Kingdom 1855–1965*, C. H. Feinstein, Cambridge University Press, Cambridge 1972, Table 6, 7, 8, 19; for 1948–1976, Economic Trends, *Annual Supplement 1977* p5.
106   Olsen and Landsberg (1975); Skolimowski (1981); Porritt (1984).
107   Nossiter (1978).
108   Thatcher (1989a [1979] p52); OECD *Main Economic Indicators* (December 1978 p144) for Japanese figures; Nevin (1983 Appendices I and IIa pp178–9). Milton Friedman explains that it takes two years for increases in the money supply to be reflected in increased retail prices (Friedman 1977 pp37–8).
109   Joseph (1975 pp8, 12), Thatcher (1977 p74); Brittan (1989 p14 fig. 1.2, citing Treasury Autumn Statement HMSO 1988); Labour Party Financial Institutions Study Group (1982 pp32–3).
110   Bacon and Eltis (1976); Joseph (1976 p22); Thatcher (1977 p95); Nossiter (1978 pp24–6); Keegan (1984 p36).
111   Joseph (1975); Pliatzky (1984 – corrects the erroneous statistics of government spending). Marquand (1988 pp250–1 Table IV) gives Public

Expenditure/GDP ratios on a standard basis for OECD member countries, 1960–80 (expressed as percentages), based on OECD and UN accounts; Nossiter (1978 pp51–4) gives summary data on welfare expenditure and taxation, citing *Public Expenditure on Income Maintenance Programmes*, OECD Studies in Research Allocation (July 1976 p17); and Revenue Statistics of OECD Member Countries (1965–75 p80).

112 Cosgrave (1975 p90); Pelling (1971, Statistical Table pp282–3) for historical data on strikes; Hyman (1989 pp33–5), cites the Report of the Royal Commission on Trades Unions and Employers Associations 1965–68 (Chairman Lord Donovan, Cmnd 3623 HMSO 1968); comparisons with other countries for 1978 are given in *Employment Gazette* (June 1989 p310 Table 1).

113 Prais (1981 Table G1 Measures of strike-proneness in Britain by size of plant 1971–73 p306).

114 Gilmour (1978 p236); Shenfield (1983 p22); Thatcher (1989a [1979] p52); Hayek (1978 p67 for the claim about closed shop as a cause of strikes); Seamen (1966); Foot (1968 pp172–8 for the discussion of the seamen's case); Smith (1910 [1776] Vol I p93). Mineworkers were paid in 1972 £33 per week compared to £32.8 per week national average; in 1974 £46.9 per week compared to £46.5 national average. Public service workers, such as NUPE members, were paid in 1978 £67.7 per week compared to a national average of £89 per week: data in New Earnings Survey Department of Employment (1988 Part A for 1972 Table 1 p25, Table 1b pp39–40). Relative pay of mineworkers is also discussed in Wilberforce (1972); Hughes and Moore (1972); Pay Board (1974); Papps (1975 Table 1 p32 shows the substantial erosion of earnings of mineworkers compared to workers in other nationalised industries). On dissatisfaction of trade unionists with a failure of investment to match wage restraint, see Tarling and Wilkinson (1977 pp412–13).

115 Joseph (1975 p52); contrast Nishiyama and Allen (1974 pp25, 45–6) and Allen (1979 pp26–30 69–70); Best and Humphries in Elbaum and Lazonick (1986).

116 Hayek (1978); Joseph (1975); Shenfield (1983 p22); Jones (1967 p124 for the reference to the need for stronger unions); Taylor (1980 for an international comparison of union benefits); Shonfield (1958 p21 for a statement by the American United Automobile Workers Union official, Nat Weinberg, on how low wage settlements perpetuate management inefficiency); Rather (1932 p29 for data on the trends in Britain's share of world trade from 1871 to 1928); Pelling (1971 pp280–3 for union membership since 1893).

117 Joseph (1975 p16); contrast Nishiyama and Allen (1974, pp15–18, 20–1, 33–5, 55–60 'Britain is at least two generations behind Japan in realising the advantages of higher education for those engaged in industry'); Allen (1979 pp34–52, 55–7, 66–70, 75–6).

118 Nevin (1983 pp69–70).

119 Gilmour (1978 p207); Thatcher (1989a [1979] p51).

120 Crosland (1964 pp226, 286); Foot (1968 pp143–8); Field (1981 pp24–5) citing Royal Commission Report No 7, Tables A1 and A2. Distribution of personal income – National Income and Expenditure 1949 to 1976/77 (after tax) 'Blue Book' HMSO.

121 Statistics given in the report of the National Executive Committee presented by Frank Allaun MP to the Labour Party Annual Conference, Brighton, October 1981.

122 Anthony Mascarenhos (1977) 'Grunwick: after 49 weeks Mrs Desai had to weep', *Sunday Times* 31 July p5; George Ward (1977), 'Why I believe the Scarman Inquiry was a political con-trick', *The Times* 1 September p14.

123 Scharfstein (1980).

124 Lipsey (1981); Flather (1985); Healey (1990 p488 – also in *Observer* 15 October 1989 p34); Abse (1989 p157); Joseph (1975 p4).

125 Lewis (1975 p14 for the 'caring' remark); Cosgrave (1975 p135) and Thatcher (1977 p52) for references to winning arguments and the battle of ideas.

126 Bevan (1978 [1952] pp124, 126).

127 Keegan (1984 p110 for reference to desire to win the election); Cosgrave (1975 p115 for reference to not being emotionally hamstrung).

128 Cosgrave (1975, p136); Thatcher (1977 p30 for reference to Labour causing inflation in 1975); Thatcher (1989a [1979] p50 for reference to Britain having the most strikes); *Guardian*, 'Thatcher bans publication of war history', 25 November 1983, p3.

129 Speech at St Lawrence Jewry, City of London, 30 March 1978, in Thatcher (1989b pp62–70).

130 Abse (1989 p23 citing interview with Robert Harris, *Observer*, 3 January 1988); Lewis (1975 p12); Cosgrave (1975 pp111, 113).

131 Junor (1983 p16 for explanation of choice of chemistry, p21 for her tutors' views of her academic abilities); Lewis (1975 p16 for her account of her failure to achieve a first-class degree); Cosgrave (1975 p79) cf Lewis (1975 p12).

132 Cosgrave (1975 pp60, 68 for quotations on the subject of lack of privilege); Thatcher (1977 [1975] p35); Junor (1983 for references to special tuition for Oxford entrance).

133 Keegan (1984 p81); Barnett (1984 p143).

134 Cosgrave (1975, especially pp22, 23, 133, 135–6, 139–40 for her philosophical interests and the significance for her of Hayek's ideas); Hayek (1979a [1944]; 1960).

135 Joseph (1975 p4).

NOTES AND REFERENCES: PART 2

1 Huhne (1990a, 1990b).

2 In an interview with Anthony Holden, *Observer*, 17 February 1980.

3 Kaldor (1983 p83).

4 Stephan (1985 pp322–3).

5 Kaldor (1983 p45).

6 eg N. M. Healey (1989 p18).

7 Kaldor (1983 p39).

8 Kaldor (1983 p53); Keegan (1984 p45).

9 Kaldor (1983 p37).

10   Keegan (1984 p142).
11   Brown (1988).
12   Hendry and Ericsson (1984).
13   Pollack (1988); see also Malcolm Coad, 'Chile's "economic miracle" rebounds on Pinochet and his supporters', *Guardian* 5 December 1989, p10; Peter Ford, 'Chile struggles to right wrongs of the poorest', *Independent* 15 September 1990, p13.
14   Huhne (1980).
15   Keegan (1984).
16   Ian Aitken, 'Talk of retreat that comes from the Tory Heart', *Guardian* 23 June 1986, p21.
17   N. M. Healey (1989).
18   Keegan (1984 p207).
19   Quoted by Huhne (1990b p14).
20   *Economic Affairs* January 1990, see Peter Wilson-Smith, 'Eureka! Economists arrive at a conclusion' *Independent on Sunday* Business on Sunday, 3 June 1990, p4.
21   Principal sources include Conservative Research Department (1989); Pirie (1989); Economic Affairs (1989).
22   Keegan (1984 pp110, 119); Labour Research (1989 p187 for unemployment statistics).
23   Brittan (1989, p12 Table 1.1, p14 Table 1.2); OECD, *Main Economic Indicators*, February 1990, p11.

24   GROSS DOMESTIC PRODUCT PER CAPITA 1988

	Dollars	UK = 100%
United States	17,965	200
Canada	15,134	168
Switzerland	15,055	167.5
Sweden	12,848	143
Japan	12,209	136
Finland	12,204	135
Germany	10,935	122
Australia	10,634	118
France	10,108	112.5
Austria	9,217	103
Netherlands	9,031	100.5
United Kingdom	8,988	100
Italy	8,133	90.5
Greece	3,496	38.9
OECD	11,807	131
EEC	8,514	95

Source: OECD *Main Economic Indicators*. Author's calculations.

25   Adrian Hain, 'Economic Commentary: Sixties scandals, sixties economics', *Tribune* 24 March 1989, p7; Christopher Johnson 'Is Britain more

productive than Japan?', *Observer* 30 April 1989, p6; William Keegan, 'Desert Island Risks', *Observer* 10 December 1989, p22; *Independent on Sunday*, 'Finance Sector Troubles', 16 September 1990, p5 – ref to shrinking manufacturing base, source Blue Book of Annual National Accounts.

26 Conservative Research Department (1989 p212 for references to profitability and investment); see also Christopher George, 'Economic Commentary: Training or a low pay economy', *Tribune* 15 June 1990, p7, and Simon Beavis, 'Ridley Denies City Short-term thinking is hampering industry', *Guardian* 26 June 1990, p9; Roberts, 'Manufacturing Investment', 3 March 1989 p2; William Keegan, 'An election road paved with good intentions', *Observer* 8 July 1990, p54 – cites a memorandum by the director general of the National Economic Development Council, Walter Eltis, on comparative levels of investment in different sectors; Coutts and Godley (1989), see also G. Wright (1989 p9); Conservative Research Department (1989 p218 for reference to investment) see also Coutts and Godley (1989) for a discussion of the accounting.

27 Roberts (19 May 1989 – Balance of Trade); Brown (1989 p26); Pirie (1989 p26).

28 Wynne Godley, 'The Mirage of Lawson's supply-side miracle', *Observer* 2 April 1989, p56; Christopher George, 'Economic Commentary: The Mess Labour is Going to Inherit', *Tribune* 22 September 1989, p7; *Independent on Sunday*, 'Finance Sector Doubles', 16 September 1990, p5; Larry Eliot, 'Shrinking Invisibles help widen the gap', *Guardian* 24 September 1990, p9.

29 Metcalf (1988); Nolan (1989); Cruddas (1990, pp1–23).

30 Peter Millar, 'Guru returns – with bad news for the ambitious', *Independent on Sunday* (Business on Sunday) 4 March 1990, p25; Mathews and Stoney (1989 p14); Bowen (1990 for an [over] optimistic view of change).

31 George Parker-Jervis, 'Rand D', *Observer* Industry. 28 January 1990, p62; Brown (1989 pp36–48); Wilkie (1989 p329); the Conservative Election Manifesto of 1987 simply denies this.

32 Thatcher (1977 p67); Angus MacPherson, 'Why a top Brain of Britain is quitting', *The Mail on Sunday* 25 March 1990, p8; Martin Ince, 'Science Brain Drain becomes a flood', *Times Higher Education Supplement* 9 February 1990, p6; 'Why the brain drainers are trying to plug the leak', *Times Higher Education Supplement* 16 February 1990, p7; Nigel Williams, 'Scientists tell P.M. to halt the Brain Drain', *Guardian* 8 February 1990, p2; P. Scott (editorial), 'The Brain Drain', *Times Higher Education Supplement*, 25 May 1990, p48.

33 Cassels (1990); NIESR (1990); Porter (1990); Jon Turney, 'Engineers may lose scholarship funds', *Times Higher Education Supplment* 22 October 1983, p6; Felicity Jones, 'Switch leaves poly (engineering) places empty', *Times Higher Education Supplement* 4 October 1985, pp1, 32; Martin Ince, 'Engineering grinds to a halt', *Times Higher Education Supplement* report of survey of engineering graduates' intentions by Imperial Ventures Limited (IVL), *Times Higher Education Supplement* 8 December 1989, p6. Edward Vulliamy, 'Businessmen cool towards City tech plan', *Guardian* 27 January 1987 p2.

34 Gray (1971 pp86–95); Kaldor (1983 pp8–97); data in personal communi-

cation to the author from Charles Coltman, Director of Strategic Planning and Market Development Rolls-Royce plc, 7 April 1990; W. T. Williams, 'Action needed to cut trade deficit', letter to *Daily Telegraph* 2 July 1988, p10.

35   Will Hutton, 'Bid for Distillers symptomatic of the takeover boom', *Guardian*, 28 August 1980, p12 (for reference to magnitude of takeover activity); Tom Wilkie (1989 p320 for data on R and D expenditure [1986] from Annual Review of Government-Funded Research and Development); Richard Thompson, Fiammetta Rocco and Peter Wilson- Smith, 'High Flyers come down with bump', *Independent on Sunday* Business on Sunday, 10 June 1990, pp10–12, for reference to British and Commonwealth Holdings.

36   Reid (1989 p54).

37   Hodgson (1986 – Lloyds); *Independent* 8 March 1990, pp1, 26, 28–9; Nick Goodway, 'The NatWest scandal', *Observer* 23 July 1989, p54; Chris Blackhurst, 'Cover-up at county, *Sunday Times* 23 July 1989, pD9; Charles Grant, 'City Shame: The NatWest scandal', *New Statesman and Society*, 2 (61), 4 August 1989, pp14–16; Lorana Sullivan, 'Barlow Clowes: the big bust up', *Observer* 19 June 1988, pp57–8; *The Guardian*, 'The Guinness Trial', 28 August 1990, pp9–12; David Hellier, 'Gold Rush', *New Statesman and Society* 1 (18), 7 October 1988, p13 (Consgold).

38   Larry Black, 'Dethroned King keeps his secrets', *Independent on Sunday* (Business) 29 April 1990, pp10–12; Richard Thompson, 'Fimbra can't police frauds', *Independent on Sunday* (Business) 17 June 1990, p2.

39   Black (ibid); Peter Large, 'Duke attacks City failings', *Guardian* 1 May 1990, p14; Melvyn Marcus and Michael Gillard, 'Ridley flies from Harrods crisis', *Observer*, 11 March 1990, p29.

40   *Observer*, 'Water Privatisation', 2 July 1989, pp1, 51–2.

41   George Parker-Jervis, 'Privatisation effect fails', *Observer* 10 September 1989 p20; Reid (1989, p53); Gordon Brown, 'Sleazing along', *New Statesman and Society* 3 (112), 3 August 1990, p6; Kevin Goldstein-Jackson, 'Sid gets the brush-off despite investors club', *Independent on Sunday* (Business) 12 August 1990, p66.

42   Brown (ibid) for estimate of undervaluation of shares.

43   Patrick Donovan, 'City offered indemnity in nuclear sale', *Guardian* 26 January 1989, p20; Andrew Glyn, 'Propped up with prejudice', *Guardian* 7 August 1984, p17; for details of the accounting of the economies of mines; Lucy Kellaway, Charles Leadbeater and Philip Stephens, 'EC tells Government to recover £44 million in illegal B.Ae subsidies', *Financial Times* 28 June 1990, p24; David Hencke, 'Secrecy on Rover cash "broke law"', *Guardian* 2 July 1990, p1.

44   Conservative Manifesto (1983 pp13–14); Manifesto (1987 p1); Mick Hodgkin, 'Britons work longer hours than other Europeans', *Tribune* 27 October 1989 p3; Mathews and Stoney (1989 p11); Jeff Covitt 'Membership decline studies', *Tribune* 27 April 1990, p2; Roberts (9 March 1990, 1 June 1990).

45   Yearbook of Labour Statistics (1988); Labour Research (1989); Keegan (1984 pp158ff); *Sunday Times*, 'Tough Thatcher defies jeers', 20 July 1990, p1; Kaldor (1983 p98 – for reference to Arthur Seldon of the IEA citing in 1982

a rise in unemployment of 1.5 million as 'the number one success' – indeed the only one of any consequence – of the Thatcher government); Ken Hyder, 'Fiddlers! How the Tories fiddled the figures', *Labour Weekly* 15 May 1987, p12; Robert Jackson, 'An unemployment myth', letter to *Independent on Sunday* 23 September 1990, p18; McLeish (1989).

46 Wynne Godley, 'Why I won't apologise', *Observer* 18 September 1988, p14.
47 Conservative Manifesto (1987); Pirie (1989).
48 Hugo Young, 'Why did the Unions commit suicide?', *Guardian* 13 September 1988, p19.
49 Quoted in Kaldor (1983 p89).
50 Adam Raphael, 'Arise, Sir Yes Man', *Observer* 3 July 1988, pp1, 6; *Telegraph Magazine*, 'Thatcher's 100', 6 October 1990.
51 Roberts (9 March 1990; 5 June 1990; 15 June 1990).
52 Crewe (1988, 1989); Rentoul (1989); Nicholas Wapshott, '79pc oppose water sale', *Observer* 2 July 1989, p1; Melvyn Marcus, Nick Goodway and Jane Renton, 'Water privatisation crisis: Voters reject Ridley's flotation plans', ibid, p51; George Pitcher, 'Public gives thumbs down to British Rail privatisation', *Observer* 29 October 1989, p19.
53 Redwood (1989 p8).
54 Conservative Manifesto (1987).
55 Mathews and Stoney (1989 p12).
56 Dilnot and Kell (1988); Christopher Huhne, 'Study discounts incentive effect of tax rate cuts', *Guardian* 29 November 1988, p15.
57 Philip Beresford, 'Can bosses justify £534,000 a year', *Sunday Times* 23 July 1989, pB5; Michael Brett, 'Beware the £500,000 bosses', *Independent on Sunday* (Business) 27 May 1990, pp10–12; John Harvey-Jones, 'High Flyers and the case for high pay', *Observer* 13 August 1989, p53; Lisa Buckingham, 'Midland Director's £398,000 pay off', *Guardian* 27 March 1990, p9 – for statement about senior boardroom salaries not being related to performance.
58 D. Lawson (1989).
59 Goffee and Scase (1979, 1990),.
60 D. Lawson (1989).
61 Hills (1989); Fabian Society (1990); Malcolm Wicks, 'Family Fortunes', *New Statesman and Society* 2 (40), 10 March 1989, p21.
62 G. Wright (1989 p18) citing National Income Accounts; Hansard, 27 June 1988, Col 104; 14 July 1988, Col 319; 10 January 1989, Col 638–642; Wicks, ibid; Hills (1989).
63 Tim Miles 'Gap between rich and poor growing, Whitehall admits', *Observer* 8 April 1990, p4.
64 Walker (1989); Hennessy (1989); Ponting (1985); Turnbull (1988).
65 Mason (1989); Young (1989); Christian Wolmar, 'Quality Services: last hope for local democracy', *Tribune* 9 February 1990, pp6–7; Hugo Young, 'Clean Hands Murky Deeds', *Guardian* 29 April 1991, p18; Nicholas Ridley, 'Why rebates are the poll tax's saving grace', *Guardian* 12 March 1991, p23; Adam Smith (1910 [1776] Vol II p324, cf p307).
66 Labour Research (1986).
67 Labour Party (1987).
68 Ron Leighton, 'Shutting up Shop', *Tribune* 12 January 1990, p4.

69 Paul Routledge, 'Mrs Thatcher shows the wrong signals', *Observer* 9 July 1989, p16.

70 Harper and Wintour (1985).

71 Northam (1988 pp52–9, 82–116).

72 Glyn (1982, 1984a, 1984b).

73 Peter Wilsher, 'What can be done for Cortonwood', *Sunday Times* 30 December 1984, p17.

74 Harper and Wintour (1985); Lynn Barber, 'The Mysteries of Mr Hart', *Independent on Sunday* (magazine) 11 March 1990, pp3–5; Northam (1988 pp52–9 for an account of the Orgreave episode); Gareth Pierce, 'How they re-wrote the law at Orgreave', *Guardian* 12 August 1985 – for an account of how television news coverage reversed the order of events at Orgreave; Joy Copley, 'Orgreave was "a frame up"', *Labour Weekly* No 700, 9 August 1985, p1; Kavanagh and Malcolm (1985, quote p8).

75 Williams, Williams and Haslam (1989).

76 Quoted by Harper and Wintour (1985).

77 Heath, Jowell and Curtice (1985 pp96–9, Table 7.5 pp117–23).

78 Gavshon and Rice (1984 pp3–32).

79 Ibid p36.

80 Ibid p210.

81 Benn (1982); Ecoropa (1982); Gould (1984); Andrew Wilson and Arthur Gavshon, 'Secrets of Belgrano revealed by documents', *Observer* 5 June 1990, p6; Belgrano Action Group (1988) Report of the Inquiry into the Sinking of the Belgrano, Cirencester; Dalyell (1988 pp37–69).

82 Quoted in Gavshon and Rice (1984 p16).

83 Dalyell (1988 p69); Roberts (24 February 1989 p2).

84 Ridley (1990 p8).

85 Adrian Hamilton, 'Euro-phobe who can't change her blind spots', *Observer* 17 December 1989, p16.

86 Edward Pearce, 'An anti-revolution outburst that was born of ignorance', *Sunday Times* 16 July 1989, pB3.

87 Peter Rogers and Christopher Huhne, 'Vicious circle of debt that must be broken', *Guardian* 27 December 1988, p11; Christopher Huhne, 'Growing debt and destruction', *Guardian* 4 August 1989, p3.

88 Cockburn (1989); Neal Kearney, 'Zone workers pay the price of freedom', *Tribune* 4 May 1990, p7.

89 John Tanner, 'Britain should give more aid – Oxfam', *Labour Weekly* 23 October 1987, p5. Since after allowing for inflation the GDP didn't increase, there was no absolute growth, apart from the proportional reduction.

90 Adam Raphael, 'PM admits aid talks linked to arms deals', *Observer* 2 July 1989, p4.

91 Dalyell (1988 p33 – quoting Hansard, 29 October 1986, Col 389).

92 Dalyell (1988 p17, 43).

93 Gavshon and Rice (1984); Gould (1984); Dalyell (1988); Belgrano Action Group (1988 see Note 81).

94 Whitelaw (1989a, 1989b pC2).

95 Cosgrave (1975 p190).

96 Ponting (1985).

97   Crick (1985).
98   Dalyell (1988 pp70–104, quote p104); James Naughtie, 'The reputations that went west with Westland', *Guardian* 25 July 1986, p16.
99   Dalyell (1988 pp143–65).
100 Ian Lee, 'Letter: Who dares say this in the name of justice', *Guardian* 14 March 1989, p18; John Hooper and Peter Murtagh, 'Spain snub over IRA operation', *Guardian* 14 March 1989, p1; Paul Lashmer and John Hooper, 'FO has "lost" key rock document', *Observer* 28 May 1989, p2.
101 Wright (1987).
102 Dalyell (1988 pp166–91); Turnbull (1988); Lord Scarman, 'A good day for the law – and a blow on behalf of the people', *Independent* 14 October 1988, p20.
103 Leigh (1988); David Leigh, 'Spycatchers who dabbled in treason', *Observer* 16 October 1988, pp33–4; David Leigh, 'MI5 and the minister's wife', *Observer* 23 October 1988, pp33–4.
104 Ramsay (1988).
105 Wallace (1990).
106 Stalker (1989); Taylor (1990).
107 Dorril (no date).
108 Andrew Vietch, 'How you have been hearing only one side of the stories', *Guardian* 13 August 1986, p11; David Hencke, 'Oxford dole fraud claims scaled down to £16,000', *Guardian* 4 January 1983; Melvyn Marcus, 'Why Ridley must go', *Observer* 27 May 1990, p28; Scrutator, 'Inspector Ridley's blind eye', *Independent on Sunday* (Business) 27 May 1990, p8; David Pallister, 'Thatcher gives spur to sanction-busters', *Guardian* 7 February 1989, p8; Hugo Young, 'The price of jobs for the cabinet boys', *Guardian* 12 June 1990, p19; Robert Harris, 'It's time to take a sharp look at the boardroom politicians', *Sunday Times* 17 June 1990, pp3, 8; Insight, 'Superrich in massive tax dodge', *Sunday Times* 21 October 1990, p1; 'The Artful Dodgers' ibid, pp1, 16–17.
109 Thatcher (1989a pp28, 83, 85, 187).
110 Home Office (1990b); Home Office (1990a).
111 Black (1980); Townsend and Davidson (1982); Health Education Council (1987).
112 Webster (1989 p170 Table 13.1).
113 Labour Party (1987b p44).
114 Kings Fund Institute (1989).
115 Roberts (17 November 1989 p2, 23 March 1990 p5).
116 Graham and Clarke (1986 p36).
117 Sunday Correspondent: Personal Finance. Janice Allan, 'Premiums soar above inflation' and Maria Scott, 'Private Health cover not a cure for all', 29 October 1989, p28; Adam Raphael, 'Exposed: The private health care rip-off', *Observer* (Open File), 8 April 1990, p6.
118 Labour Party (1987b pp41–6); Annabel Ferriman, 'Waiting lists soar despite £30 million blitz', *Observer* 9 October 1988, p3; Jeremy Laurance and Jo Reville, 'Hospital waiting lists rising again', *Sunday Times* 13 November 1989, pA1; Michael Durham, 'Queue at the hospitals grows to record 1 million: One in five has to wait a year for NHS operation', *Sunday Times* 21 October 1990, pp1, 3.

119 David Utting, 'The Policies that lead to destitution', *Sunday Correspondent* 12 November 1989, p12; Roberts (9 February 1989 p4 – Homelessness); Christian Wolmar, 'Revealed: Rising Tide of Homelessness', *Observer* 6 November 1988, p8.

120 Wolmar ibid; Platt (1989); Roberts (23 March 1990 p5 – House Building); Murie (1989 p221).

121 Edward Pickering, 'Dwindling Rights of Teenagers', *Observer* Sunday 26 March 1989, p6; Shelter (1988); Maev Kennedy, 'Disabled lose in "survival of fittest" housing policy', *Guardian* 7 June 1988, p6.

122 Roberts (22 December 1989 p2 – Council rent arrears); Roberts (5 May 1990 p5 – Mortgages); Platt (1989 ref repossessions).

123 Department of the Environment (1989); Alan Travis, 'Creeping improvement in state of nation's houses', *Guardian* 29 November 1989, p2; Roberts (7 April 1989 p2 – Renovation Grants).

124 Thatcher (1989a p130); Roberts (22 December 1989 p2 – House Prices); Murie (1989 p217 Table 16.2).

125 Letter from 7 Directors of Housing, *Guardian* 31 May 1988, p18.

126 Plender (1990).

127 Wright (1977 pp190–7); Reynolds and Sullivan (1987); Reynolds (1987).

128 Tomlinson (1989 p191 – pupil–teacher ratios); Roberts (7 July 1989 p2 – Teachers); Liz Lightfoot, 'Scandal of our Schools' *Daily Mail* 27 May 1990, pp1–2; Roberts (21 April 1989 p2 – Education Capital Investment); Tomlinson (1989 p190).

129 Nick Wood, 'Sir Keith to keep exams nuclear free' *Times Education Supplement* 18 March 1983; Judith Judd, 'History dons object to PM's interference' *Observer* 2 August 1989, p2; Auriol Stevens, 'Lessons Japan can teach the West', *Observer* 19 December 1982, p24.

130 Roberts (23 March 1990 p5 – Youth Training); *Independent on Sunday* (Business) Focus 28 January 1990, p17.

131 UNESCO (1987 4.11–4.17).

132 Data: OECD (March 1986); SIPRI (1989) – author's calculations.

133 Cited in Abse (1989 p24).

134 Cited in Gellner (1968 [1959] p273n).

135 Burgess (1977).

136 Warnock (1989).

137 Scott (1989).

138 Conrad Russell, 'Baker's fig-leaf fails to hide flaws in loan scheme for students', *Sunday Times* 13 November, 1988, p112; Judith Judd, 'Student loans will not pay for 100 years', *Observer* 2 July 1989, p4.

139 James Meikie, 'University job cuts feared as Bristol reveals debts of £4 m.', *Guardian* 20 November 1990, p1.

140 Manwaring and Sigler (1985); Labour Party (1987b); Rentoul (1987); Brown (1989).

141 Brown (1989 p132).

142 Brown (1989 p137).

143 Brown (1989, p126).

144 Roberts (24 March 1990 p4 – Supplementary Benefit).

145 Labour Party (1987b pp99–103 for pensioners); Office of Population Censuses and Surveys (1988), also Annabel Ferriman, 'Four Million

disabled live in poverty', *Observer* 6 November 1988, p2; Nikki Knewstub, 'Responses soon to Griffiths report', *Guardian* 27 June 1990, p5 – on Care in the Community; Stephen Cook, 'Community care is a farce inquest told', *Guardian* 9 October 1990, p2; Victor Smart 'Gilmour Slams Tory "Hypocrisy"', *Observer* 6 November 1988, p2; Patrick Wintour, 'Changing attitudes shake family values', *Guardian* 9 October 1990, p6.

146   Adam Raphael 'Scandal of the real scroungers', *Observer* 23 October 1988, p8; Roberts (21 April 1989 p2 – Family Credit Uptake).

147   Sarah Lonsdale 'Charities axe staff as councils cut cash aid' *Observer* 16 September 1990, p7; Charities Aid Foundation (1989); Madelaine Bunting, 'Firms cutting donations to charities', *Guardian* 7 November 1989, p2; Tim Miller, 'Charities hit by volunteer shortages', *Observer* 12 November 1989, p4; Tim Kelsey, 'The rattle of tins fall on deaf ears', *Independent on Sunday* 25 November 1990, p8.

148   Colin Brown, 'Howe stresses need to raise standards in social services', *Independent* 5 June 1989, p8.

149   Brown (1989 pp119–23).

150   Christopher Huhne, 'Gap between high and low pay greatest since 1886', *Independent* 30 September 1990, p1; Department of Employment (1990).

151   Wilson (1989 pp13–21).

152   *Daily Telegraph* editorial, 'Intrusive Body', 14 May 1983, p14; *Daily Telegraph* editorial, 'MPs' Pay', 9 July 1983, p12; Julian Critchley, 'Your MP – you pay for what you get', *Daily Telegraph*, 3 May 1986, p14.

153   *Sunday Times* editorial, 'The under-valued engineer', 29 July 1981, p13.

154   *Sunday Times* (1990 p33); *Guardian*, 'The working class lives on says judge', 27 November 1990, p8.

155   Conservative Manifesto (1987); Jenkins (1987); Crewe (1989 p244).

156   Nicholas Wapshott, Sarah Lonsdale and William Keegan, 'UK dives into recession', *Observer* 23 September 1990, p1; David Bowen, 'Rate of business failures highest for 10 years', *Independent on Sunday* (Business) 25 November 1990, p3.

157   Crewe (1989 pp246–8 – for 1979 data); Gallup Poll '9 out of 10 say put more money into the health service' *Daily Telegraph* 28 October 1983, p12.

158   Crewe (1988); Crewe (1989); King (1989); Rentoul (1989); Jacobs and Worcester (1990).

159   Crewe (1988, p36 – for unemployment versus inflation); Crewe (1989 – for guarantees of a steady job, and privatisation data); Crewe (1989 p248 – for views on trade unions; p242 – for views on rewards for caring, and collective welfare provision); Crewe (1989 – on council house building); Crewe (1988 p34 – for social welfare benefits; p41 – for national pride data).

160   Jacobs and Worcester (1990); see also *The Times* 4 July 1990, p9, 'Mrs Thatcher's crusade against socialism has failed'; Crewe (1988 p41); Rentoul (1989 p27); *Independent on Sunday* NMR Poll, 4 November 1990, p20.

161   Murie, (1989 p224); John Willock, 'Inner City renewal programme wound down', *Guardian* 9 October 1990, p20; Hugh O'Shaughnessy and Geoffrey Lean, 'Britain to be sued over dirty water', *Observer* 17 September 1989, p1; Roberts (7 April 1989 p2 – River Pollution).

162   Roberts (7 July 1989 p2 – food safety); Roberts (24 March 1989 p2 – Health and Safety Inspectors).

163   David Wastell and Robert Porter, 'Report on Piper Alpha damning', *Sunday Telegraph* 11 November 1990, p1; Christopher Leake, 'Fatal Flaws in Piper Alpha', *Mail on Sunday* 11 November 1990, p6; Roberts (8 December 1989 p2 – Rail Collisions); David Norris, 'Crash wiring at fault', *Daily Mail* 17 December 1988, p9; Roberts (9 June 1990 p3 – British Rail subsidy); Maeve Kennedy, 'British transport the worst in Europe', *Guardian* 15 May 1990, p1; George Pitcher, 'Transport policy off the rails', *Observer* 14 January 1990.

164   Neil Ascherson, 'I'll show you something that'll make you change your mind', *Independent on Sunday* 8 July 1990, p19; Mick Brown, 'Begging: the latest free market growth industry', *Sunday Times* 18 September 1988, p113; Thatcher (1977 p4).

165   Church of England (1985, 1990); Susannah Herbert and David Hughes, 'Church damns Tory reforms', *Sunday Times* 28 January 1990, p1; Alison Smith and Richard Palmer, 'Church and State clash on poor', *Sunday Times* 26 November 1989, pA2; *Observer*, 'Methodist attacks MP', 25 June 1989, p2; Walter Schwartz, 'Voice of urban protest heard in the wilderness', *Guardian* 27 December 1988, p16.

166   Thatcher (1989b, pp249–55); Raban (1989).

167   *Constitutional Reform* (1986); *New Statesman and Society* (1988): Charter 88; *Samizdat* (1988); Neuberger (1987); Thornton (1989); Hillyard and Percy-Smith (1989).

168   Julian Rollins, 'Scientists gagged in supermilk row', also Comment, *Today* 8 August 1989, pp12, 10; editorial, 'Secrets Bill: Publish and be jailed', *Observer* 5 February 1989, p12; Norton-Taylor (1985).

169   Editorial, 'Keepers of secrets, tellers of tales', *Observer* 11 September 1988, p14; Ken Hyder, 'Government Taps 30,000 phone lines', *Observer* 30 October 1988, p12; Hollingworth and Norton-Taylor (1988).

170   Dalyell (1988 pp61–9); Shenfield (1989 pp26–8); Dowd (1990).

171   Adam Raphael, 'Cabinet rift over secrecy', *Observer* 19 June 1988, p6; Jenkins and Hutchings (1988).

172   Raphael (ibid).

173   Common Voice (1990); Zander (1985); IPPR (1990).

174   Nairn (1981, 1988); Campaign for a Scottish Assembly (1988); *New Statesman and Society* (1988); Wilson (1989); Charter 88 (1990); Ascherson (1990); Benn (1990).

175   Personal communications to the author from Patrick Cormack 31 January 1990; Reg Prentice 1 February 1990; Max Beloff 17 January 1990; Alun Gwynne-Jones 22 January 1990; Kingsley Amis 18 January 1990; Hugh Thomas 20 January 1990. Other material in: John Mortimer interview with Kingsley Amis, 'Would you take a man like him', *Sunday Times* 18 September 1988, pG8; Edward Pearce, 'An anti-revolution outburst that was born of ignorance', *Sunday Times* 16 July 1989, pB3; Edward Pearce, 'Icons of the Right: Heseltine', *Samizdat* No 10 May/June 1990, p27; Johnson (1990).

176   Ref: Cormack ibid; Prentice ibid; Beloff ibid; Amis ibid; Amis quoted in Mortimer ibid; Pearce in *Samizdat* ibid; Thatcher (1989a p85).

177   Patrick Cormack, 'End of term for the Atlee of the Tories', *Independent* 8 August 1989, p15.

178   Michael White, 'Howe assault puts PM on the alert', *Guardian* 4 November 1990, p1.

179   The events were comprehensively covered in all newspapers on 23 November, especially *Daily Telegraph, The Times, Daily Mail, Independent* and *Guardian*.

180   Andrew Grice and David Smith, 'Tories still support Thatcher's European Stance', *Sunday Times* 4 November 1990, p1.12; Julia Langdon and David Wastell, 'Heseltine ready to fight Thatcher', *Sunday Telegraph* 4 November 1990, p1; Stephen Castle, 'Voters want Thatcher to quit', *The Independent on Sunday* 4 November 1990, pp1, 20 (NMR Poll); Andrew Grice, 'Polls say Tories would do better under Heseltine', *Sunday Times* 18 November 1990, p1; Peter Dobbie and Richard Heller, 'Marginals say no to Thatcher', *Mail on Sunday* 18 November 1990, pp1, 3; ref Castle (ibid) for data on voters' views of Margaret Thatcher; *Sunday Times* editorial, 18 November 1990, p3.7; Nicholas Wapshott, 'Booming Lib-Dems cast more gloom over Thatcher', *Observer* 18 November 1990, p2.

181   Norman Macrae, 'Tarzan's government of all the apes', *Sunday Times* 18 November 1990, p3.6 for views on insulted MPs; Thatcher (1977 p54); Robert Harris, 'Thatcher is now for burning – win or lose', *Sunday Times* 18 November 1990, p3.6.

182   Quoted in Nicholas Wapshott, 'She will be winged and bleeding', *Observer* 18 November 1990, p21.

183   Heseltine, in an interview with Michael Jones, 'Rough, Radical and Ready for Action', *Sunday Times* 18 November 1990, p1.15.

184   Jacobs and Worcester (1990).

185   Honderich (1990).

186   Lipsey (1981).

BIBLIOGRAPHY

Abse, L. (1989) *Margaret, daughter of Beatrice: A Politician's Psycho-Biography of Margaret Thatcher*, Cape, London.

Allen, G. C. (1979) *The British Disease: A short essay on the causes of the nation's lagging wealth (1976)*, Hobart Paper 67, Institute for Economic Affairs, London.

Allison, L. (1986) *Right Principles: A Conservative Philosophy of Politics*, Blackwell, Oxford.

Anderson, M. J. (1986) *The Unfinished Agenda: Essays on the political economy of government policy in honour of Arthur Seldon*, Institute for Economic Affairs, London.

Armytage, W. H. G. (1961) *A Social History of Engineering*, Faber & Faber, London.

Ascherson, N. (1990) 'The only safe way of handling power is to distribute it', *Independent on Sunday* 15 July, p21.

Bacon, F. (1975) *The Advancement of Learning*, Armstrong, William A. (ed), Athlone Press, London.

Bacon, R. & Eltis W. (1976) *Britain's Economic Problem: Too Few Producers*, Hutchinson, London.

Barnett, A. (1984) 'The Failed Consensus', in Curran (1984), pp138–47.

Barry, B. (1989) *Does Society Exist? The Case for Socialism*, Fabian Society, Tract 536, London.

Barry, N. et al. (1984) *Hayek's 'Serfdom' revisited*, Institute for Economic Affairs, London.

Barry, N. (1987) *The New Right*, Croom Helm, London.

Barry, N. (1988) *The Invisible Hand in Economics and Politics*, Hobart Paper No 111, Institute for Economic Affairs, London.

Barth, H. (1976) *Truth and Ideology*, University of California Press, London.

Belsay, A. (1986) 'The New Right, Social Order and Civil Liberties', in Levitas (1986), pp167–97.

Benn, T. (1979) *The Case for a Constitutional Premiership*, Institute for Workers' Control, Pamphlet No 67, Nottingham.

Benn, T. (1980) *Arguments for Socialism*, Penguin, Harmondsworth.

Benn, T. (1982) *Tony Benn on the Falklands War*, Spokesman Pamphlet No 79, Nottingham.

Benn, T. (1990) *The Commonwealth of Britain Bill*, Draft 4: Manuscript,October.

Benne, K. C. (1970) 'F.S.C. Northrop and the Logic of Ideological Reconstruction', *Educational Theory* (20), Spring, pp99–120.

Benton, S. (1987) 'The Hardening on the Right', *New Statesman*, Vol 113 (2919), 6 March, pp19–22.

Benton, T. (1982) 'Realism, power and objective interests', in Graham, K. (1982) *Contemporary Political Philosophy*, Cambridge University Press, Cambridge.

Beresford, P. (1990) 'Britain's Rich: The Top 200', *Sunday Times Magazine* 8 April, pp33–65.

Berlin, I. (1958) *Two Concepts of Liberty*, Clarendon Press, Oxford.

Bevan, A. (1978) *In Place of Fear* [1952], Quartet, London.

Black, D. (1980) *Inequalities in Health*, Department of Health and Social Security, London. Typescript, restricted circulation. Ref Townsend and Davidson (1982).

Blackburn, R. (1967) 'The Unequal Society', in Blackburn and Cockburn (1967), pp15–55.

Blackburn, R. & Cockburn, A. (1967) *The Incompatibles: Trade Union Militancy and the Consensus*, Penguin/New Left Review, London.

Booker, C. (1970) *The Neophiliacs*, Fontana, London.

Bosanquet, N. (1983) *After the New Right*, Heinemann, London.

Bottomore, T. (1970) *Elites in Society*, Penguin, Harmondsworth.

Bowen, D. (1990) *Shaking the Iron Universe*, Hodder & Stoughton, London.

Brittan, S. (1975) *Participation without Politics*, Hobart Paper Special 62, Institute for Economic Affairs, London.

Brittan, S. (1988) *A Restatement of Economic Liberalism* (1973), Macmillan, London.

Brittan, S. (1989) 'The Thatcher Government's Economic Policy', in Kavanagh and Seldon (eds) (1989), pp1–37.

Brown, G. (1988) 'Some Miracle', *Labour Party News* No 12, November/December, p19. (Abridged from Hansard.)

Brown, G. (1989) *Where There is Greed* ... Mainstream, Edinburgh.

Buchanan, A. E. (1982) *Marx and Justice: The Radical Critique of Liberalism*, Rowland & Allanhead, Totowa, N. J.

Buchanan, A. E. (1985) *Ethics, Efficiency and the Market*, Clarendon Press, Oxford.

Buchanan, J. M. (1968) *The Demand and Supply of Public Goods*, Rand McNally, Chicago.

Buchanan, J. M. (1981) 'An American Perspective: From "Markets Work" to Public Choice', in Seldon (1981), pp79–97.

Bulmer, S. (ed) (1989) *The Changing Agenda of West German Public Policy*, Dartmouth, Aldershot.

Burgess, T. (1977) *Education After School*, Penguin, Harmondsworth.

Burke, E. (1969) *Reflections on the Revolution in France* [1770], in O'Brien, C. C. (ed), Penguin, Harmondsworth.

Burton, J. (1983) *Picking Losers ...? The Political Economy of Industrial Policy*, Institute for Economic Affairs, London.

Butler, E. (1983) *Hayek: His contribution to the political and economic thought of our time*, Temple Smith, London.

Butler, E., Pirie, M. & Young, P. (eds) (1989) *The Omega File*, Adam Smith Institute, London.

Cairncross, A. (1985) *Years of Recovery: British Economic Policy 1945–51*, Methuen, London.

Campaign for a Scottish Assembly. (1988) *A Claim of Right for Scotland*, Report of the Constitutional Steering Committee, Scottish Constitutional Convention, July, Edinburgh.

Casey, J. (1978) 'Tradition and Authority', in Cowling (1978), pp82–100.

Cassels, J. (1990) *Britain's Real Skills Shortage*, Policy Studies Institute, London.

Cecil, H. Lord. (1912) *Conservatism*, Williams & Norgate, London.

Charities Aid Foundation. (1989) *Charity Trends* (12th edn), Charities Aid Foundation, Tonbridge, Kent.

Charter 88. (1990) *Make a Date with Democracy*, Proceedings of Charter 88's first Constitutional Assembley, London, 14 July, 1990. Charter 88, London.

Church of England (1985) *Faith in the City*, Church House Publishing, London.

Church of England (1990) *Living Faith in the City*, Church House Publishing, London.

Clarke, W. (1967) *The City in the World Economy*, Penguin, Harmondworth.

Cliff, T. (1975) *The Crisis: Social Contract or Socialism*, Pluto, London.

Cockburn, A. (1989) 'Scenes from an Inferno', *New Statesman and Society*, 2 (49), pp14–15.

Collard, D. (1968) *The New Right: A Critique*, Fabian Tract 387, Fabian Society, London.

Common Voice. (1990) *The Intelligent Persons Guide to Electoral Reform*, Common Voice/New Statesman and Society, London.

Cmnd 3888. (1969) *In Place of Strife: A Policy for Industrial Relations*, HMSO, London.

Congdon, T. (1978) *Monetarism: An Essay in Definition*, Centre for Policy Studies, London.

Conservative Central Office. (1979) *The Conservative Manifesto 1979*.

Conservative Central Office. (1983) *The Conservative Manifesto 1983*.

Conservative Central Office. (1987) *The Conservative Manifesto 1987*.

Conservative Research Department. (1989) *The Economy*, Politics Today No 13, London.

Constitutional Reform Society. (1986) *The Quarterly Review, Constitutional Reform*, Vol 1 No 1, Spring 1986, London.

Cooper, M. H. & Culyer, A. J. (1968) *The Price of Blood*, Hobart Paper 41, Institute for Economic Affairs, London.

Cormack, P. (ed) (1978) *Right Turn: Eight men who changed their minds*, Leo Cooper, London.

Correspondent. (1989) 'The Decade of Extremes', *The Sunday Correspondent*, 24 December.

Cosgrave, P. (1975) *Margaret Thatcher: Prime Minister*, Arrow, London.

Coutts, K. & Godley, W. (1989) 'The Economic Record of Mrs Thatcher', *Political Quarterly*, 60 (20), pp137–51.

Cowling, M. (ed) (1978) *Conservative Essays*, Cassell, London.

Cowling, M. (1989) 'The Sources of the New Right', *Encounter*, Vol LXXIII No 4, November, pp3–13.

Crewe, I. (1982) 'The Labour Party and the Electorate', in Kavanagh, D. (ed) *The Politics of the Labour Party*, Allen & Unwin, London.

Crewe, I. (1988) 'Has the electorate become Thatcherite?' in Skidelski (1988 pp25–49).

Crewe, I. (1989) 'Values: The Crusade that Failed', in Kavanagh and Seldon (eds) (1989), pp239–50.

Crick, B. (1985) '3 out of 10 for McCowan', *New Statesman*, 109 (2814) 22 February, pp16–17.

Crosland, C. A. R. (1964) *The Future of Socialism* [1956], Cape, London.

Crossland, B. (1989) 'The life-long education and training of mechanical engineers' (1988 George Stephenson Lecture), *Proceedings of the Institute of Mechanical Engineers*, Vol 203, pp139–44.

Cruddas, J. (1990) *Restructuring Work Relations in the 1980s*, unpublished PhD. dissertation, University of Warwick.

Culyer, A. J. (1981) 'The IEA's Unorthodoxy', in Seldon (ed) (1981), pp99–119.

Curran, J. (ed) (1984) *The Future of Socialism*, Polity/New Socialist, London.

Dahrendorf, R. (1976) 'This Britain', *Observer*, 4 January, p7.

Dahrendorf, R. (1982) *On Britain*, British Broadcasting Corporation, London.

Dalyell, T. (1988) *Misrule*, New English Library/Hodder and Stoughton, London.

Day, P. (1986) 'Is the concept of freedom essentially contestible?' *Philosophy*, No 61 (235), January, pp116–23.

Deakin, G. (ed) (1986) *The New Right: Images and Reality*, Runimede Trust, London.

Dennis, N. & Halsey, A. H. (1988) *English Ethical Socialism*, Oxford University Press, Oxford.

Department of Employment. (1988) *New Earnings Survey*, Department of Employment, London.

Department of the Environment. (1989) *English House Condition Survey*, Department of the Environment, London.

Dilnot, A. & Kell, M. (1988) 'The effect of reduction of income tax on incentives', *Fiscal Studies*, Vol 9 No 4, Institute for Fiscal Studies, London.

Dorril, S. (no date) 'Blood revenge: The aftermath of the assassination of Airey Neave', *Lobster*, No 8, pp18–22.

Dowd, K. (1990) 'Keynes: The Story So Far', *Review of Macroeconomic Policy* by Weale, M. et al. (1989), Unwin Hyman, London. *Times Higher Education Supplement*, 11 May, p24.

Eatwell, R. & O'Sullivan, N. (1989) *The Nature of the Right: European and American Political Thought since 1789*, Pinter, London.

Eccleshall, R. (1978) *Order and Reason in Politics*, University of Hull Press, Oxford.

Eccleshall, R. (1984a) 'The World of Ideology', in Eccleshall et al. (1984), pp7–36.

Eccleshall, R. (1984b) 'Conservatism', in Eccleshall et al. (1984), pp79–114.

Eccleshall, R. (1990) *English Conservatism since the Restoration: An Introduction and Anthology*, Unwin Hyman, London.

Eccleshall, R., Geoghegan, V., Jay, R. & Wilford R. (1984) *Political Ideologies*, Hutchinson, London.

Economic Affairs. (1989) *Mrs Thatcher's Decade*, Economic Affairs, Vol 10 (2), December/January, Institute for Economic Affairs, London.

Economist Editorial. (1990) 'The Modern Adam Smith', *Economist*, 316 (7663), pp11–12.

Ecoropa. (1982) *Falklands War: The Disturbing Truth*, Ecoropa Information Sheet II, Powys.

Edgar, D. (1984) 'Bitter Harvest', in Curran (1984), pp39–57.

Edgeley, R. (1978) 'Education for Industry', *Radical Philosophy*, (19), Spring, pp18–23. Reprinted from *Educational Research*, 20 (1), November 1977, pp26–32.

Einzig, P. (1969) *Decline and Fall? Britain's Crisis in the Sixties*, Macmillan, London.

Elbaum, B. & Lazonick, W. (eds) (1986) *The Decline of the British Economy*, Clarendon, Oxford.

Emden, C. S. (1962) *The People and the Constitution*, Oxford University Press, Oxford.

Entreves, A. P. de. (1970) *Natural Law*, Hutchinson, London.

Evans, P., Rueschmeyer, D. & Skocpol, T. (1985) *Bringing the State Back In*, Cambridge University Press, Cambridge.

Fabian Society. (1990) *The Reform of Direct Taxation: Report of the Fabian Taxation Reform Committtee*, Fabian Society, London.

Fay, S. & Young, H. (1978) 'The Day the Pound Nearly Died', *Sunday Times*, 14, 21, 28 May.

Field, F. (1981) *Inequality in Britain*, Fontana, London.

Finer, H. (1946) *The Road to Reaction*, Dennis Dobson, London.

Flather, P. (1985) 'High Priest, Mad Monk, or Seeker after Truth?', *Times Higher Education Supplement*, 11 January, p11.

Flew, A. G. N. (1981) *The Politics of Procrustes*, Temple Smith, London.

Flew, A. G. N. (1989) *Equality in Liberty and Justice*, Routledge, London.

Floorsman, S. C. (1976) *The Existential Pleasures of Engineering*, Barrie & Jenkins, London.

Foot, P. (1968) *The Politics of Harold Wilson*, Penguin, Harmondsworth.

Forbes, I. & Smith S. (eds) (1983) *Politics and Human Nature*, Francis Pinter, London.

Forsyth, M. (1988) 'Hayek's Bizarre Liberalism: A Critique', *Political Studies*, XXXVI (2), pp235–50.

Franco, P. (1990) *The Political Philosophy of Michael Oakshott*, Yale University Press, London.

Friedman, I. (1972) *Inflation: Worldwide Disaster*, Hamish Hamilton, London.

Friedman, M. (1962) *Capitalism and Freedom*, Chicago University Press, Chicago.

Friedman, M. (1970) *The Counter-Revolution in Monetary Theory*, Occasional Paper No 33, Institute for Economic Affairs, London.

Friedman, M. (1974) *Monetary Correction*, Occasional Paper No 41, Institute for Economic Affairs, London.

Friedman, M. (1977) *From Galbraith to Economic Freedom*, Occasional Paper No 49, Institute for Economic Affairs, London.

Friedman M. & Friedman R. (1980) *Free to Choose*, Secker & Warburg, London.

Fuller, R. (1980) *Inflation: The Rising Cost of Living on a Small Planet*, Worldwatch, London.

Gallie, B. (1956) 'Essentially Contested Concepts', *Proceedings of the Aristotelian Society*, 56, 12 March, pp167–98.

Gamble, A. (1988) *The Free Economy and the Strong State*, Macmillan, London.

Garner, L. (1979) *The NHS: Your Money or Your Life*, Penguin, Harmondsworth.

Gavshon, A. & Rice, D. (1984) *The Sinking of the Belgrano*, Secker and Warburg/New English Library, London.

Gellner, E. (1968) *Words and Things* [1959], Penguin, Harmondsworth.

Gilmour, I. (1978) *Inside Right: A Study of Conservatism*, Quartet, London.

Gilmour, P. (1976) 'The Tax Backlash', *Sunday Times*, 16 May, p17.

Girvin, B. (1987) 'Conservatism and Political Change in Britain and the U.S.A.', *Parliamentary Affairs*, No 40, April, pp154–71.

Glyn, A. (1982) *Economic Aspects of the Coal Industry Dispute*, National Union of Mineworkers, Barnsley.

Glyn, A. (1984a) 'Propped up with prejudice', *Guardian*, 7 August, p17.

Glyn, A. (1984b) *The economic case against pit closures*, National Union of Mineworkers, Sheffield.

Godley, W. (1988) 'Why I won't apologise', *Observer*, 18 September, p14.

Goffee, R. & Scase, R. (1979) 'Have the Tory gurus got it right?', *Guardian*, 14 September.

Goffee, R. & Scase, R. (1990) *Reluctant Managers: their work and lifestyles*, Unwin Hyman, London.

Goldthorpe, J., Llewellyn, C. & Payne, C. (1980) *Social Mobility and Class Structure in Modern Britain*, Clarendon Press, Oxford.

Gorer, G. (1966) *The Danger of Equality*, Cressett, London.

Gould, B. (1985) *Socialism and Freedom*, Macmillan, London.

Gould, D. S. (1984) *On the Spot: The Sinking of the Belgrano*, Cecil Wolf, London.

Gould, D. S. (ed) (1988) *Report of the Assessors on the Belgrano Inquiry*, Belgrano Action Group, Cirencester.

Graham, D. & Clarke, P. (1986) *The New Enlightenment*, Macmillan/Channel 4 TV, London.

Grant, R. A. D. (1988) 'Michael Oakshott', in Scruton (1988a), pp275–94.

Gray, J. (1989) *Limited Government: A positive agenda*, Hobart Paper 113, Institute for Economic Affairs, London.

Gray, R. (1971) *Rolls on the Rocks: The Story of Rolls-Royce*, Panther, London.

Green, B. (1986) *Monetarism and Morality*, Centre for Policy Studies, London.

Green, D. G. (1987) *The New Right: The Counter Revolution in Political, Economic and Social Thought*, Harvester, Brighton.

Green, T. H. (1931) *Lectures on the Principles of Political Obligation*, Longmans, Green, London.

Green, T. H. (1969) 'The Limits of Lassez-Faire' in Kauvar, G. B. & Surendon, G. C. (èds), *The Victorian Mind*, Cassell in association with the Victorian Society, London, pp156–65.

Griffiths, B. (1982) *Morality and the Market Place*, Hodder and Stoughton, London.

Grisewood, H. (1966) *Ideas and Beliefs of the Victorians* [1949], Dutton, New York.

Hailsham, Lord. (1976) 'Elective Dictatorship' (Dimbleby Lecture), *Listener*, Vol 96 (2480), pp16–17.

Hailsham, Lord. (1978) *The Dilemma of Democracy*, Collins, London.

Hall, S. & Jacques, M. (eds) (1983) *The Politics of Thatcherism*, Lawrence & Wishart, London.

Halsey, A. H. (1978) *Change in British Society*, Oxford University Press, Oxford.

Halsey, A. H., Heath, A. F. & Ridge, J. M. (1980) *Origins and Destinations: family, class and education in modern Britain*, Oxford University Press, Oxford.

Harper, K. & Wintour, P. (1985) 'The bitter battle that ended an era', *Guardian*, 5 March, pp15–18.

Harris, L. (1966) *Long to Reign Over Us? The status of the Royal family in the 1960s*, William Kimber, London.

Harris, R. (1980) *The Challenge of a Radical Reactionary*, Centre for Policy Studies, London.

Harris, R. (1986) *Morality and Markets*, Centre for Policy Studies, London.

Harris, R. (1989) *The Conservative Community*, Centre for Policy Studies, London.

Harris, R. & Seldon, A. (1977) *Not from Benevolence ... 20 Years of Economic Dissent*, Hobart Paperback No 10, Institute for Economic Affairs, London.

Haseler, S. (1976) *The Death of British Democracy*, Elek, London.

Haseler, S. (1989) *The Battle for Britain: Thatcher and the New Liberals*, I. B. Tauris, London.

Hattersley, R. (1987) *Choose Freedom: The Future of Democratic Socialism*, Penguin, Harmondsworth.

Hayek, F. A. (no date) *Rules, Perception and Intelligibility*, Proceedings of the British Academy, Vol XLVIII, London, pp321–44.

Hayek, F. A. (1955) *The Counter Revolution in Science*, Collier-Macmillan, London.

Hayek, F. A. (1960) *The Constitution of Liberty*, Routledge & Kegan Paul, London.

Hayek, F. A. (1968) *The Confusion of Language in Political Thought*, Occasional Paper 20, Institute for Economic Affairs, London.

Hayek, F. A. (1973a) *Economic Freedom and Representative Government*, Occasional Paper 39, Institute for Economic Affairs, London.

Hayek, F. A. (1973b) *Law, Legislation and Liberty: Vol I: Rules and Order*, Routledge & Kegan Paul, London.

Hayek, F. A. (1975) *Full Employment at Any Price?* Occasional Paper 45, Institute for Economic Affairs, London.

Hayek, F. A. (1976) *Law, Legislation and Liberty: Vol II: The Mirage of Social Justice*, Routledge & Kegan Paul, London.

Hayek, F. A. (1978) *A Tiger by the Tail: The Keynesian Legacy of Inflation* (2nd edn), Hobart Paperback 4. Institute for Economic Affairs, London.

Hayek, F. A. (1979a) *The Road to Serfdom* [1944], Routledge & Kegan Paul, London.

Hayek, F. A. (1979b) *Law, Legislation and Liberty: Vol III: The Political Order of a Free People*, Routledge & Kegan Paul, London.

Hayek, F. A. (1983) *Knowledge, Evolution and Society*, Adam Smith Institute, London.

Hayek, F. A. (1986) 'The Moral Imperative of the Market', in Seldon, A. (ed) (1986) *The Unfinished Agenda*, Institute for Economic Affairs, London, pp143–9.

Hayek, F. A. (1988) 'The Weasel Word "Social"', in Scruton (1988b), pp49–54.

Healey, D. (1990) *The Time of My Life*, Penguin, Harmondsworth.

Healey, N. M. (1989) 'Is Monetarism Dead at Last?' in *Economic Affairs* Vol 10 (2), January/December, pp18–23.

Health Education Council. (1987) *The Health Divide*, Health Education Council, London.

Heath, A., Jowell, R & Curtice, J. (1985) *How Britain Votes*, Pergamon, Oxford.

Hendry, D. F. & Ericsson, N. R. (1984) *Assertions without empirical basis: An economic appraisal of 'Monetary Trends in ... the United Kingdom' by Milton Friedman and Anna Schwartz*, Bank of England, London.

Hennessy, P. (1989) 'The Civil Service', in Kavanagh and Seldon (eds) (1989), pp114–23.

Heseltine, M. (1989) *The Democratic Deficit: The Balance in Europe for Britain to Redress*, Centre for Policy Studies, London.

Hills, J. (1989) *Changing Tax*, Child Poverty Action Group, London.

Hillyard, P. & Percy-Smith, J. (1988) *The Coercive State*, Fontana, London.

Himmelfarb, G. (1987) *Victorian Values and Twentieth-century Condescension*, Centre for Policy Studies, London.

Hirst, P. (1987) 'Can Socialism Live?', in *New Statesman*, Vol 113 (2919), 6 March, pp6–10.

Hirst, P. (1989) *After Thatcher*, Collins, London.

Hirst, P. & Zeitlin, J. (1988) 'Crisis, What Crisis?' in *New Statesman*, Vol 115 (2973), 18 March, pp10–12.

Hobhouse, L. T. (1911) *Liberalism*, Oxford University Press, Oxford.

Hodgson, G. (1986) 'How the upper class gets away with it', *New Statesman*, Vol 111 (2882), 20 June, pp10–11.

Hogg, Q. (1947) *The Case for Conservatism*, Penguin, West Drayton.

Hollingworth, M. & Norton-Taylor, R. (1988) *Blacklist: The inside story of political vetting*, Hogarth Press, London.

Home Office. (1990a) *The Police and Public in England and Wales*, Home Office Research Study 117, HMSO, London.

Home Office. (1990b) *Trends in crime and their interpretation: a study of crime in post-war England and Wales*, Home Office Research Study 119, HMSO, London.

Honderich, T. (1990) *Conservatism*, Hamish Hamilton, London.

Hudson Institute. (1974) *The United Kingdom in 1980: The Hudson Report* (The Hudson Institute Europe), Associated Business Programmes, London.

Hughes, J. & Moore, R. (1972) *A Special Case*, Penguin, Harmondsworth.

Huhne, C. (1980) 'Chilly wind from Chicago', *Guardian*, 1 March, p15.

Huhne, C. (1983) 'Why Milton's monetarism is bunk', *Guardian*, 15 December, p19.

Huhne, C. (1990a) *Real World Economies: Essays in Imperfect Markets*, Macmillan, London.

Huhne, C. (1990b) 'The sons of Adam Smith seek path to new enlightenment', *Independent on Sunday*, 15 July, pp12–14.

Hume, D. (1970) *Moral and Political Philosophy*, Aiken H. D. (ed), Hafner, New York.

Hyman, R. (1989) *Strikes*, Macmillan, London.

IEA. (ed) (1974) *The Long Debate on Poverty*, Institute for Economic Affairs, London.

IEA. (ed) (1989) *Ideas, Interests and Consequences*, Institute for Economic Affairs, London.

IISS. (1990) *Miltary Balance 1989–90*, International Institute for Strategic Studies, Brasseys, London.

Illich, I. (1973) *Deschooling Society*, Penguin, Harmondsworth.

ILO. (1978) *Year-Book of Labour Statistics: 1978*, International Labour Organisation, Geneva.

IPPR. (1990) *A British Bill of Rights*, Constitution Paper No 1, Institute for Public Policy Research, London.

Jacobs, E. & Worcester, R. (1990) *We British: Britain Under the Microscope*, Weidenfeld & Nicolson, London.

Jenkins, J. & Hutchings, V. (1988) '88 Ways to lose your liberty', in *New Statesman and Society* Vol I (26), pp31–4.

Jenkins, P. (1987) *Mrs Thatcher's Revolution: The Ending of the Socialist Era*, Jonathan Cape, London.

Jessop, B., Bromley, S. & Ling, T. (1988) *Thatcherism: A Tale of Two Nations*, Polity, Cambridge.

Johnson, P. (1978) 'Farewell to the Labour Party' in Cormack (1978), pp75–87.

Johnson, P. (1990) 'A Woman for all seasons', *Daily Mail*, 23 November, pp6–7.

Jones, J. (1967) 'Unions Today and Tomorrow', in Blackburn and Cockburn 1967, pp121–32.

Joseph, K. (1975) *Reversing the Trend*, Barry Rose, Chichester.

Joseph, K. (1976) *Stranded on the Middle Ground*, Centre for Policy Studies, London.

Joseph, K. (1979) 'The Class War' (Gilbraith Lecture), in *Guardian*, 18 July, p7.

Joseph, K. & Sumption, J. (1979) *Equality*, John Murray, London.

Jouvenel, B. de (1952) *The Ethics of Distribution*, Cambridge University Press, Cambridge.

Jouvenel, B. de. (1957) *Sovereignty*, Cambridge University Press, Cambridge.

Junor, P. (1983) *Margaret Thatcher*, Secker & Warburg, London.

Kaldor, N. (1982) *The Scourge of Monetarism*, Oxford University Press, Oxford.

Kaldor, N. (1983) *The Economic Consequences of Mrs Thatcher*, Duckworth, London.

Kamenka, E. (1969) *Marxism and Ethics*, Macmillan, London.

Kavanagh, D. & Seldon, A. (eds) (1989) *The Thatcher Effect: A Decade of Change*, Oxford University Press, Oxford.

Kavanagh, S. & Malcolm, R. (1985) 'Riot and Unlawful Assembly', *Legal Action*, September, pp6–8.

Keegan, W. (1984) *Mrs Thatcher's Economic Experiment*, Penguin, Harmondsworth.

Keynes, J. M. (1936) *The General Theory of Employment Interest and Money*, Macmillan, London.

King, A. (1989) 'Thatcher: the tide turns', *Sunday Telegraph*, 30 April, pp1, 25.

King, D. (1987) *The New Right: Politics, Markets and Citizenship*, Macmillan, London.

Kings Fund Institute. (1989) *Efficiency in the N.H.S.*, Kings Fund Occasional Paper No 2, Kings Fund Institute, London.

Kolakowski, L. & Hampshire, S. (1977) *The Socialist Idea: A Reappraisal*, Quartet, London.

Kropotkin, P. (1939) *Mutual Aid*, Penguin, Harmondsworth.

Kuhn, T. (1970) 'The Essential Tension: Tradition and Innovation in Scientific Research' [1963] in Hudson, L. (ed) *The Ecology of Human Intelligence*, Penguin, Harmondsworth, pp342–56.

Labour Party. (1982) *The City: A Socialist Approach*, Report of the Labour Party Financial Institutions Study Group, London.

Labour Party. (1987a) *Company Donations to the Conservative Party and other Political Organisations*, Information Paper No 77, Labour Party Policy Directorate, October.

Labour Party. (1987b) *The Tory Record*, Labour Party, London.

Labour Party Defence Study Group. (1977) *Sense About Defence*, Quartet, London.

Labour Research. (1986) 'Political fund ballots: a multiple victory', *Labour Research*, May, pp22–4.

Labour Research. (1989) *Fact Service*, Vol 51 No 47, 23 November.

Lane, T. (1983) 'The Tories and the Trade Unions: Rhetoric and Reality' in Hall and Jacques (1983), pp169–87.

Laski, H. (1933) *Liberty in the Modern State*, Penguin, Harmondsworth.

Lawson, D. (1989) 'How the bosses help themselves', *The Spectator*, Vol 262 (8397), pp9–11.

Lawson, N. (1980) *The New Conservatism*, Centre for Policy Studies, London.

Lawson, N. (1988) *The New Britain*, Centre for Policy Studies, London.

Leadbeater, C. (1990) 'Back to the Future', *New Statesman and Society*, Vol 3 (99), 4 May, pp17–18.

LeGrand, J. & Estrin, S. (1989) *Market Socialism*, Oxford University Press, Oxford.

Leigh, D. (1988) *The Wilson Plot*, Heinemann, London.

Letwin, S. B. (1978) 'On Conservative Individualism' in Cowling (ed) (1978), pp52–68.

Letwin, W. (ed) (1983) *Against Equality*, Macmillan, London.

Levitas, R. (ed) (1986) *The Ideology of the New Right*, Polity, Cambridge.

Lewis, R. (1975) *Margaret Thatcher: A Personal and Political Biography*, Routledge & Kegan Paul, London.

Lipsey, D. (1981) 'Why Sir Keith can only blame himself', *Sunday Times*, 13 May, p14.

Littlechild, S. C. (1986) *The Fallacy of the Mixed Economy* (2nd edn), Hobart Paper 80, Institute for Economic Affairs, London.

Lubasz, H. (1976) 'Marx's Initial Problematic', *Political Studies* XXIV (1), pp24–42.

Macpherson, C. B. (1962) *The Political Theory of Possessive Individualism: Hobbes to Locke*, Oxford University Press, Oxford.

Macpherson, C. B. (1977) *The Life and Times of Liberal Democracy*, Oxford University Press, Oxford.

Macpherson, C. B. (1981) *Burke*, Oxford University Press, Oxford.

Maine, H. S. (1986) *Ancient Law* [1861], Dorset Press, USA.

Maistre, J. de. (1965) *The Works of Joseph de Maistre*, Lively J. (ed), Allen & Unwin, London.

Manning, Cardinal. (1934) *The Dignity and Rights of Labour*, Burnes, Oates & Washbourne, London.

Manwaring, T. & Sigler, N. (1985) *Breaking the Nation: A Guide to Thatcher's Britain*, Pluto Press/New Socialist, London.

Markovic, M. (1974) *From Affluence to Practice*, University of Michigan Press, Ann Arbor.

Marquand, D. (1988) *The Unprincipled Society: New Demands and Old Politics*, Fontana, London.

Marshall, G., Newby, H., Rose, D. & Vogler, C. (1988) *Social Class in Modern Britain*, Hutchinson, London.

Marx, K. (1842) 'Debates on the Law on Thefts of Wood', *Works* Vol 1, pp224–63.

Marx, K. (1843) 'Justification of the Correspondent from Mosel', in Karl Marx and Friedrich Engels (1975) pp332–58. *Collected Works: Volume 1. Marx: 1835–1843*, Lawrence & Wishart, London.

Mason, D. (1989) 'Local Government', in Pirie (1989) pp45–63.

Mathews, K. & Stoney, P. (1989) 'Explaining Mrs Thatcher's Success', in *Institute for Economic Affairs*, Vol 10 (2), December/January, pp10–16.

McLeish, H. (1989) *The jobs miracle that never was*, Labour Market Briefing No 1, December, Labour Party, London.

Metcalf, D. (1988a) 'Water Notes Dry Up', Discussion Paper 314, Centre for Labour Economics, London School of Economics, London.

Metcalf, D. (1988b) *Trade Unions and Economic Performance: The British Experience*, London School of Economics, London.

Micklethwaite, B. (1986) 'Privatise the Royal Family?' *Economic Affairs*, 6(4), April–May, p50.

Mill, J. S. (1975) *Three Essays*, Oxford University Press, Oxford.

Miller, D. (1976) *Social Justice*, Clarendon Press, Oxford.

Miller, D. (1989) *Market, State and Community*, Oxford University Press, Oxford.

Miller, D. (1990) 'Trusting the Market', *New Socialist*, 65 February/March, pp29–31.

Milner, H. (1989) *Sweden: Social Democracy in Practice*, Oxford University Press, Oxford.

Ministry of Labour. (1966) *Statistics on Incomes, Prices, Employment and Production*, No 18, September HMSO, London.

Minogue, K. (1978) 'On Hyperactivism in Modern British Politics', in Cowling (1978), pp117–30.

Minogue, K. (1989) *The egalitarian conceit*, Centre for Policy Studies, London.

Mitchell, W. C. (1988) *Government As It Is*, Hobart Paper 109, Institute for Economic Affairs, London.

Moore, R. & Beddoe, R. (1975) *Low Pay: The Record Since 1964*, Trade Union Research Unit, Ruskin College, Oxford.

Mount, F. (1987) 'All Anarchists Nowadays', *Spectator*, 25 April, p24.

Mount, F. (1990) 'Small Mind and Less Logic' (see also Honderich 1990), *Spectator*, 265 (8453), 14 July, pp23–5.

Mountbatten, P. (1983) *A Question of Balance*, Sphere, London.

Murie, A. (1989) 'Housing and the Environment', in Kavanagh and Seldon (eds) (1989), pp213–25.

Nairn, T. (1981) *The Break-up of Britain*, Verso, London.

Nairn, T. (1988) *The Enchanted Glass: Britain and its Monarchy*, Hutchinson Radius, London.

Neuberger, J. (1987) *Freedom of Information – Freedom of the Individual*, Macmillan, London.

Nevin, M. (1983) *The Age of Illusions*, Gollancz, London.

New Statesman. (1987) 'Socialism – A Future?' *New Statesman*, Vol 113 (2919), 6 March.

New Statesman and Society. (1988) 'Charter 88', *New Statesman and Society*, Vol 1 (26), 2 December.

NIESR. (1990) 'Productivity, Education and Training: Britain and other Countries Compared', *National Institute Economic Review*, National Institute of Economic and Social Research, London.

Nishiyama, C. & Allen, G. C. (1974) *The Price of Prosperity: Lessons from Japan*, Hobart Paper No. 58, Institute for Economic Affairs, London.

Nolan, P. (1989) 'Walking on Water? Performance and Industrial Relations under Mrs Thatcher', *Industrial Relations Journal*, Vol 20 (2), pp81–92.

Northam, G. (1988) *Shooting in the Dark: Riot Police in Britain*, Faber & Faber, London.

Northrop, F. S. C. (1948) 'The Neurological and Behaviouristic Psychological Basis of the Ordering of Society by Means of Ideas', *Science*, 107, 23 April, pp411–17.

Northrop, F. S. C. (1959) *The Logic of the Sciences and the Humanities* (1947), Meridan, New York.

Northrop, F. S. C. (1960) *Philosophical Anthropology and Politics*, Macmillan, New York.

Northrop, F. S. C. (1971) *Ideological Differences and World Order*, Yale University Press, reprinted Greenwood Press, Westport, Connecticut.

Northrop, F. S. C. (1978) *The Complexity of Legal and Ethical Experience* [1959], Yale University Press, reprinted Greenwood Press, Westport, Connecticut.

Norton-Taylor, R. (1985) *The Ponting Affair*, Cecil Wolf, London.

Nossiter, B. D. (1978) *Britain: A Future that Works*, Andre Deutsch, London.

Nozick, R. (1974) *Anarchy, State and Utopia*, Blackwell, Oxford.

Oakley, B. & Owen, K. (1990) *Alvey: Britain's Strategic Computing Initiative*, Massachussetts Institute of Technology Press, London.

Oakshott, M. (1962) *Rationalism in Politics*, Methuen, London.

Oakshott, M. (1975) *On Human Conduct*, Oxford University Press, Oxford.

Observer. (1989) 'Thatcher's Monuments', *Observer Magazine Special Issue*, 23 April.

Observer. (1989) 'Ten Years at Number Ten', *Observer Special Supplement*, 30 April.

OECD. (various dates) *Main Economic Indicators*, Organisation for Economic Co-operation and Development, Paris.

Office of Population Censuses and Surveys. (1988) *The Financial Circumstances of Disabled People*, OPCS, London.

Olsen, M. & Landsberg, H. H. (eds) (1975) *The No-Growth Society*, Woburn Press, London.

O'Neill, J. (ed) (1973) *Modes of Individualism and Collectivism*, Heinemann, London.

Orwell, G. (1981) *The Lion and the Unicorn: Socialism and the English Genius* [1941], in *George Orwell*, Book Club Associates in Association with Secker & Warburg and Octopus, pp527–64.

Oxford University Socialist Discussion Group. (ed) (1989) *Out of Apathy*, Verso, London.

Papps, I. (1975) *Government and Enterprise*, Hobart Paper No 61, Institute for Economic Affairs, London.

Parekh, B. (1986) 'The New Right and the Politics of Nationhood', in Deakin (1986), pp33–44.

Partington, J. Orlick, T., Salmela, J. (1982) *Sport in Perspective*, SIP Inc., Coaching Association of Canada, Ottowa.

Patten, C. (1983) *The Tory Case*, Longman, London.

Paul, J. (ed) (1981) *Reading Nozick: Essays on Anarchy, State and Utopia*, Blackwell, Oxford.

Pay Board. (1974) *Relative Pay of Mineworkers: Special Report*, Cmnd 5567, HMSO, London.

Pelling, H. (1971) *A History of British Trade Unionism* (2nd edn), Penguin, Harmondsworth.

Pimlott, B. (ed) (1984) *Fabian Essays in Socialist Thought*, Heinemann, London.

Pirie, M. (ed) (1987) *Hayek: On the Fabric of Human Society*, Adam Smith Institute, London.

Pirie, M. (ed) (1989) *A Decade of Revolution: The Thatcher Years*, Adam Smith Institute, London.

Plamenatz, J. (1970) *Ideology*, Macmillan, London.

Plant, R. (1974) *Community and Ideology*, Routledge & Kegan Paul, London.

Plant, R. (1978) 'Community: concept, conception, ideology', *Politics and Society*, January, pp79–107.

Plant, R. (1984) *Equality, Markets and the State*, Tract 494, Fabian Society, London.

Platt, S. (1989) 'The Forgotten Army', *New Statesman and Society*, 2 (41), 3 November, pp12–15.

Playfair, H. (1885) 'Science and Technology as Sources of National Power', in Basalla, G., Coleman, W., Kargon, R. H. (eds) (1970) *Victorian Science*, Doubleday Anchor, New York; Bell, London, pp60–83.

Plender, J. (1990) 'Home to Roost', *New Statesman and Society*, 3 (86), pp14–15.

Pliatzky, L. (1984) *Getting and Spending: public expenditure, unemployment and inflation*, Blackwell, Oxford.

Polanyi, G. & Wood, J. B. (1974) *How Much Inequality?* Research Monograph 31, Institute for Economic Affairs, London.

Polanyi, M. (1958) *Personal Knowledge*, Routledge & Kegan Paul, London.

Polanyi, M. (1966) 'Continuity and Contrast', in Grisewood (1966) pp433–45.

Polanyi, M. (1967) *The Tacit Dimension*, Doubleday Anchor, New York.

Polanyi, M. (1969) *Knowing and Being*, Routledge & Kegan Paul, London.

Pollack, B. (1988) 'The iron heel of economics: 15 years of Pinochet's Chile', *Times Higher Education Supplement*, 9 September, p14.

Pollard, S. (1989) *Britain's Prime and Britain's Decline: the British Economy 1870–1914*, Edward Arnold, London.

Ponting, C. (1985) *The Right to Know*, Sphere, London.

Popper, K. (1957) *The Poverty of Historicism*, Routledge & Kegan Paul, London.

Popper, K. (1969) *Conjectures and Refutations*, Routledge & Kegan Paul, London.

Porritt, J. (1984) *Seeing Green*, Blackwell, Oxford.

Porter, M. (1990) *The Competitive Advantage of Nations*, Macmillan, London.

Prais, S. J. (1981) *Productivity and Industrial Structure*, Cambridge University Press, Cambridge.

Pratten, C. (1990) 'Why sterling has to go', *Financial Times*, 18 July, p15.

Prebble, J. (1969) *The Highland Clearances*, Penguin, London.

Pym, F. (1985) *The Politics of Consent*, Sphere, London.

Raban, J. (1989) *God, Man and Mrs Thatcher*, Counterblast 1, Chatto & Windus, London.

Ramsay, R. (1988) 'Smears that speak volumes about the secret state's techniques', *Tribune*, 22 July, p6.

Rand, A. (1961) *The Virtue of Selfishness*, Signet, New York.

Rand, A. (1964) *For the New Intellectual*, Signet, New York.

Raptis, M. (1980) *Socialism, Democracy and Self-Management*, Allison and Busby, London.

Rather, A. W. (1932) *Is Britain Decadent?* Sampson Low Marton, London.

Raw, C. (1977) *Slater Walker*, André Deutsch, London.

Redwood, J. (1989) 'The Thatcher Economic Record', in Pirie (1989), pp6–18.

Ree, J. (1974) *Descartes*, Allen Lane, London.

Reid, M. (1989) 'Mrs Thatcher and the City', in Kavanagh and Seldon (eds) (1989), pp49–63.

Reimer, E. (1971) *School is Dead*, Penguin, Harmondsworth.

Rentoul, J. (1987) *The Rich get Richer: The Growth of Inequality in Britain in the 1980s*, Unwin Hyman, London.

Rentoul, J. (1989) *Me and Mine: The Triumph of the New Individualism*, Unwin Hyman, London.

Revolutionary Communist Party of Britain (Marxist-Leninist). (1981) *For the unity of the workers in struggle for democratic rights, against Capitalist exploitation and class collaboration and for an end to wage slavery*, RCPB (M-L), London.

Reynolds, D. (1987) 'A selective mis-reading of the facts', *Guardian*, 12 May, p13.

Reynolds, D. & Sullivan, M. (1987) *The Comprehensive Experiment*, Falmer, London.

Ridley, N. (1990) 'Saying the Unsayable About the Germans', *Spectator*, Vol 265 (8453), 14 July, pp8–10.

Roberts, G. (1989/90) 'Fact File: facts and figures from Parliamentary Proceedings', *Tribune*, London.

Rogers, G. F. C. (1983) *The Nature of Engineering: A Philosophy of Technology*, Macmillan, London.

Rorty, R. (1989) *Contingency, Irony, and Solidarity*, Cambridge University Press, Cambridge.

Rothbard, M. (1978) *For a New Liberty: The Libertarian Manifesto*, Collier–Macmillan, London.

Rothstein, A. (1950) *A History of the U.S.S.R.*, Penguin, Harmondsworth.

Russell, B. (1941) 'The Ancestry of Fascism' [1935], in *Let the People Think*, Watts, London, pp61–79.

Ryan, A. (1984) 'Left Standing', *New Society*, 28 November, p334.

Samizdat. (1988) *Samizdat* Vol 1 No 1, November/December.

Sampson, A. (1977) 'The Gambler', *Observer*, 16 October, p19.

Scharfstein, B. A. (1980) *The Philosophers: Their Lives and the Nature of their Thought*, Blackwell, Oxford.

Schon, D. (1967) *Invention and the Evolution of Ideas* (first published as *Displacement of Concepts* [1963]). Social Science Paperbacks, Tavistock, London.

Schumpeter, J. A. (1987) *Capitalism, Socialism and Democracy* [1943], Unwin Hyman, London.

Scott, P. (1989) 'Higher Education' in Kavanagh and Seldon (eds) (1989), pp198–212.

Scruton, R. (1980) *The Meaning of Conservatism*, Penguin, Harmondsworth.

Scruton, R. (ed) (1988a) *Conservative Thinkers*, Claridge, London.

Scruton, R. (ed) (1988b) *Conservative Thoughts*, Claridge, London.

Seamen. (1966) *Would you work 56 hours for £14?*, National Union of Seamen.

Seidentop, L. (1990) 'Thatcherism's inconsistency', *Financial Times*, 6 November, p25.

Seldon, A. (ed) (1978) *The Coming Confrontation: Will the Open Society Survive to 1989?*, Institute for Economic Affairs, London.

Seldon, A. (ed) (1981) *The Emerging Consensus?*, Institute for Economic Affairs, London.

Sen, A. (1987) *On Ethics and Economics*, Blackwell, Oxford.

Shelter. (1988) *Freedom to lose: Housing Policy and People wih Disabilities*, Shelter, London.

Shenfield, A. (1983) *Icarus: or the fate of Democratic Socialism*, Adam Smith Institute, London.

Shenfield, A. (1986) *What Right to Strike?*, Hobart Paper 106, Institute for Economic Affairs, London.

Shenfield, A. (1989) 'Mrs Thatcher: Hammer and Reformer of the Unions', in Pirie (1989), pp19–32.

Shonfield, A. (1958) *British Economic Policy Since the War*, Penguin, Harmondsworth.

Siegfried, A. (1931) *England's Crisis*, Harcourt Brace, New York.

Silver, H. (1965) *The Concept of Popular Education*, Macgibbon and Kee, London.

SIPRI. (1989) *Yearbook 1990*: 'World Armaments and Disarmament', Stockholm International Peace Research Institute, Oxford University Press, Oxford.

Skidelsky, R. (ed) (1988) *Thatcherism*, Chatto & Windus, London.

Skolimowski, H. (1981) *Eco-Philosophy*, Marion Boyars, London.

Smith, A. (1910) *The Wealth of Nations* [1776], 2 vols. Dent, London.

Stalker, J. (1989) *Stalker*, Penguin, Harmondsworth.

Stephan, A. (1985) 'State Power and the Strength of Civil Society in the Southern Cone of Latin America', in Evans, Rueschmeyer and Skocpol (1985), pp317–43.

Stephen, J. F. (1967) *Liberty, Equality, Fraternity*, Cambridge University Press, Cambridge.

Stevenson, L. (1974) *Seven Theories of Human Nature*, Oxford University Press, Oxford.

Stigler, G. (1981) *The Pleasures and Pains of Modern Capitalism*, Occasional Paper 64, Institute for Economic Affairs, London.

Strachey, J. (1937) *The Theory and Practice of Socialism*, Gollancz, London.

Stretch, L. (1986) *Engineering: Mechanical or Moral Science?* Becket, London.

Sunday Telegraph. (1989) 'Thatcher's Britain'; Telescope Review; Analysis, *Sunday Telegraph*, 30 April, pp1, 13–15, 25.

Sunday Times. (1989) 'Her First Ten Years', *Sunday Times Magazine*, 30 April.

Sunday Times (1990) 'Britain's Rich: The Top 200', *Sunday Times Magazine*, 8 April.

Tarling, R. & Wilkinson, F. (1977) 'The Social Contract: post-war incomes policies and their inflationary impact', *Cambridge Journal of Economics*, 1, pp395–414.

Taylor, K. (1990) *The Poisoned Tree: The Untold Truth About the Police Conspiracy to Discredit John Stalker and Destroy Me*, Sidgwick, London.

Taylor, R. (1980) *The Fifth Estate: Britain's Unions in the Modern World*, Pan, London.

Thatcher, M. (1977) *Let Our Children Grow Tall; Collected Speeches 1975–1977*, Centre for Policy Studies, London.

Thatcher, M. (1989a) *Speeches to the Conservative Party Conference 1975–1988*, Conservative Political Centre, London.

Thatcher, M. (1989b) *The Revival of Britain: Speeches on Home and European Affairs 1975–1988* (compiled A. B. Cooke), Aurum, London.

Thomas, G. (1985) *Mr Speaker*, Century, London.

Thomas, H. (1979) *History, Capitalism and Freedom*, Centre for Policy Studies, London.

Thompson, P. (1990) *Sharing Success*, Collins, London.

Thornton, P. (1989) *Decade of Decline: Civil Liberties in the Thatcher Years*, National Council for Civil Liberties, London.

Tocqueville, A. de. (1956) *Democracy in America*, Mentor, London.

Tomlinson, J. (1988) *Can Government Manage the Economy?*, Tract 524, Fabian Society, London.

Tomlinson, J. (1990) *Hayek and the Market*, Pluto, London.

Tomlinson, J. R. G. (1989) 'The Schools', in Kavanagh and Seldon (eds), (1989), pp183–97.

Townsend, P. (1979) *Poverty in the United Kingdom*, Penguin, Harmondsworth.

Townsend, P. & Davidson, N. (1982) *Inequalities in Health*, Penguin, Harmondsworth.

Trevelyan, G. M. (1959) *A Shortened History of England*, Penguin, Harmondsworth.

Tullock, G. (1976) *The Vote Motive*, Hobart Paperback No 9, Institute for Economic Affairs, London.

Turnbull, M. (1988) *The Spycatcher Trial*, Heinemann, London.

Tyrell, R. E. (1977) *The Future that Doesn't Work: Social Democracy's Failures in Britain*, Doubleday, New York.

UNESCO (1987) *Statistical Yearbook*, United Nations Educational Social and Cultural Organisation, Geneva.

Venable, V. (1964) *Human Nature: The Marxian View*, Dennis Dobson, London.

Walker, D. (1989) 'The Civil Service', in Pirie (ed) (1989), pp33–44.

Wallace, C. (1990) 'The Honour of lying for Queen and Country', *Independent on Sunday*, 4 February, p23.

Waltzer, M. (1989) 'The Good Life: the Civil Society Argument', *New Statesman and Society*, Vol 2 (70), 6 October, pp28–31.

Warnock, M. (1989) *Universities: Knowing Our Minds*, Counterblast No 8. Chatto & Windus, London.

Watkins, K. W. (ed) (1978) *In Defence of Freedom*, Cassell, London.

Weber, M. (1964) *The Theory of Social and Economic Organisation*, Collier-Macmillan, London.

Webster, C. (1989) 'The Health Service', in Kavanagh and Seldon (eds) (1989), pp166–82.

Weiner, M. (1981) *English Culture and the Decline of the Industrial Spirit 1850–1980*, Cambridge University Press, Cambridge.

Whitelaw, W. (1989a) *The Whitelaw Memoirs*, Aurum, London.

Whitelaw, W. (1989b) 'The bitterness of politics', *Sunday Times*, 30 April, C1–2.

Whittle, F. (1957) *Jet: The Story of a Pioneer*, Pan, London.

Wigham, E. (1961) *What's Wrong with the Trade Unions?* Penguin, Harmondsworth.

Wilberforce, Lord. (1972) *Report of the Commission of Inquiry into a dispute between the NCB and the NUM*, Cmnd 4903, HMSO, London.

Wilkie, T. (1989) 'The Thatcher Effect on Science', in Kavanagh and Seldon (eds) (1989), pp316–29.

Williams, K. Williams J. & Haslam, C. (1989) 'Pitfalls in the power game', *Times Higher Education Supplement*, 3 March, p17.

Williams, S. (1981) *Politics Is For People*, Penguin, Harmondsworth.

Wilson, E. (1979) *The Mental as Physical*, Routledge & Kegan Paul, London.

Wilson, E. (1989) *The Myth of British Monarchy*, Journeyman/Republic, London.

Wilson, H. (1977) *A Prime Minister on Prime Ministers*, Weidenfeld & Nicolson, London.

Worsthorne, P. (1977) 'The Case for the Monarchy', in Penguin Special, *The Queen*, Penguin, Harmondsworth, pp165–84.

Worsthorne, P. (1978) 'Too much Freedom', in Cowling (1978), pp141–54.

Worsthorne, P. (1979) 'When Treason can be Right', in *Sunday Telegraph*, 4 November, p16.

Worsthorne, P. (1984) 'Danger: Tory Gurus at Work', *Sunday Telegraph*, 11 March, p16.

Worsthorne, P. (1988) *The Politics of Manners*, Centre for Policy Studies, London.

Worsthorne, P. (1990) 'The grace of class', *Sunday Telegraph*, 2 December, p27.

Wright, G. (ed) (1989) *ABC of Thatcherism*, Fabian Society, London.

Wright, N. (1977) *Progress in Education*, Croom Helm, London.

Wright, P. (1987) *Spycatcher*, Viking, New York.

Wrong, D. (1979) *Power: Its forms, bases and uses*, Blackwell, Oxford.

Young, H. (1989) *One of Us: A biography of Margaret Thatcher*, Macmillan, London.

Young K. (1989) 'Local Government', in Kavanagh and Seldon (eds) (1989), pp124–32.

Zander, M. (1985) 'Towards a Bill of Rights', *New Society*, Vol 74 (1197), pp413–14.

INDEX